THE EAST INDIA COMPANY

STUDIES IN MODERN HISTORY

General editors: John Morrill and David Cannadine

This series, intended primarily for students, will tackle significant historical issues in concise volumes which are both stimulating and scholarly. The authors combine a broad approach, explaining the current state of our knowledge in the area, with their own research and judgements; and the topics chosen range widely in subject, period and place.

Titles already published

FRANCE IN THE AGE OF HENRY IV (2nd Edn) *Mark Greengrass*

VICTORIAN RADICALISM *Paul Adelman*

WHITE SOCIETY IN THE ANTEBELLUM SOUTH *Bruce Collins*

BLACK LEADERSHIP IN AMERICA: FROM BOOKER T. WASHINGTON TO JESSE JACKSON (2nd Edn) *John White*

THE TUDOR PARLIAMENTS *Michael A. R. Graves*

LIBERTY AND ORDER IN EARLY MODERN EUROPE *J.H. Shennan*

POPULAR RADICALISM *D. G. Wright*

'PAX BRITANNICA'? BRITISH FOREIGN POLICY 1789–1914 *Muriel E. Chamberlain*

IRELAND SINCE 1800 *K. Theodore Hoppen*

IMPERIAL MERIDIAN: THE BRITISH EMPIRE AND THE WORLD 1780–1830 *C.A. Bayly*

A SYSTEM OF AMBITION? BRITISH FOREIGN POLICY 1660–1793 *Jeremy Black*

BRITANNIA OVERRULED: BRITISH POLICY AND WORLD POWER IN THE 20TH CENTURY *David Reynolds*

POOR CITIZENS: THE STATE AND THE POOR IN TWENTIETH-CENTURY BRITAIN *David Vincent*

THE HOUSE OF LORDS IN BRITISH POLITICS AND SOCIETY 1815–1911 *E.A. Smith*

POLITICS UNDER THE LATER STUARTS: PARTY CONFLICT IN A DIVIDED SOCIETY 1660–1715 *Tim Harris*

BRITAIN AND LATIN AMERICA IN THE NINETEENTH AND TWENTIETH CENTURIES *Rory Miller*

THE EAST INDIA COMPANY: A HISTORY *Philip Lawson*

THE BRITISH IN THE AMERICAS 1480–1815 *Anthony McFarlane*

PUTTING BRITAIN FIRST: PARTY COALITION AND THE IDEA OF A NATIONAL GOVERNMENT; 1885–1987 *G.R. Searle*

THE EAST INDIA COMPANY: A History

Philip Lawson

Longman
London and New York

Addison Wesley Longman Limited,
Edinburgh Gate,
Harlow, Essex CM20 2JE, England
and Associated Companies throughout the world.

Published in the United States of America
by Addison Wesley Longman, New York

First published 1993
Third impression 1997

ISBN 0582 07386 3 CSD
ISBN 0582 07385 5 PPR

British Library Cataloguing-in-Publication Data

A catalogue record for this book is available from the British Library

Library of Congress Cataloging in Publication Data

Lawson, Philip.
The East India Company : a history / Philip Lawson.
p. cm. -- (Studies in modern history)
Includes bibliographical references and index.
ISBN 0-582-07386-3 -- ISBN 0-582-07385-5 (pbk.)
1. East India Company--History. 2. Great Britain--Commerce
–India--History. 3. India--Commerce--Great Britain--History.
4. India--History--1500–1765. I. Title. II. Series: Studies in modern history (Longman (Firm))
DS465.L38 1993
382'.094205' 0903-dc20 92–44920
CIP

Set 7B in 10/11 pt Bembo
Produced by Longman Singapore Publishers (Pte) Ltd.
Printed in Singapore

Contents

List of Maps

Preface

The East India Company's history is central to the British experience of trade and territorial expansion overseas. Its longevity, spanning over two and a half centuries from its founding in 1600, and critical role in bringing India and other eastern lands into the British empire, mark the Company out as unique in the nation's history. No less important, those involved in this enterprise have provided a romantic anthology of tales and legends for succeeding generations to pore over. The poetry of Kipling, the prose of Henty and the celluloid stars of the twentieth century in the Bengal Lancers fighting exotic rulers of kingdoms in the Orient, have carried historical fact into fantasy and folklore. National heroes have been carved out of the military exploits of men such as Clive, Hastings and Wellesley, and, in the process, a cult of the Raj developed which has been impossible to eradicate from the mass of literature published on the Anglo-Indian past.

Why this pattern or manner of writing about the East India Company developed is not so surprising from an academic viewpoint. The Company's involvement in the East was an epic story on a grand scale. Moreover, the one thing the Company's history possesses in abundance is archival and secondary material documenting its development. The sheer volume of manuscripts, scholarly books, articles, popular histories and pot-boilers conveying some aspect of the Company's past defies description. It would take several lifetimes to read all that exists today on the East India Company's history and nothing suggests the production will cease in the near future. Scholars on four continents are presently devoted to revealing every detail of the Company's advance, from its humble seventeenth-century origins to full-blown agent of imperialism by 1857.

Faced with such an established regimen of specialized enquiry into the East India Company's history, it might seem out of place to offer a more compact survey. The purpose of this study, however, is to take stock of what has gone before, synthesizing the old and new research and making the whole story accessible to readers of all backgrounds and interests. The logic of the chapters that follow is driven by the need to tell the story of a trading company in all its facets and contexts – east and west. I have sought, therefore, to emphasize the impact of the East India Company's history not only in its Indian context but also the British setting. The evolution of the Company's trade policy over its long contact with the East had ramifications for British society, especially in the eighteenth and early nineteenth centuries, that should no longer be neglected. In encompassing the trade and then territory of India, the East India Company changed its own *raison d'être* and introduced profound change to the subcontinent and the part played by Britain in the global trade and diplomatic networks of the time. This experience, I believe, proved to be a novel one in British history and its analysis is of no little matter to understanding the evolution of relations between East and West since the Company's demise in 1858.

It goes without saying that in preparing this survey and the message it contains, I owe a great debt to all those who have previously worked in this field, producing the superb histories that have made writing this study so enjoyable. In thanking them I also acknowledge that any errors in synthesis or abridgement remain mine. The organization of the study is chronological, within which I have deliberately set out to give each period of the Company's development its due, avoiding the traditional inclination to emphasize the last century of its existence. The organization of the sources for the survey takes two forms. Modern secondary sources – books, articles and the like – are run into the text, while printed primary sources or older documentation are cited in endnotes, appearing after each chapter. This course was followed to encourage any reader interested in a particular aspect of the Company's history to investigate the matter further, using the sources provided, old and new. For this reason manuscript citations are not part of the book's structure, although it will be obvious that I have relied on my knowledge of the archival sources in several areas of the study.

A last few words of thanks are reserved to all those who have assisted and endured my persistent enquiries and obsessions with all things to do with the East India Company over the past decade. The expertise of Huw Bowen, in particular, and the words of wisdom of Peter Marshall, in a general sense, have proved invaluable. The work of K.N. Chaudhuri and Chris Bayly has also been indispensable to the completion of this project. I would like, in addition, to express gratitude to the Central Research Fund at the University of Alberta for supporting my research, to my students for putting up with it and to Linda Bridges for her perseverance and care. Last, to Doug Owram goes the credit for allowing me the time and to my family the burden of tolerance for which I am so grateful – again!

For Eileen

CHAPTER ONE

England and the East in the Sixteenth Century

THE NAME OF THE GAME: CONTEXT TO BRITISH TRADE IN THE EAST

Any discussion of the European and Asian trading world within which the East India Company emerged in 1600, needs to be prefaced with a word about context. In particular it is necessary to appreciate some basic English assumptions about establishing links between London and the East in the sixteenth century. The first concerns the term East, and its close relations, like the East Indies, Asia and India. These terms were, to all intents and purposes, interchangeable in the context of the sixteenth-century debate about the grand design of England gaining direct access to eastern markets. The East could mean a number of geographical locations from which exotic oriental products emanated. Few of the written records that exist promoting a trading enterprise to the East in this period display a serious concern with geographical detail.

In retrospect this haziness is understandable. Modern methods of cartography were in their infancy, and the sea-borne trading world of the East into which Europeans had thrust their mariners at the end of the fifteenth century proved a diverse place indeed (M. Bowen 1981: 34–6). Centuries-old networks of exchange existed in the East Indian islands, north to China and Japan, west to the Indian sub-continent, and even further west into the Indian Ocean, the Persian Gulf and Red Sea. This huge area witnessed trade in all manner of raw and manufactured products, and, rather than discriminate in accounts of the nations and peoples involved in this cycle of exchange, the English tendency until well into the eighteenth century was to refer to all these places with the generic term – the East.

There existed a similar lack of focus when it came to the question of just what it was that the English wanted from the East. In the chapters that follow, analysing the history of the East India Company over 250 years or so, economic themes loom large. This is not surprising for a trading organization of this type, economic motives provided this Company and others with a *raison d'être* in good times and bad. Before 1600, however, the reasons for looking East did not appear so reductionist or clear cut. Interest in the Orient was not concentrated solely on trade. There were those encouraging voyages to the East for purely nationalistic reasons; to outdo the Spanish and Portuguese. Others wished to sail around Africa and make landfall in India for religious reasons; to spread Christianity and encircle the Islamic powers of the region (Scammell 1989: 68). In addition there existed a good deal of interest in sailing the eastern seas for plunder and piracy; and both these factors would blight the orderly development of the East India Company's position in the East over the next century. Last, but by no means least, a great motivating factor behind the desire to go East was the simple thirst for knowledge and adventure in unknown seas. The phenomenal propaganda success of Sir Francis Drake's circumnavigation of the globe from 1577 to 1580 provides a perfect illustration of this fact. His exploits captured the imagination of English people because they were presented with the right blend of Protestant national fervour triumphing over Catholic perfidy on the high seas, and the more personal story of native seamen surviving the uncharted but perilous waters of the unknown world. The lure of such adventures cannot be neglected as an important element in encouraging England's eastern design in the late sixteenth century. The more mundane, and narrowly focused, diplomatic efforts at breaking into eastern markets in these years clearly drew inspiration from the support and interest aroused by the actions of figures such as Drake and his fellow circumnavigator, Sir Thomas Cavendish (Morison 1978: 719–21; Rabb 1967: 19–22).

A related factor in this context of England's perceived desire of the East concerns trade goods themselves and modes of exchange. By the end of the sixteenth century the English had knowledge of many eastern products, most of which could be described as exotic luxuries. These included precious stones, expensive spices, ceramics and silks. Such products were not the necessities of life, but they made it more bearable and fashionable, especially for the élite. No less important, they could be the avenue to quick riches for those merchants and middlemen fortunate enough to handle this merchandise. In such an economic framework of supply and demand it would obviously pay the English merchants to have direct access to eastern products rather than rely on other Europeans to bring them in. Nevertheless, it should not be assumed that a simple causal relationship occurred whereby the English wanted and then suddenly achieved direct access to eastern markets. Far from it: until the 1580s few Englishmen knew where direct access to these goods could be secured either by land or sea. Popular literature, which politicians, merchants and the reading public readily assimilated, circulated stories of fabulous wealth and kingdoms in the Orient (Lawson 1989). But there was nothing of either physical or practical use in these images for opening up a trade. The English first invented an East that bore no relation to the reality of the temporal or spatial imperatives of trading there. Only when fragments of information from actual voyagers and travellers began circulating in the 1580s and 1590s did they see the error of their ways. Accounts by Drake and Cavendish, for example, not only contradicted all romantic notions of dealing with native and European powers in the East but also revealed the sheer logistical magnitude of the task facing English captains and their fleets. In the last two decades of the century, therefore, England's role in these trading patterns of the Orient had to be reinvented.

In the 1580s and 1590s this process got under way with a systematic approach to educating the English about the eastern enterprise, evident in the work of writers such as Richard Hakluyt and translators like Thomas Hickock (Parker 1965: 129–33). Hakluyt, in particular, believed that England's future survival and greatness as a nation lay in developing a colonial and trading empire overseas. He himself undertook the mammoth task of gathering and disseminating all available information about the Orient to further this aim. Personal interviews, translations from foreign travel accounts, folklore and any relevant histories all fell within his purview, and it is not surprising that with such expert knowledge he became an adviser to those planning a trading company to the East by a sea route around the Cape of Good Hope. This tinge of reality that observers such as Hakluyt brought to the English view of the East was certainly welcome and very timely, and yet it would be an exaggeration to say that old impressions of eastern geography and civilizations were eradicated overnight. Put bluntly, by 1600 the English were ready to sail east around the Cape, but the ultimate destination of the voyage remained unclear. No one quite knew what would happen when an

English fleet entered the Indian Ocean and the seas beyond. The first royal charter granted to the East India Company echoed all these uncertainties, and simply hedged around the question of a specific destination; its operations were to be global, comprising

> the said East-Indies, in the Countries and Parts of Asia and Africa, and into and from all the Islands, Ports, Havens, Cities, Creeks, Towns, and Places in Asia and Africa, and America, or any of them, beyond the Cape of Bona Esperanza to the Straits of Magellan, where any Trade of Traffick or Merchandize may be used or had . . .[1]

The lesson to be learned from such documentation is that initially the English had no particular interest in the Indian subcontinent. A perception emerged in the late sixteenth century that the best oriental markets (and thus profits) lay in the East Indian islands of Java, Sumatra, the Bandas and Moluccas to which India might prove a stepping-stone. The whole enterprise was no more certain than this, and the fact that any fleets set sail in the first years of the seventeenth century represents an enormous tribute to the spirit and courage of the seamen involved.

In the event the English risked all and eventually succeeded after 1600 in finding a niche in the trade networks of the East. However, one further complication had to be resolved before the rules of this trading game were mastered. Again it stemmed from inexperience. Of those promoting this eastern design in the late sixteenth century, few had bothered to consider what sort of trade patterns would develop, if all other obstacles to direct access could be overcome. On the surface this appeared to be the least of the worries related to establishing an oriental trade, and yet it presented a fundamental problem for the simple reason that English export products, principally woollen cloth, lead and tin, proved very expensive and not in great demand in the markets of the East. The only cargo of real interest to the merchants of the East was silver bullion which could be of benefit to the English in any exchange because of its higher value in Asia compared to Europe. Yet under existing English law, its exportation was forbidden. Consideration of this practicality then opened the door on to other imponderables: could a dispensation on the bullion restriction be had? If so, would the straight import value of an eastern cargo recoup the initial outlay or would the English have to become involved in the inter-port carrying trade of the Indian Ocean? And, finally, might it be necessary to develop a re-export trade to Antwerp from England of eastern goods to make the enterprise viable? Any one of these questions left unanswered was capable of bringing the whole eastern design down, and all three were crucial factors in the policy of fits and starts that characterized English contact with the East in the early seventeenth century. Up to the 1590s the salient experiences of England's designs in the East had proved to be uncertainty, lack of focus, inexperience and misconception. There was much to learn in this context, therefore, but so little time to enjoy the lesson with European competitors, like the Dutch, on the horizon. That such a legacy was overcome in the seventeenth century says a great deal about the hopes and aspirations of the English; not least because other, more immediate, problems had still to be solved – in particular, the establishment of a trading company to fulfil these long-held goals in the East.

HOPES AND ASPIRATIONS OF A COMPANY TRADING TO THE EAST

To explain the appearance and early success of the East India Company on the international trading scene after 1600 used to be a simple matter. The phenomenon of a trading company becoming an imperial power over the span of 250 years or so was rooted in the glories of the Elizabethan age. The accession of Queen Elizabeth I in 1558 seemed to later generations of writers and scholars the very point when the most debilitating constraints on English overseas expansion receded. This Protestant heroine became in the words of one seventeenth-century MP (Sir John Eliot), 'Elizabeth, that glorious star, glorious beyond any of her predecessors'. A cult of the invincible *Gloriana* grew up in English writing, originating in the work of writers such as Spenser and Shakespeare, and lasting well into the twentieth century. And in the making of this mythology about Elizabeth's reign, the eastern design played its part. Sir George Birdwood, who did much to publicize the records of the old India Office Library in the late nineteenth and early twentieth century, captured this heritage perfectly when he lamented that 17 November, the day of her accession or, as it was known, 'Queen Elizabeth's Day', was no longer a public holiday: 'it should still be so observed, at least in the India Office, and in British India', he wrote in 1886, 'in praise perennial of Her Imperious Majesty's heroic memory.'[2]

The misleading assumptions embodied in this unashamedly

nationalistic cult have only come to be questioned in the later twentieth century. It is not difficult to see why. The story of a warrior queen taking the fight for the spoils of new worlds outside Europe to her Catholic enemies has enduring emotional appeal, especially when it is dressed up in the heroic exploits of men such as Drake, Cavendish and Hawkins. However, in an age that has seen the collapse of empire and the state's economic might, such interpretations of English overseas expansion are now considered inadequate. Heroic exploits and bellicose nationalism in traditional histories encapsulate a singular and uncomplicated vision of the nation's past; one in which the state controls its own destiny. Thus, when Elizabeth and her ministers wished to trade with the East, they simply chartered a company for the purpose, and ensured its success through aggressive diplomacy, and, if necessary, force of arms. Such a narrow vision of the East India Company's emergence in English history may be attractive reading but it is an incomplete analysis of this dynamic in expansion to the East. Modern historical research on the sixteenth and seventeenth centuries illustrates that the so-called glories of the Elizabethan moment played but one small part in the quest and eventual organization of an overseas trade to the Orient. By the sixteenth century there existed a backdrop of European and global exchange that the English could neither avoid nor ignore if they wished to take a role in the drama. And it is within this broader supra-national context that a revised view of the East India Company's foundation and early experience has evolved.

This process of reinterpretation begins with an acceptance of the fact that the formation of the East India Company was not a novel event in itself, but the culmination of almost a hundred years of erratic attempts at securing direct access to eastern markets. Indeed, the founding of the 'Company of Merchants of London, Trading into the East Indies . . . ', as it was described in the royal charter of 1600, could be termed a last desperate throw in England's efforts to gain those eastern markets the produce of which was then controlled in Europe by Portugal, Spain and Holland. The English enjoyed the fruits of European trade with the East throughout the sixteenth century, but they paid a higher price for these products because of its control by foreign middlemen, and supply could prove unreliable for the same reason. This economic disadvantage in relation to eastern trade irked successive English monarchs, their councils, parliaments and merchant élites from Henry VII's reign onwards. Yet there existed few practical means by which to remedy this ailment. The English state and its trade structures were backward in comparison to its European competitors. Its rulers faced the constant prospect of wanting to break into a trading network that saw European ships making successful voyages to the East Indies, while lacking the resources to do so. First the Portuguese, then the Spanish and Dutch all had an edge on the English when it came to sea-borne trade to the East. Their superiority covered straightforward sailing technology right through to the financial organization and support for expensive, hazardous, deep-sea voyages in tropical waters (Parry 1981: 38–114). In consequence, these European nations, not England, led the way in innovation and the adaptation of medieval techniques used in the short-haul trade routes which eventually resulted in the great merchant marines of fair-skinned sailors in the East by 1600.

Nevertheless, the fact that the English knew nothing in detail of this trading world, and could not provide the resources before 1600 to find a toe-hold in its structures, does not mean they did not try. England's interest in the trade of the East began a century before the founding of the East India Company. This interest never amounted to much in practical terms, principally because of England's weakness in the framework of European power politics of the sixteenth century. After the epic voyages of Columbus across the Atlantic and da Gama around the Cape of Good Hope to India in the 1490s, the two Catholic powers, Spain and Portugal, decided to partition the world. Their basic intent was simply to avoid conflict and monopolize trade routes to the East, which, in the contemporary European view of the world, would lead to untold wealth. This partition received papal sanction, and was formalized in diplomatic terms with the treaty of Zaragossa in 1529 between Spain and Portugal. Trade patterns soon developed in the wake of these agreements in which these two nations seized the initiative in deep-sea voyaging beyond Europe. Portuguese control and influence on the high seas became focused on bases down the coasts of Africa, on to the west coast of India and then into the East Indian islands of modern-day Indonesia. Conversely, Spanish power in the New World became concentrated in the Caribbean, central and south America, and eventually across the Pacific to the Philippines.

By the early sixteenth century this structure had excluded the English from the East along the sea routes plied by Spanish and Portuguese vessels, and this dominance looked secure for the foreseeable future. From England the situation looked grim and raised the question of what could be done (in the absence of financial and naval resources) to break this mould. At first the English thought that circumventing the problem would resolve the exclusion issue. In short, the state supported the idea of discovering a sea route to the East by sailing from Europe either north-east or north-west in waters not frequented by Spanish and Portuguese ships. If a route to the eastern markets could be found by voyaging in either of these directions, the Iberian monopoly would be breached without a direct challenge to the existing, and overwhelming, power of Spain and Portugal.

It is this theme that dominates English thinking on the eastern design for seventy-five years or so after Henry VII's accession in 1485. In fact it appeared in Henry VII's own 'Letters Patent' to John Cabot in 1496, as he set sail north-west from Bristol to find a sea-route to the East. The king charged Cabot 'to seek out, discover, and find whatsoever isles, countries, regions or provinces of the heathen and infidels whatsoever they be, and in what part of the world soever they be, which before this time have been unknown to all Christians'.[3] Such endeavours took on an almost missionary zeal in the first half of the sixteenth century, as the English became obsessed with discovering routes to the East safe from Spanish and Portuguese influence. As late as 1553, when Sir Hugh Willoughby's and Richard Chancellor's expedition set sail to find a north-easterly route to Cathay around Norway and Russia, circumventing the Iberian powers remained uppermost as a motivating factor behind the whole enterprise.

All the hopes and moneys invested in opening up these routes in the frigid northern seas proved in vain. By the mid-sixteenth century, therefore, the English had certainly avoided a major conflict with Spain and Portugal, but the long-held desire for direct access to eastern markets was no nearer to fulfilment than it had been under Henry VII. It is at this point in traditional accounts of English expansionism that the Elizabethan period (1558–1603), assumes a special importance in putting an end to those national frustrations at the control exercised by the Iberian powers over eastern trade. Under the leadership of a dynamic new queen, proclaimed many generations of admiring historians, the English state was transformed and its people eventually found the resources and sea power to meet the Spanish and Portuguese threat head on. Elizabeth's apotheosis came in 1588 with the defeat of the Armada. In its wake, England began to send its sailors and merchant-men into the very eastern waters so long controlled by the Portuguese. Royal actions in this period embodied a new spirit of endeavour and national enterprise. The crown supported two circumnavigations of the globe: Francis Drake's in the years 1577–80 and Thomas Cavendish's, during 1586–88. Charters were granted to merchants who wished to trade in the Mediterranean and Africa, and royal encouragement was given to aristocrats who wanted to establish

English settlers in America. Here, at last, was a leader and her people in accord, dismissing the uncertainties of the previous age, and thrusting England into the European and, through this, world trading structures.

Did it happen this way? Was there a simple cause and effect in this historical context to deal with a pressing problem in Tudor trade aspirations? The answer must be, not really: only the simple chronology of voyages and grants by the crown is accurate in accounts such as the one outlined above. The rest requires severe qualification and revision. True, Elizabethan England was undoubtedly a place of change, both in its domestic affairs and dealings with foreign powers. Yet it would be folly to say that the state and its ruling élites controlled this change or that it was beneficial to the people as a whole. Indeed, many of the latest opinions on Elizabethan governance and economic management present a very unflattering picture of this period in England's past, with some historians believing that Elizabeth allowed the state to become 'ungovernable' altogether (Guy 1984: 264). In this light it can be seen that the benefits from trade expansion which did accrue to the nation and its mercantile communities over the last part of the sixteenth century frequently had more to do with luck and happenstance than deliberate planning.

Two or three of these factors affecting England's trade performance are worthy of note in illustrating this point. First there were unpredictable changes within the state itself that provided a solid basis for a more concerted attack on the Spanish–Portuguese monopoly. The spectacular growth of London as a great port and financial centre, in particular, had a profound impact on England's ability to raise the money and ships required for long high-risk voyages to the East. London's growth also provided a huge market for exotic products brought in from abroad, and, in turn, the town served as a distribution centre for the domestic markets already developing in response to the advent of agricultural reform and population growth (Wrigley and Schofield 1989: 208–9, 472). Recent scholarship has illustrated that in the sixteenth and seventeenth centuries the English economy with its expanding agricultural production, markets and mining was a unique case in comparison to other European economies. The country was spared the worst aspects of decline and crisis that afflicted Spain and France, especially in the period 1600–40, and then, later on, Holland (Brenner 1976; 1982 and Levine and Wrightson 1991). True, the English merchant community was hardly homogenous. Tensions existed between London and the outports over control and distribution of goods from abroad and the granting of monopolies to favourites and royal benefactors at home. Nevertheless, trade and profit on the sea-routes to the East represented a new frontier of economic opportunity in the view of many English merchants at this time, and with the growth of the City's financial and commercial power came the confidence to exploit it. Outlets for investment were limited and the desire for profits did not always lead into legitimate pursuits for wealth on this frontier. Unregulated privateering and piracy, as the pioneering research of Andrews has shown, proved no less important in the push for English overseas expansion than the mere public trading and settlement companies (Andrews 1978). Activity of this sort often became an embarrassment to the state rather than a benefit, as the economic rewards of piracy could be offset by a diplomatic crisis, leading, as it did in 1588, to war.

A second exogenous factor in the changes within the state was the remarkable interest in the activities and adventures of English mariners that arose in this period. A wave of propaganda about opportunity in the new worlds of the Atlantic and East Indies found expression in anthologies, pamphlets, ballads and translations. Richard Hakluyt is the most famous author of this genre, but he represents only the tip of an iceberg promoting English enterprise overseas. The scholar who documented the development of this literature pointed astutely to the fact that a 'literary empire' existed in England long before the trading or territorial empires (Parker 1965). All this printed documentation, some of it fact some of it fiction, educated and excited people, creating an atmosphere in which there was sympathy and encouragement for the push to break the Iberian strangle-hold on extra-European trade routes. The attraction of the literary empire in the late sixteenth century was that it possessed the right mix of nascent nationalistic fervour, religious zeal and economic determinism. Herein was offered the broadest appeal to English ambitions overseas with least offence to traditional mercantile interests.

A third factor over which the English government had no control, but which undoubtedly assisted the interests of its traders, was the decline of Portuguese power in the East. The zenith of Portugal's empire in the East occurred in the early sixteenth century, but by the late Elizabethan period it had suffered a severe eclipse. The amalgamation of the Spanish and Portuguese crowns in 1580; a small population, a lack of capital, and resources spread far too thinly from Africa to the Moluccas took its toll on Portugal's will over the sixteenth century. By 1600 the Portuguese found it impossible to give full financial and military support to its imperial administrators in the face of European competition and the open hostility of those suffering the rough hand of Portugal's direct rule around the globe (Boxer 1969; 1980). To say that there was a power vacuum in the structure of European trade to the East would be overstating the case; there appeared, however, an opportunity for supplanting this ailing power in eastern waters. Whether or not the English could exploit this opportunity was a matter for conjecture. On the surface the pre-conditions for an aggressive mercantile policy in the East did exist. The ministers of state could rely on the support of their subjects for bold policy initiatives, and the expertise involved in raising capital, commanding long deep-sea voyages and providing logistical support for these enterprises had more or less been mastered by 1600. By dint of good timing and developments beyond the government's control, in fact, the necessary elements for fulfilling the dream of direct access to eastern markets seemed to have dropped in England's lap by the end of the sixteenth century.

In the event, nearly all these advantages were thrown away. Rather than the English exploiting these opportunities, it was the Dutch who seized the initiative in the East and prospered at Portugal's expense. In the period from 1580 to 1689, the history of Dutch enterprise in developing a trading empire in the East Indies is one of unmitigated success. The commercial and cultural fluorescence that drove Holland into prominence in the trans-oceanic trading worlds of this era has lately been revealed in its entire illuminating detail, and termed a 'Golden Age' (Schama 1987). This success would offer a stark contrast to the English experience over the same era. Despite a small population and a constant struggle against Spanish dominance, the Dutch not only engineered the ships, the sailors and capital investment required to dislodge Portugal in the East but also expanded their position over the next century to monopolize the most profitable of all markets sought after by Europeans – spices. Where the Dutch were aggressive at the end of the sixteenth century in pushing their eastern design, the Elizabethan government proved timid. The expertise of the English merchants and their mariners did not receive the official encouragement enjoyed by their competitors. It is often assumed that this official indifference was irrelevant in the general economic development of the early modern English state; that such matters resolved themselves in the market place over the *longue durée*. This is too modern an interpretation. Foreign policy, and the concomitant foreign trade relations of the period, were in the firm control of the crown. Deep-sea sailors from England instigating trade in foreign waters without official sanction, did so at their peril. No one doubted then that treaties with European powers and grants to chartered trading companies controlled by the crown were inextricably linked, for the simple reason that good relations with a country like Portugal or Spain depended so clearly on a lack of friction in trading concerns either in Europe or the wider world. Such concerns produced, in their turn, an overtly cautious approach in English diplomatic dealings with Spain up to 1588 (and arguably beyond), and they certainly infected the ministerial view of whether or not to support an aggressive trade policy in the East.

It would be straightforward to place the responsibility for this timidity solely on fear of the Iberian, and, later, Dutch navies, which was real enough even after the dispersal of the Armada in 1588. However, the cautious official Elizabethan view of developing a direct trade to the East was a little more complicated than this. The neglected element in this story is that at first the crown chose the wrong vehicle with which to reach its goal in the East between 1588 and 1600. Before this period, the English experience of securing direct access to Eastern markets had revolved around developing sea routes to the north-west and north-east. This design had proved a miserable failure and by mid-century the English were confronted with the choice between accepting permanent exclusion from these markets or rethinking the whole approach to Eastern trade. It is the belief of leading scholars on early modern Europe that, under Elizabeth, exclusion was no longer acceptable to her merchant classes, who demanded an aggressive foreign policy of the type being pursued by the Dutch. Elizabeth and her ministers were willing to go some way down the road to meeting these demands, but not the whole distance. Instead of favouring trade development to the East by sea voyaging, the crown chose to focus English endeavour on the old overland routes, running from the Mediterranean ports of modern Lebanon, south-east to the Persian gulf, then on to India and the spice islands.

This policy initiative did not originate with Elizabeth but under her predecessor, Mary I, when she granted a royal charter to the Muscovy Company in 1555. This charter not only ratified the specific, though, at this time, negligible trade contacts with Russia, but, significantly, also sought to gain a more secure access to Eastern products coming overland through territories under Russian influence. Elizabeth and her ministers saw the merits of this policy and continued to provide official encouragement for the overland trade. In 1566 the Muscovy Company received a grant of new monopoly rights to trade in Persia, Armenia and the Caspian Sea region; subsequently, in 1581, all pretences at concealing England's real intentions in the Middle East were abandoned with the founding of the Levant Company. The sole purpose of the Levant Company was to raise English involvement in the trade of products from eastern markets by any means possible, and this mission attracted serious attention from the state and merchants alike. Two of the Company's own adventurers, Ralph Fitch and John Newberry, themselves actually travelled overland to India and on to the Moluccas between 1583 and 1591 in pursuit of this goal. In theory there seemed nothing untoward in this policy decision. The English had long had experience of securing eastern products along these routes. This access represented the safe political and economic choice for Elizabeth and her ministers, and, furthermore, it appeared the least hazardous and provocative in the existing state of European power politics.

Unfortunately for the crown and its ministers, this policy carried a couple of basic flaws when it came to enactment, in that the overland route proved neither safe nor profitable. At almost the very moment that the Levant Company came into being to expand and exploit the market for eastern goods via the caravan routes from India, the whole trade appeared on the verge of ruin. Two concerns loomed large in English despair for the future. First, the Levant Company simply did not have the resources to protect its products on the journey from south-east Asia and India to the Mediterranean. Second, in the 1580s and 1590s it became apparent that the Dutch had begun to secure a sea route to the eastern spice islands at the expense of Portugal. If not checked, it would only be a matter of time before Holland seized control of the European market in eastern products. Worse still, the recognizably superior naval technology and financial organizations of the Dutch state could guarantee any monopoly acquired in the East for some time to come. It could be said, therefore, that by the 1590s the English had progressed no further towards fulfilling the dream of direct access to eastern markets since Cabot set sail a hundred years earlier.

SEA AND SPICES

The choices facing the English crown in the light of rising Dutch hegemony in eastern trade at the end of the sixteenth century were thus stark and uninviting. As faith in the viability of the overland route to the East evaporated in the 1590s, it became imperative to address the central issue of combating another era of exclusion. At first

Elizabeth and her ministers dithered. In government circles the hope of avoiding expense and foreign hostility lingered, but by the end of the century no safe choices existed on this matter. The north-west and north-east passages to the East had been found wanting, and the favoured overland enterprise, despite the best efforts of the Muscovy and Levant Companies, proved inadequate. A belated attempt to revamp the Levant Company occurred in 1593 to meet these deficiencies. The queen issued a new charter, granting the Company permission to gain direct access to eastern trade goods by either 'land or sea', in areas already under the influence of other Europeans.[4] This grant represented an important philosophical break with past thinking on access, but meant little without the right financial and logistical backing. The logic of the situation pointed towards eschewing traditional remedies and accepting the previously unpalatable necessity of focusing English efforts on the development of a long sea route to the East, with all the economic and diplomatic pitfalls that might entail.

This logic at first impressed the London mercantile community rather more than the queen and her Council. The merchants proved keener on a new approach to eastern trade because they had bitter practical experience of past failings, and an awareness that a concerted effort between the state and its traders was the only policy left to break the cycle of exclusion. In fact some merchants were not prepared to wait for the crown to come around to their way of thinking in the 1590s. At least two small fleets were fitted out by London merchants involved with the Levant Company for trading to the East, and both ended in disaster. Of the two, James Lancaster's voyage in 1591 is the best known because records exist to show that he actually traded in the East Indies. However, none of his three ships or crew returned, only Lancaster himself after a tortuous journey that ended in the West Indies where a French privateering vessel brought him home in 1594. The other fleet, under Robert Dudley, set sail in 1596, and though it made landfall in the East, none of the ships or their crews are known to have returned to England, excepting for one man rescued by the Dutch from Mauritius in 1601 (Williamson 1961: 122–3).

The inadequacy of such high-risk private voyages, combined with the underlying English misconceptions about eastern trade, convinced the London merchants once and for all that a single organization, boasting considerable resources, was now required. To convince the City merchants of a change of approach was one thing, to persuade the crown of the efficacy of this way of proceeding was quite another. In effect, what the merchants wanted in establishing a trading company for the East by royal charter was a declaration of economic war on Spain and Holland. Viewed from the royal perspective this looked like a recipe for eternal expense and a diplomatic denouement. Nevertheless, the merchants pulled it off. Right at the last moment, it seemed, the crown threw off a century of attachment to the safe and cautious policies in a last-gasp effort to break the mould of exclusion from eastern markets.

What caused this royal conversion to supporting the idea of one organization reliant on a sea route for access to eastern markets? In answering this question it is necessary to examine the position of both the crown and the merchants. From the royal court's vantage point, the granting of monopolies was attractive because monopolies provided much-needed capital to a monarchy verging on bankruptcy. In addition, the economy was depressed and allowing the creation of monopolistic trading companies proved an inexpensive way of stimulating economic activity and enterprise (Guy 1988: 399–401). To the merchants and their allies in London the view was somewhat different from the politicians' whose faith in the failed traditional routes had prolonged the indecision on alternative policies. There were two interlocking elements to the merchants' campaign in the 1590s to bring the crown into line with their designs in the East: the first was propaganda, and the second, an assiduous cultivation of connections and influence at the Elizabethan court. In view of the nature of overseas trade, it is not surprising that the propaganda element in this campaign concentrated on the monetary value of sea-borne trade in the East.

When petitions for an eastern trading company began arriving in the queen's council chamber in 1599–1600, they contained remarkably precise figures about what trade to the East would be worth to an English company, and, by implication, to the state through the taxes levied on imports. This information was gleaned from different and diverse sources, including documentation and manifests from Portuguese East Indiamen captured in 1588 and 1593, along with statistical information contained in a translation of the Dutch author van Linschoten, who had resided in India for six years before publishing his findings on the economics of trade between Europe and the East in 1595–96. The message carried in these documents and published work could not be ignored. There was a vast market in Europe for eastern products, particularly spices; the profits to be had from such a trade could be enormous; and if all went well, the state could only enrich itself from being involved in such an enterprise.

The merchants took no chances with their campaign, and sought the advice of Richard Hakluyt when compiling the case for an eastern trading company out of London. Hakluyt performed this public relations duty well because he had the literary skills, and made use of his contacts at court, such as the Earl of Cumberland and Sir Thomas Smith, who had the ear of the queen and her advisers. The thrust of their argument to the crown about the necessity for a new trading company bore, as ever, on the value of the commerce to the state in times of trouble with the traditional overland routes. They also stressed the fact that immediate action was required to avoid falling prey to Dutch control of the European market in eastern goods, especially spices. The new company was to be an offshoot of the Levant organization; not unnaturally, because its sponsors and trading designs overlapped. What these petitioners to the crown had in mind was that the Levant Company would continue to import durable goods such as textiles, gems, silks and the like from the traditional overland routes, while the new company's ships would sail directly to the East Indian islands to gain direct access to the spice markets.

All in all it proved a powerful case, and the more difficult to resist in 1600 when it became public knowledge that the Dutch fleets had beaten the English to the punch. The return of six Dutch ships from the East Indian islands in 1599, laden with a vast array of oriental commodities, set off what could only be described as a panic amongst London traders connected with the Levant and its products. These English observers had visions of the planned eastern enterprise for developing a direct trade by sea collapsing around their ears (Chaudhuri 1965: 11–13). Under the auspices of the Lord Mayor of London in the autumn of 1600, the London merchants and their political allies decided upon a collective action to meet the Dutch threat to their plans. They decided to petition the crown for backing in the struggle to outmanoeuvre the Dutch and establish British trade in the East. After several meetings between September and December 1600, these merchant bodies presented a great petition to Queen Elizabeth, requesting the formation of a new trading company. The motive and intent behind these actions, and eventual resolutions, took aim squarely at Dutch pretensions in the East. The English petitioners told the queen that they had been

> induced by the success of the voyage performed by the Dutch nation and being informed that the Dutchmen prepare for a new voyage . . . stirred up no less affection to advance the trade of their native Country . . . and upon that affection have resolved to make a voyage to the East Indies if her majesty will be pleased to add to their intention the better to perform the enterprise.[5]

It was under such immediate pressure and the financial contingencies mentioned earlier that Elizabeth and her ministers finally gave in on the quest for the Cape sea route on 31 December 1600, granting a charter establishing 'The Governor and Company of Merchants of London, Trading into the East-Indies'.

NOTES

1. Madden and Fieldhouse, *Select Documents*, I, 235–6.
2. The comments are made in the Introduction to Stevens, *The Dawn of British Trade to the East Indies*, p. xxiv. Similar sentiments can be found in Sainsbury's introduction to the *Calendar of State Papers: East Indies 1513–1616*, II, pp. viii-ix.
3. Madden and Fieldhouse, *Select Documents*, I, 212.
4. Cawston and Keane, *Early Chartered Companies*, p. 73.
5. Stevens, *The Dawn of British Trade to the East Indies*, p. 8.

CHAPTER TWO

The Formative Years: 1600–60

There has been a tendency in modern scholarship that concerns itself with English expansionism in the seventeenth century to treat the first sixty years of East India Company history as an aside. The push into the northern Atlantic and Caribbean has received more scholarly attention, and, as a result, assumed more importance in both general and specialized studies dealing with early modern European expansionism. It was not always so. In the late nineteenth and first half of the twentieth century several worthy volumes told the detailed story of the perseverance and enduring initiative that turned the East India Company into a world-wide trading and territorial power in the century and a half after its founding (e.g. Hunter 1899–1900 and Foster 1933). The fact that such accounts have been neglected in the post-war world is a matter of regret, but this oversight can be explained by recognizing that such histories presented a picture of England's past somehow divorced from the mainstream accounts of the nation's past. The development of the imperial school of history, into which the story of the East India Company fell most readily, created the impression that the Company's experience belonged solely in the category of overseas ventures that possessed their own imperatives and context.

Of late these artificial divisions of the nation's history have been challenged, and less tolerance shown for delineating the overseas experience as somehow separate from the domestic scene of the early modern period (Lawson 1986; Cressy 1987; Bayly 1989; Bowen 1991). This revision appears a very positive development because it provides a means of marrying the excellent pre-war studies on the East

India Company to the more modern pioneering work of social, economic and political historians of seventeenth-century England. Indeed, in what follows it is intended to explore the argument that the East India Company's formative years are inextricably bound up with mainstream developments in the English state. As England's fortunes at home and abroad rose and fell, so did those of the Company, and three eras characterize the East India Company's experience in the first sixty years of its existence. First came two enthusiastic decades in which prospects and optimism about performance appeared at a premium. This era then gave way to two decades (1620–1640) that were not so bright, being smitten with internal and external crises and threats to disband the whole enterprise. The last twenty years of this formative period to 1660 proved unique and complicated to say the least, including as they did civil war and republican government in England. Nevertheless, just when the Company reached the brink of extinction in the 1650s, Oliver Cromwell initiated a new beginning for the eastern enterprise, laying the foundations for future expansion and prosperity.

THE MAKING OF THE EAST INDIA COMPANY

To explain why the first twenty years of operations proved so rewarding and exciting for 'the Company of Merchants of London trading into the East Indies' it is necessary to look at the specific actions taken by the Company itself. Those entrepreneurs involved in the organization's initial experiences certainly seized the moment. The decline of Portuguese power in the East, and a trade upturn in northern Europe provided a perfect setting for an assertive approach to building the English company from scratch. There was no room for faint hearts because long-distance trade to the Orient was a precarious business operation. Contemporary observers and commentators were well aware of the dangers awaiting navigators in eastern seas. The English would first have to overcome the enormous physical privations of such voyaging, and then deal with the endemic menace of Dutch competitors, piracy and shipwreck. After surmounting these hurdles, the problem of breaking into centuries-old trading patterns had still to be confronted. And, to make matters worse, there was little demand for English products in these markets.

That any trading organization could overcome such inauspicious prospects says much about those involved in its foundation. The initial accomplishment lay in the nature and wording of the original charter granted by the crown to those petitioning for an eastern trading company. Whereas certain clauses relating to structure and ownership were common to other chartered ventures of the time, trading and colonizing overseas, the East India Company was exceptional in that it received privileges which were not permitted to other concerns such as the Muscovy or Levant Companies.[1] First of all, enacting clauses in the charter ensured that the Company would be a restricted trading concern whose focus lay entirely on trade and profit, not conquest and colonization. The arming of vessels involved in the eastern trade was as belligerent as the Company could be at this stage. Indeed, to give the trading imperative added weight, the Company was granted a monopoly of all trade from England to the East. Second, financial organization of the Company's structure would be based on a joint-stock concept rather than the more common medieval practice of regulated trading concerns. Third, the Company could carry bullion out of the realm to exchange for trade goods in the East contrary to all existing laws regarding such movements of the nation's wealth. Fourth, and last, the internal organization of the Company's administration was laid down in the charter. In subsequent years, the Governor, with a deputy, and the committee men were to be elected annually by a ballot in the general assembly of shareholders (known as the Court); and the Court could remove the Governor by a vote, if it so wished.[2]

Of these four unique factors, the joint-stock concept has commonly been emphasized as the real breakthrough in trading practice, leading the Company to success. It seems to represent the singular innovation that divides the medieval from the modern approach to modes of international exchange. Such views require correction however. In theory the joint-stock concept of pooled risk appeared an innovative solution to investing in eastern trade. The idea was borrowed from the experience of the Venetians and Dutch, who saw the benefit of many small investors in the state sharing the burden of supporting this sort of unpredictable, long-distance trade enterprise. In good times dividends would be paid and everyone would benefit, in bad, no individual investor with a small stake in the project would go bankrupt because of a business downturn or failure. The old regulated companies had not worked in this fashion. Three or four large investors had combined to support one specific voyage, sometimes investing all their wealth in the venture. If the venture succeeded, the profits were divided amongst the three or four investors and huge fortunes could be made. If the regulated project failed, however, the cost could be enormous to individual investors, resulting most often in personal ruin and penury for the family concerned.

In this context, it can be seen why the idea of pooling risk in the form of joint stock to support a trading venture of some three years' duration appealed to East India Company investors. The majority recognized that the old regulated company practice of drawing up one subscription per outward voyage, with any profit being divided amongst the subscribers on its return, simply would not do for the long-haul trade to the East Indies. Yet it would be naive to expect the merchants of England to abandon the habits of a lifetime overnight; no matter what it said about joint-stocks in the East India Company's charter. The move from regulated to joint-stock practices, therefore, proved an understandably gradual process. The East India Company began as an adjunct to the 'regulated' operations of the Levant Company, and the same rules of investment practice applied to the junior partner at the outset of its operations. For the first twelve voyages to the spice islands between 1601–13, East India Company subscribers behaved like regulated company investors, committing money to one voyage only and awaiting its return before reinvesting. Only in 1614 did the first joint-stock voyage take place, and even then it was limited to a four-year subscription (Chaudhuri 1965: 226–27). In fact, not until 1657 can it actually be said the Company became a genuine joint-stock endeavour – that is continuous, unlimited investment taking place without reference to individual voyages, and stocks being valued and traded accordingly at the Company's headquarters in Leadenhall Street, London.

Eschewing this traditional focus on joint stocks then, it is more helpful in an analysis of the Company's early success to look at the administrative structure of the organization and its trading privileges. The English may have been slow in coming to terms with the practicalities of eastern trade, but they soon mastered the fundamental business skills of trading-company capitalism after 1601. The Company that evolved from the original charter succeeded because it possessed a sophisticated administrative structure that paid attention to details, and a mandate that everyone understood as being focused on trade and profit. The governor and committee system permitted speedy executive decisions to be taken; an absolute necessity in a trading endeavour where resources were tied so closely to fleets returning from voyages of over two years' duration. There were twenty-four individual Directors responsible for the same number of 'committees', reporting directly to the Governor and his deputy. This structure encouraged stability and strong leadership in the organization. The work of each Director covered the day-to-day business of operating the Company's workshops and ships, as well as its central administration. This meant that the executive could always be in touch with the most mundane Company activity, ranging from the slaughterhouse to the number of silver rials required for the next voyage. The early records of the Company are replete with the administrative minutiae necessary to the running of any successful business, and it is this attention to detail which explains the East India Company's early rise to profitability.[3]

Thus the Company was modern because of its command structure rather than its investment practices. Nothing was left to chance in the decision-making process. The Company's assets also boasted a very efficient postal system and a splendid headquarters in the heart of London, accessible to the investors and in close proximity to wharves and warehouses owned and controlled by the organization (Foster 1924). No less important in this story of building a sophisticated company was the practice of keeping meticulous records and open book accounts, along with Court procedures of debate and voting modelled after those in parliament. Such modes of proceeding lent an air of confidence and optimism which proved invaluable to raising and sustaining capital in this new endeavour. Projecting the image of a solid company with good prospects persuaded investors to put up the requisite sums of money to launch the early trade ventures. This proved no small matter. The amount subscribed for the first voyage in 1601 totalled around £70,000 – a huge sum for an undeveloped financial market like that of early seventeenth-century England. London itself, the capital city, lacked a large bank at this time and enjoyed no tradition of providing large-scale monetary support for this sort of mercantile enterprise.

The underpinning for this confident outlook, that made such drawbacks seem irrelevant to investors, can be found in the nature of the relationship the Company shared with the state through its royal charter. The crown created the initial and essential investor confidence in the Company by its grant of certain privileges. First there was the monopoly of importing oriental products, and, more significantly, the right to enforce the monopoly against interlopers in the trade. This grant was not novel in itself, but it was seen as an indispensable element of long-distance trade to guard against the unofficial or piratical voyager able to disrupt all the Company's efforts. Second, the charter allowed the Company to export bullion out of the realm to buy goods in the ports of the Indian Ocean; these could then be used for barter and exchange in the spice islands. In an age of economic theory which measured a nation's wealth in terms of hard currency or metal this was a dispensation truly worth having (Jack 1977: 46–60). This privilege made the Company's task of breaking into the pattern of trade in spices that much easier; not least because the transported silver rials were worth three or four times their European value in the East. Third, and last, the very fact of the crown granting the charter to the Company implied official sanction, which proved crucial in overcoming early doubts over which direction trade policy should take. No one questioned the belief that the state wished this enterprise to succeed for reasons of revenue enhancement. Eventually this close relationship between the English government and the Company would be seen to have both positive and negative aspects; but, for those involved at the launch of the Company's trade, proximity to the councils of state was viewed in the most positive light.

The cause of this enthusiasm is not difficult to identify in view of the practical problems facing the Company in its formative period of operation. The fact that the crown had chartered the Company not only gave a welcome boost to morale to all involved in it but also necessitated the specific duties of issuing commissions for every voyage undertaken, providing warrants for each shipment of bullion, and assisting in a judicial or administrative capacity on such diverse matters as defaulting investors and dereliction of duty by the Company's seamen.[4] The East India Company was not a quasi-national endeavour like its main competitor, the Dutch East India Company, because the English charter licensed a company of individual adventurers to manage their own affairs and trade in the East, under their own coat of arms and colours. This Company would only be checked if such activity threatened national diplomatic goals and priorities. Yet the state and the English Company remained enmeshed in this endeavour over the next two centuries partly for the obvious reason that both hoped to profit from it but, no less importantly, for the simple reason, as Hunter elegantly put it so long ago, that the Company 'drew its very existence from Royal prerogative' (Hunter 1899–1900, I: 256). The Company's founders and their successors never lost sight of this reality, and exploited it to the full. The needs of the crown and its ministers had to be considered because privileges granted by charter could just as easily be taken away by the same agency. All that was required was three years' notice.

THEORY VERSUS REALITY

Did the early voyages live up to such high expectations? The answer is yes and no. Many facets of the Company's performance in the first twenty years or so of its existence can, and at the time were, considered to be an unmitigated success. Establishing a viable and profitable trade seemed to fulfil all the promise expressed in the wording of the original charter. Achieving this viability did involve a great deal of trial and error, however, because it soon became apparent to the Company and its captains that a bilateral mode of exchange between England and the spice islands was not feasible. There were not only the predilections of the native rulers and merchants to consider but also the open hostility of Dutch and Portuguese traders towards English interference in their theatres of operation. These European powers had a much greater influence, even control, over the local rulers in the Moluccas and Banda islands, where the sought-after cloves, nutmegs and peppers originated, than the London Company bargained for. Thus the Company's seamen quickly adapted and moulded their trading aspirations to meet these local realities. By the 1620s such adaptation had developed a revised trade pattern which, with certain variants, was modelled on Portuguese practices in the East. In its simplest form, this trade involved fleets leaving London with cargoes of bullion and trade goods, some of which were produced in England while others were obtained from exchanges in other European markets. These cargoes would be taken first to parts of the Red Sea, Persian Gulf or western mainland India and traded for textiles or related products. With these cargoes aboard, the East India Company ships would then proceed to East Indian islands such as Java or Sumatra, seeking to trade the textiles for spices. More often than not, the bulk of the cargo on the homeward journey would be pepper supplemented, by the 1630s and 1640s, with sugar, saltpetre, textiles and indigo. In the early sixteenth century there existed an enormous demand for pepper, in particular, and the early success of the Company rested on its importation and sales.

The Company's own records reveal the evolving pattern of exports and imports over the first forty years or so of trade activity. In 1601, £21,742-worth of bullion was exported and £6,860-worth of other trade commodities. These goods included woollen cloth, lead and tin originating in England, but the cargoes were also supplemented with exports such as ivory, iron, coral and quicksilver picked up in trade with other Europeans. Up to 1633 the ratio between exported bullion and commodities varied drastically only in certain years. In 1614–15, for example, approximately £50,000 worth of goods were sent east, as opposed to £40,000 of bullion. On average, the ratio heavily favoured bullion. In 1610 it was £19,200 to £28,508; in 1633 £115,900 to £45,800 and between 1633 and 1640 only bullion was sent. No commodities at all appear in the records.

The pattern that evolved for imports displays similarities to these trends in that one cargo, pepper, dominated Company trade over the first twenty-five years or so of its activity. By 1630 the total value of pepper imports to the Company had surpassed £1 million dwarfing all other trade goods in terms of profit. Pepper was an attractive cargo because of its light weight, easy transportation, but high value. The Company only sold a fraction of the pepper cargoes in Britain itself, making most of its money on re-exports to European markets, especially in the Baltic. There seemed for this brief period no limit to the appetite for this spice as a flavouring and preserving agent in the European diet. However, the bounty was shortlived because the English were not the only nation meeting this demand from the East. The Dutch had also reaped vast profits from the pepper trade, but by 1630 the market was saturated and the price collapsed. The situation was made worse by the general economic and credit crisis afflicting Europe at the time (Keay 1991: 111–29). It is after this point that the Company saw the sense of diversifying and other products began to figure more largely in the import ledgers. Spices other than pepper, like cloves, nutmeg, mace and cinnamon from the East Indian islands became more profitable. But more important were products from the Indian mainland, such as indigo, used in the dyeing industry, and saltpetre, used in preserving meats, gunpowder production and medicines. In addition, light textiles from India, such as calicoes and silk, became common items in the cargoes of Company imports to Britain. Many of these goods not only revolutionized consumer taste and manufacturing in Britain but, as time went on, lessened the necessity for so much bullion to be exported to the East.

To support this evolving trade pattern and ensure a constancy of supply when the Company's fleets went east, resident factors in charge of warehouses (factories) were introduced in the various ports of call. The factor's task was simply to establish the warehouse system so that when Company ships arrived they could exchange required trade goods without waiting for deals to be made with local merchants. These factors and their warehouses or factories fell under the control of the Factor General, who in the early years of the Company's operations was the extremely able and efficient administrator, Sir

William Keeling. His organizational skills alone did much to bring to fruition the goal of creating what Chaudhuri described as an 'interregional and integrated' trading system in place of the quickly discredited bilateral ideal (1965: 47). Rather than invite exclusion or conflict, the Company intended to slip into the nooks and crannies in the eastern trade structures which the native traders and other Europeans had ignored. The policy appeared to work well at first, as the scale of Company operations after only two decades bears witness. By the early 1620s the English Company had factories established in the Red Sea ports, like Muscat; on the Indian mainland at places such as Surat in the West and Masulipatam in the East; in nearly all the East Indian spice islands trading with Europeans, and even in Japan at Hirado – from which base it was expelled in 1623.

No less impressive in this exercise of trial and error were the diplomatic efforts that went into securing this position. Several examples could be cited where such efforts led to success for the Company's trade, but there is none better perhaps than that of obtaining permission to establish a factory on the Indian mainland. The Company's initial concern with a base at Surat on the north-west coast could hardly be described as overwhelming. The Portuguese had bases on this coast at places such as Goa, Calicut and Diu, and the English perceived their use as transition points in trade to the spice islands not, as would transpire later, centres for all Company activity in the region. To achieve the privilege of a base at Surat, however, meant dealing directly with the Mogul Empire which ruled most of northern and central India at that time. Indeed, the gift of allowing foreigners trading rights on territory under Mogul control lay with the Emperor himself. Coming to terms with this eastern power of which they had little experience proved no straightforward affair for the English Company; and it involved a strategy of four painstaking stages before a secure base was granted. To start with, the Company had to educate itself about the nature of Mogul power in India at the beginning of the seventeenth century. From the outside this Indian dynasty appeared like any other imperial power known to Europeans. The Moguls, or as they were originally known, Mongols, had invaded India from the North over a century earlier, and by 1600, under the leadership of the great Emperor, Akbar, brought about 75 per cent of the sub-continent under their control, including most of the ports favoured by Europeans. Yet superficial judgements could be misleading, for when the Company's representatives made a closer inspection of Mogul power they soon realized that it was exercised in a particular manner. Most important of all, the influence of the Islamic rulers did not pervade Indian Hindu society or institutions, as might be expected from such a powerful dynasty – a lesson the English learned well much later. The Moguls used client rulers in conjunction with imperial agents to undertake the basic administrative goal of the Royal Court at Agra, which was always the raising of revenue. In general terms the Islamic Mogul rulers remained quite remote from the mass of alien peoples under their charge; points of contact were restricted in the main to the visits of tax collectors and occasionally the courts that supported their work (Wolpert 1989: 126–49).

As the Company became acquainted with these practicalities, it did not take long to further realize the necessity of opening a direct negotiation with the Mogul Court. Again, this was not a straightforward matter because the Portuguese, from the beginning, proved hostile to English entreaties. Portugal's long-established presence in Agra gave them sufficient influence to persuade the Emperor to dismiss approaches from what they described as a minor European power out to disturb the peace in this eastern trading world. The Company switched its tactics, therefore, and in the third phase of its strategy canvassed a direct relationship between the English monarchy and the Mogul Emperor. In 1608 King James I fell in line with this plan, and granted William Hawkins an embassy to the Emperor, Jahangir, with the aim of obtaining approval for permanent English factories on Indian soil. Hawkins arrived at the Mogul Court in 1609, and proved a good choice for the mission. He spoke Turki, the language of the Emperor, and possessed a good understanding and knowledge of the ways this imperial power operated. Not even Hawkins, however, could overcome Portuguese hostility and their anti-English sentiment at the court. After two years in Agra, Hawkins left India with a bride, an official, though honorary, title, a lot of goodwill, but precious little else. The East India Company fleet that arrived in Surat after his mission was rebuffed in its attempt to trade, and dealings with the Mogul Court looked destined to end in frustration and failure.

It was at this point that East India Company strategy moved into an unexpected fourth and decisive phase. In 1613 two Company ships commanded by Thomas Best anchored downstream from Surat at a place known as Swally Roads. Best's purpose was to trade with native merchants when the opportunity arose, but the Portuguese decided to resist this move with armed force. In the prolonged naval engagement that ensued, however, Best forced the Portuguese to withdraw and completed his trading mission. Two years later a similar altercation took place at this spot, and with the same result, when Nicholas

Downton defeated a large fleet under Portuguese command. These events had a profound impact on the Emperor and his advisers who were not slow to see the evidence of a change in European power-broking, taking place before their own eyes. The Mogul Empire had no regular navy of its own and had always favoured the client sea power of the Portuguese for policing trade in the area. Now the Emperor's policy options appeared to need revision. If the English guns were to predominate at sea, the Emperor needed to bring them within his imperial orbit. In the aftermath of these victories it came as no surprise that the official permission, or *firman,* was sent from the Emperor's court, allowing the East India Company to post factors and build warehouses in the Mogul's dominions. In 1617 the Emperor also received a resident English ambassador, Sir Thomas Roe, at his court, as a courtesy to King James I. None of these privileges took the form of what Europeans would recognize as treaty obligations. These grants by the Emperor represented favours to foreign minions or, as Jahangir put it more politely in his letter to James I, favours to a junior partner in 'this league of friendship'.[5]

To the Company in London such detail was of no immediate concern because it had secured the sought-after bases in India which at the time appeared an invaluable stepping stone to the spice island trade. For historians, however, the implications of what had happened at Surat are worthy of discussion in the broader context of the Company's development. It was an inescapable fact that the East India Company's diplomacy had only succeeded because of its armaments. In strict theoretical terms such actions contradicted the Company's mandate and should have been censured at the very least. Yet the engagements of Surat and others at Ormuz less than a decade later, in 1622, when Company forces combined with the local Persian ruler to force the Portuguese from this Gulf base, provided a simple illustration of how the demands of local emergencies could override directives from London. Whether or not the Company intended or concocted a deliberate policy of aggression in these years is impossible to say from the evidence extant. But with the passage of time it has not stopped scholars from debating the point. At one extreme there are those who view the Company's actions as a classical example, in Marxist terminology, of the rise of European usury capitalism. The more powerful financial and technological resources of the West exploited and then distorted the legitimate aspirations of the Indian people (Mukherjee 1974). More restrained versions of this thesis point out that whether or not the English Company designed an aggressive policy, everyone could see that the use of force could result in more profit. It was axiomatic, therefore, that when the opportunity arose, force would be used (Chaudhuri 1978). The ultimate logic of the framework within which the Company operated was that the trade would be an armed trade.

At the other end of the spectrum of modern historical analyses of these events are the more pragmatic views. Of these, the most dominant interpretation in western scholarship at present admits that force was used by the English Company, but usually with very little thought given to its longer-term impact on trading policy (Marshall and Williams 1982). A second hybrid of this pragmatic school posits the very practical and sensible argument that clearly many instances of English aggression occurred, but it is equally clear that in most cases of armed conflict the Company was on the receiving end of local or European hostility. The logistics of policing and expanding eastern trade by force of arms was simply beyond the Company's capabilities, and made it impossible even to respond to small provocations (Watson 1980a). The limited armaments on Company ships evolved in the defence against pirates and interlopers, not as the cutting edge of aggressive trade expansion. On the whole the Company's captains remained true to the instructions issued in London never to initiate hostilities. The scholars canvassing these views of English restraint have a point when they maintain that talk of a planned, armed expansionism by the East India Company badly misconstrues the place of seventeenth-century trade priorities and policies within the context of the state's available resources. This debate has to be addressed by anyone dealing with the Company's development, but it is doubtful that it will ever be resolved to everyone's satisfaction because of the underlying ideological prejudices each scholar brings to the subject. One thing is certain, however: the debate cannot be ignored for it casts such a long shadow over the later history of the Company when it moved from being a trading organization to a territorial power.

To contemporary observers the only consideration that mattered after two decades of Company operations was profit, and in this matter there existed satisfaction all round. It has been estimated that in the period 1601–12, the Company invested £517,784 in capital and saw a return of 155 per cent profit on the original sum. In the years 1613–23 this performance declined somewhat as the Company's fixed costs in the East grew; nevertheless, the return was still healthy. On £418,691 of invested capital, average profit over the ten-year period came to some 87 per cent (Chaudhuri 1965: 22). If such a performance could be maintained, the future looked prosperous for both Company and investors alike. The East India Company's ability to adapt to the inter-port trade of the Indian Ocean and East Indian islands had the appearance of a master-stroke; with the bases on the Indian mainland offering welcome security to the vagaries of the spice trade. No less important, the high-powered London mercantile élite running the Company enjoyed support at the highest levels of government which was utilized to the full. Prince Charles, the king's son and heir, symbolized the closeness of this arrangement when he subscribed £6,000 of East India stock himself. By 1623 the Company seemed to have all eventualities in terms of organization and planning well covered.

THE COMPANY'S COMING OF AGE

Unfortunately for everyone involved in this enterprise, these figures and the Company's early performance flattered to deceive. The first two decades of growth and promise were followed by two of doubt and uncertainty. Company activities slumped; in the years 1628–31 its ships went no further East than the Persian Gulf, and there was talk of suspending trade operations altogether until matters improved. What caused this drastic turn-round in Company fortunes? First there were the intangible factors over which the Company had no control. Most prominent of these was a trade recession that struck the maritime nations of northern Europe particularly hard. The Company's trade had been buoyed by the economic upturn of the early seventeenth century, but it soon discovered the brutal reality of how quickly a recession could affect this rosy picture. The figures spoke for themselves: between the years 1617 and 1632 £1,629,040 of invested capital produced an average profit of 12 per cent – a reduction of some 73 per cent on the previous decade's performance. This downturn affected all parts of the domestic economy as well as overseas trade. The mass of evidence presented to parliament on this 'Decay of Trade' in the 1620s and 1630s, coupled with the published work on the slump, reveal the deep wounds inflicted on the nation's economy during this crisis.[6] To make domestic matters worse, the plague returned to England in 1625 and a dearth afflicted many parts of the country until 1631. The general European situation offered no relief from this gloom because of the destabilizing effect on trade of the Thirty Years War then being waged on the continent. A final unexpected blow to the Company's operations in this period arrived with the news of war and an horrendous famine in the state of Gujarat after 1630. This area around the Surat factory became so devastated that the Company had, for a time, to move its base of operations to Masulipatam on the east coast, with a consequent deleterious effect on performance and returns.

Against this perilous economic scene, the Company was obliged to undertake an immediate reassessment of all its trading and administrative procedures. Like any business organization today, this Company's early success had been fuelled by prospects of continued growth and expansion which appeared reasonable on the first twenty years' performance. Growth and expansion, however, had entailed a massive increase in capital costs, including factors' salaries, factory construction or provision, more armed escorts and much more manpower all round. When the recession occurred the Company found itself overextended. It had too many bases of operation in the East, often staffed by corrupt factors, producing insufficient returns for capital invested and dividends paid. From the 1620s onwards the Company sought to remedy this situation by a retrenchment and reorganization of its trade operations in the East. Bases were abandoned as a result, factors brought to account, and a far more conservative voyaging policy was initiated (Chaudhuri 1965). Through such measures the Company made it easier for its operations to survive the worst years of economic crisis, but in such years as 1627–28 and 1631, the severity of trade downturn emphasized the tenuous nature of both the Company's financial position and its future development. Nothing could be taken for granted within the economic framework in which the Company conducted its business.

Two or three other issues are worthy of note in this context of the Company's coming of age, as they shed light on the seriousness of the situation facing the whole enterprise at this juncture. Of these, the most familiar threat to the Company's viability was Dutch competition. The danger stemmed from the intrinsic superiority of the Dutch East India Company in its day-to-day operations. From its founding in 1602 the Dutch Company had been better financed, equipped with better fleets and given an explicit mandate to use any means available to secure and defend a monopoly of the eastern spice trade to Europe. This mission put real teeth into Dutch activity in the East, making it very unpleasant for other Europeans who crossed their path (Parker 1988: 132). The English Company simply could not compete on an equal footing with the Dutch, and this fact was made painfully obvious to those in London after the incident at Amboina in 1623 when ten Englishmen, among others, were tortured and put to death by the local Dutch commander. The issue became a *cause célèbre* in England and, eventually, a matter of national shame because, try as they might over the next twenty years, the English achieved nothing by way of redress. The Company base at Amboina was a legitimate operation, and yet the Dutch were powerful enough to treat all efforts at gaining recompense with contempt (Hunter 1899–1900, I: 383–434). Not until the 1650s and Cromwell's success in the Dutch wars was compensation for the relatives of Amboina's victims extracted from the Dutch East India Company.

The reverse at Amboina also became a symbol of the English Company's sudden lack of commitment to the spice island trade, for after 1623 there occurred a marked shift in the concentration of voyages away from the islands to the Indian mainland. It is still a matter of dispute whether or not this shift happened because of the Amboina incident or whether it simply represented the culmination of a process begun earlier in response to the downturn in trade. Whatever the reason, it cannot be denied that after 1623 the East India Company did redirect a great deal of its trade to Surat and Masulipatam, and contemporaries perceived this as the result of overwhelming Dutch strength rather than the Company's choice (Parry 1981: 200). From this point on the East India Company was forced to open trade and make money where it could rather than where it wished to. In practice, this meant the Company would operate in those areas of no interest or use to the Dutch.

Dutch success in trade competition with England leads naturally into a second factor that made life difficult for the East India Company, and this was the behaviour of the Stuart monarchy in the years 1603–40. It has been customary to present the early Stuarts' dealing with trade affairs in a wholly negative light. Scott, for example, wrote of James I in his great history of joint-stock companies that 'few sovereigns have restricted and disorganized trade more than he did, by the numerous and ill-considered burdens he laid upon it' (1910, I: 133). What little research and writing that has been done on this subject since Scott's magisterial study suggests that this judgement may be harsh. Davies probably gave a more accurate summary of trade policy under the early Stuarts when he portrayed it as 'a curious medley of inconsistencies' (1959: 334). There were, as this quotation intimates, good and bad aspects of crown policy on trade from 1603–40. It is a mistake to assume that neither James I nor Charles I had no appreciation of the East India Company's worth. On the contrary, in this period the monarchy was chronically short of funds to carry out the functions of governance expected of it, and it well knew that one source of wealth that flowed directly into royal coffers came from customs and imposts on overseas trade. In theory, the wealthier the East India Company became, the more money would accrue to the crown. James I and Charles I did appreciate this crucial fact about the Company's importance to the state's financial condition. By 1621 various royal levies on the Company's operations produced in the region of £20,000 per annum, and it was obviously in the crown's interest to ensure that this prosperity continued. Royal support for the Company manifested itself on many levels; as in the supremely important reaffirmation of the East India charter throughout these years and the protection of the pepper monopoly by Proclamation in 1609. In the darkest years of 1627–31 Charles I even offered to become a shareholder in the Company himself, in order that his 'favour and protection' might tide the troubled eastern trade over the recession.

These positive aspects of royal policy were, however, marred by other actions highly detrimental to the East India Company's fortunes in these years. James I and Charles I certainly wanted trade to the East to prosper, but from their viewpoint, surveying a depleted Treasury, it simply was not fulfilling the revenue demands expected from the enterprise. In particular, revenues from the punitive import duties levied on spices and peppers proved disappointing. This disappointment convinced the early Stuarts and their advisers that the eastern trade could be exploited to the further benefit of crown finances. An examination of the actions taken by James I and Charles I reveals an underlying scheme to persevere with the East India Company as the main agent of eastern trade while supplementing this enterprise with other private efforts under royal warrant. Two examples, one from each reign, demonstrate how disastrous this way of proceeding could be for the Company's trade and profit. The year 1618 was a desperate one for royal finances, and James I sanctioned one trade endeavour which he thought might help rescue the situation: he granted a charter to a group of petitioners led by Sir James Cunningham for the formation of a Scottish East India Company. The English Company, not surprisingly, looked upon the prospect of competition and duplication from an organization in its sister kingdom with horror, and lobbied the crown and anyone with influence at court to have the patent withdrawn. Such was the outcry at the idea of a Scottish Company that James acceded to the request for withdrawal of the patent, but only on condition that Cunningham be suitably indemnified and the East India Company 'lend' the king £20,000 – money that was never seen by the Company again. This piece of Jacobean statecraft cost the East India Company much in terms of hard cash and investor confidence, underlining the point that political contacts at court could not be neglected for a minute because the Company's fate was, at times like these, so closely bound up with that of the state.

Charles I was, in many ways, more proficient at exploiting untapped sources of revenue for the Royal Treasury than his father, and the eastern enterprise did not escape his own efforts at seeking supplementary levies from trade activity. The most poignant incident in this search came in 1637 when Charles I granted a private group of merchants, under the leadership of William Courteen and Endymion Porter, a patent to trade in those areas of the East not frequented by East India Company ships. This royal involvement in the Courteen Association, as it became known, was predicated solely on the belief that money could be raised for the crown in this risky endeavour. Charles I had every right to use his prerogative power in this manner, but the East India Company certainly believed that he had offended the spirit of the original charter to no good effect. And, as it happened, the Company was proved correct. Courteen's merchantmen operated in the Indian Ocean and China Seas for over fifteen years, but brought neither wealth nor honour to the English crown. The Association's activities frequently collapsed into piracy because of its inability to break into the established trading patterns in the East so fiercely guarded by other Europeans. These depredations, in turn, gave rise to a great deal of local hostility toward English traders generally, as it proved very difficult for native powers to distinguish between Courteen's vessels and seamen and those of the East India Company. Thus the crown's willingness to consider such surrogate trade organizations in the East again did nothing to promote confidence in the Company's future among investors at home. The patent for Courteen's Association ran out in the Interregnum, but by then the East India Company had expended a lot of money and manpower repairing the damage this band of freebooters inflicted on the eastern trade.

The last factor to be discussed in this story of the Company's coming of age did not carry the pure practical threat of either Dutch competition or Stuart statecraft, and yet the outcry against the East India Company's monopoly and trading privileges proved just as menacing to its survival. There were two main thrusts to the campaign on this front: the first had to do with political and philosophical objections to grants of monopolies as an abuse of prerogative power and a restriction of personal freedom; the second concentrated on the trading privileges granted to the Company. In short, many critics believed that the exclusive clauses of the Company's trading privileges had caused all manner of economic ills in early seventeenth-century England. Some of these complaints were reasonable, some bizarre, ranging from too little corn in the realm to the ruination of English shipping through long voyages in warm seas resulting in worm-eaten hulls!

Of the former argument, evidence of how dangerous criticisms of monopolies could be may easily be gleaned from the well-documented parliamentary campaigns on this subject over the first half of the seventeenth century. The matter came to the fore in 1604, in the so-called 'Free Trade Committee' of the House of Commons, and did not fade from prominence as an issue in any debate on the state of national trade up to 1660 and beyond.[7] The East India Company survived this direct assault on its monopoly by pleading that its organizational needs and trade goals represented a special case. The Company's supporters put forward the opinion, in both parliament and the press, that England's competitors secured monopolies in this trade for the very good reason that no other framework of exchange in the East could succeed. This case proved to be the winning position in the argument; but only just, and only with regard to the East India Company. Recent research has shown that the general concept of monopoly was offensive to many Englishmen on both practical and ideological grounds (Sacks 1990). In the case of the East India Company, for example, its critics made the very sensible and practical point, then and after, that the Company monopoly restricted the free and equitable involvement of merchants and towns outside London (the outports) in eastern trade because royal prerogative dictated that this should happen and precluded any means of redress. Attacks of this nature struck home, and the Company itself was frequently compelled to answer its critics. Typical of such work was the published petition to the House of Commons written by Thomas Mun on behalf of the Company of Merchants of London Trading to the East Indies. In this tract (of 1628) the 'privileges and immunities' enjoyed under the charter were presented as essential to the 'Strength, Wealth, Safety, Treasure and Honour' which the Company's activities bestowed on the nation. Contemporary recognition of the organization as a special case proved an enormous advantage to the Company's trade and competitive edge, but, like its relationship with the state, monopoly status had to be protected and cultivated for many years to come.

Scholars have usually placed less emphasis on the second thrust of this campaign – the attacks on the Company's trading privileges – in explaining its troubles during these formative years. However, this approach needs some qualification. Public and private documents on the economic crises in the reigns of James I and Charles I show an almost obsessive concern with the East India Company's privilege regarding the export of bullion. Critics saw this privilege as an evil common to all the country's economic ills. Company practice on this point came under the most severe attack at Westminster in the 1620s. For example, export of bullion was condemned in debates on 'The Cause of the Want of Money in England and Wales' in 1621; it appeared as one of eight factors that caused the whole trade depression also discussed in the Commons in 1621, and the export of bullion again figured as a principal grievance during the debates of 1624 on 'The Decay of Trade of the Outports' in 1624.[8] Few historians now dispute that theory on a well-managed economy in this period revolved around the ideal of favourable trade balances producing hard currency reserves for the nation (Keirn and Melton 1990). And it was in the context of such convictions that the East India Company's metal export practices fell under suspicion. What the Company had to do was to convince its critics that carrying bullion out of the country did not impoverish the economy. This provided a severe challenge to the Company's supporters, for it entailed a campaign to demonstrate that previous methods of measuring the nation's wealth were incorrect.

Fortunately for the East India Company it found the most able writers for the task at hand: for example, Dudley Digges and Thomas Mun. Mun's work, in particular, became most influential in defending and justifying the Company's innovative role in English trade expansion.[9] At the heart of Mun's defence of the East India Company against its critics lay two interlocking propositions. The first of these maintained that the Company's operations augmented the whole nation's wealth, not just that of London, through the re-export of eastern products to Europe from Britain. The second proposition argued that the Company's entire operation produced immense spin-off benefits to the nation's economy in areas such as shipbuilding, seamanship, victualling and all manner of banking and insurance services. Mun stressed repeatedly that although it appeared the export of bullion weakened the country's economic position, closer examination of the statistics illustrated that this type of trade exchange produced quite the opposite result. Indeed, numerical evidence was the inherent strength of Mun's analysis. His figures showed, for example, that England had saved some £75,000 up to 1621 by being involved directly in the spice trade: they also illustrated how

£100,000-worth of bullion spent in the East could result in £494,223 gross being returned to the English economy after straight sales of imports and re-exports of spices to Europe had been tabulated (Mun 1621: 23–4). It was to the Company's relief that none of its critics could match the sophistication of Mun's econometric postulations.

Such a brief summary cannot do justice to the scope of the theoretical and ideological battles over the role of the Company's monopoly and privileges in these years. But it is possible to deduce from just a cursory glance at the press and parliamentary debates how the East India Company's affairs pervaded national economic concerns. They influenced opinion on England's role as a trading nation and, in turn, had an impact on the organization of the internal economy at this formative stage in its development (Barber 1975: 5–28). By the mid-seventeenth century it had become apparent that this Company was not a simple trade body that could be left to its own devices. Its relationship with the crown through the monopoly charter grant made the Company an exception to the rules that governed other such companies. Moreover, its affairs were discussed openly at Westminster and in the press; and among its shareholders was a large body of MPs who took an active interest in ensuring the success of the eastern enterprise. These characteristics had played their part in helping the Company to weather the fierce storms of the first four decades of operation. By 1640 here was a sophisticated trade organization, hardened and matured by past experience, proclaiming in the annual report 'that affairs in India have never before been in a more hopeful condition . . . ' Little did anyone connected to the Company suspect that things could get worse over the next fifteen years or so.

TURMOIL AND TRIUMPH

The last twenty years of this period to 1660 proved traumatic for the nation, its people and institutions, and, in turn its economy and trade. The English, divided over religious and constitutional issues, were at war among themselves, and with Scotland, from 1642 to 1649. They then experimented with republican government until it collapsed in acrimony at the beginning of 1660. The Company did not escape involvement in these momentous events: it soon found itself convulsed with internal political wrangles and external threats bent on destroying its monopoly privilege. The national crisis created an atmosphere in which trade organizations had to survive in their day-to-day business dealings by any means available. For fifteen years or so the precepts of the overseas trading game were changed to drastic effect, producing distortion and dislocation of the eastern trade structure with England in its wake.

There are obvious general points that help to explain why the years 1642–49 damaged the East India Company's interests at home and abroad: civil war was not conducive to ordered commercial development; capital sharing suffered; food supplies to London were precarious; merchant ships were commandeered for the naval war; and, most serious of all, the Company's investors and high officials split into factions of Royal and Parliamentary supporters. These groups waged a verbal and procedural war in the Company's ranks, and as parliament's forces gained the upper hand in the 1640s over the country at large, so did its supporters within the East India Company. At the end of the 1640s Royal supporters were purged from positions of responsibility within the Company and most of its ships took to helping the Parliamentary cause.

In straightforward business terms this reorientation looked to be a healthy development for the East India Company. After Charles I's execution in January 1649 and the triumph of the Parliamentary army, the Company might have expected reward for backing the winning side. Such hopes were soon dashed. The Company's leaders quickly discovered that parliament was as ready to exploit the organization's financial resources, through forced 'loans', as the early Stuarts had ever been. In addition the Company realized that parliament's political leaders and their supporters were not committed to maintaining monopoly privileges in eastern trade. Some of this antipathy was due to what might be called the outport's revenge; the Civil War presented an opportunity to reduce the power of the London Company and give all England's traders a chance in the competition for eastern spoils. More serious still for the Company, was the belief common among parliament's leaders that trade monopolies represented the rough edge of Stuart despotism in the commercial world. In consequence, it became increasingly apparent after 1649 that the Company operated under parliamentary sufferance, surviving for the most part because of its ability to pay the loans demanded by the republic.

Underlying this self-knowledge of its precarious existence, was a constitutional dilemma facing the Company which complicated matters considerably. The point at issue was straightforward: after the king's execution in 1649 by whose authority did the Company operate? No precedent for parliamentary grants of charters existed, and this cast doubt on the question of the East India Company's charter renewal due in 1654. The omens were not good. During the Civil War both sides had frequently ignored the Company's monopoly, granting private trading rights to anyone willing to risk a voyage in unfamiliar eastern waters. Most endeavours ended in failure, but it proved extremely frustrating for the Company to witness its diplomatic and trading efforts in the East being harmed by the actions of a few free-booters. Moreover, the damage done in England to confidence in the Company's future proved so severe that it caused a paralysis of will over trade policy decisions in the early 1650s. Two views emerged about the future from within the Company's ranks: the first sought an accommodation with the critics through joint voyages, some of which, like that under Lord Fairfax in 1649, took place; the second recommended a suspension of the joint stock indefinitely, awaiting Cromwell's decision on the renewal of the charter. The result of this divided purpose was an economic disaster for the Company, and when Cromwell decided in 1653 not to renew the charter it appeared that the last nail had been hammered into the organization's coffin. The eastern trade now lay open by official decree and the Company's prized monopoly disappeared.

Little is known of the background to Cromwell's decision on the renewal, but it seems fair to say that it could not have been an easy one to take. In all other cases Cromwell's approach to overseas trade and settlement was consistently aggressive. In 1651, for example, the Rump Parliament passed the Navigation Acts which, in effect, sought to create a monopoly of the import–export carrying trade for Commonwealth ships. At the Peace of Westminster in 1654, which ended the first Anglo-Dutch War, Cromwell also pressed for the best financial terms in recompense for damage done to the East India Company's trade and possessions, dating back to Amboina in 1623. No less significant, the great expansion of ship-building and naval activity in the period underscores parliament's desire to enlarge and protect English overseas trade and settlement. To explain Cromwell's reluctance to renew the charter in 1653, therefore, requires an appreciation of the residual resentment towards the Company and its monopoly privileges. Cromwell's supporters included those with practical and ideological prejudices against continuing with a policy based originally on royal prerogative, and so commonly linked in their minds to abuses of power by the Stuart kings, James I and Charles I. The voices against exclusion from the eastern trade arose at the moment the Company experienced its lowest point of resistance, and for the first time, the state took the critics' side with regard to policy on its future.

It is difficult to measure how difficult and, as it happened, how pragmatic Cromwell's decision on the renewal proved to be by the speed with which it was rescinded. From 1653 to 1657 eastern trade became a shambles for English traders, in which neither the merchants nor the state found profit. This free-for-all had, as in the past, resulted in complete dislocation of eastern patterns of exchange, and aroused the hostility of many local rulers to the point where they refused any further dealings with the English. Cromwell did not deliberate long over this dire financial situation for the Company and the state, and in 1657 issued a new monopoly charter for the London East India Company. The new charter itself has been lost to posterity, but it is known from commentaries by seventeenth-century observers that it differed little from its predecessors. In fact, it provided an example of solid continuity in the state's relationship with the eastern enterprise from one form of national government to another. The republican Cromwell might seem an unlikely saviour of a royally chartered company with monopoly privileges, and yet his decision to renew engendered the most favourable prospects for trade to the East since the Company's founding. Everyone connected with this enterprise, whether Royalist or Parliamentarian in sympathy, now accepted that the East India Company alone was the most efficient commercial vehicle for realizing the dreams of an expanded and profitable trade in the East. Open trade had been tried and found wanting, silencing critics of the monopoly for some time to come. On 19 October 1657 the huge sum of £740,000 was subscribed in a new and permanent joint-stock venture, illustrating once and for all the confidence that both investors and the Company had in its long-term future. It was not misplaced: the special-case status of the East India Company endured and the Cromwellian charter ushered in a golden age of English trade in the East.

NOTES

1. Madden and Fieldhouse, *Select Documents*, I, 229–66.
2. *The Laws or Standing Orders of the East India Company 1621.*
3. Stevens, *The Dawn of British Trade to the East Indies*; Birdwood and Foster, *East India Company Letterbook 1600–1619; Calendar of State Papers: East Indies 1513–1621*, I–IV, VI and VIII.

4. The material covered in Stevens, *The Dawn of British Trade to the East Indies* is replete with such matters.
5. Birdwood and Foster, *East India Company Letterbook 1600–1619*, p. 479.
6. Thirsk and Cooper, *Seventeenth-Century Economic Documents*, pp. 473–7.
7. Ibid., pp. 436–44, 506.
8. Ibid., pp. 12–13; 471–2, 477–9.
9. Two of Mun's three major publications on eastern trade published in London 1621, 1628 and 1664, and cited in the bibliography below, are also reproduced in full in McCulloch, *Early English Tracts on Commerce.*

CHAPTER THREE

The Restoration of the Company and its Trade: 1660–1709

With the restoration of Charles II to the English throne in 1660, the ultimate destiny of the eastern enterprise began to unfold. It is not for nothing that recent scholarship covering the late seventeenth and early eighteenth century has chronicled a previously undocumented but fundamental transformation in the English state and its economy during this period. The dating of the modern fiscal and bureaucratic infrastructure, seen as unique to England's development as an industrial nation and leader on the world stage, has now been pushed back over a hundred years.

During this process a severe re-evaluation of some old assumptions about modernism and its fabrications in the country's governance has arisen (Brewer 1989). To students familiar with the East India Company's early development such new perspectives and conclusions about this age may not be so novel. The Company was a modernizing force in English society and its economy, pioneering the break with the nation's medieval trading past over the first sixty years of its business activity. It had the efficient internal organization and meticulous record-keeping any present-day government department would envy; after 1657 the Company boasted a permanent joint stock of the sort which most public corporations float their business endeavours of pooled risk and limited liability today; last, but by no means least, the Company proved dynamic and aggressive, looking to expand its operations and influence at the expense of its competitors. The Company's successes in these years were not an exact mirror of the rise of the English state at home and abroad, but the minor distortions hardly obscure the view of a continuing close bond between the two.

Indeed, this symbiosis has profound implications for any interpretation of the temporal development of the modern English fiscal state. For historians looking at the Company's history it means that this period will have to be judged on its own merits, as important in its own right rather than a stepping-stone to the more favoured stories of eighteenth- and nineteenth-century territorial expansion. Such an approach is long overdue, and in this chapter, it will be argued that this period proved to be, at one and the same time, the most fateful and yet most enterprising in the East India Company's history.

There were, as always, two sides to the coin. On the one side, an overview of these years reveals that the Company prospered as a trading organization, building a strong relationship with the crown in the years to 1688 and then overcoming both internal and external enemies by 1709. By this date the Company's impact on the English state, its people and capital city was manifest. On the other side of the coin, it can also be seen how much Company activity bore witness to the fact that the organization became overambitious and reckless in its expansionary phase of the 1680s. These ambitions, in turn, made the Company vulnerable to rivals at home who found new opportunities with the changed monarchy after 1688 to bring down the East India Company. For a brief period between 1694 and 1701, it had to suffer a vicious campaign against the trade monopoly in the East and the depredations of two competing companies. In the end the East India Company's prosperity was assured but the integrity of its charter and mandate up to 1709 looked decidedly shaky at times. Modernism and innovation had their price in a changing world, and the cost was paid increasingly in the public eye where the facts about Company operations were laid bare, open for a novel scrutiny and debate.

ONWARD AND UPWARD TO 1688

To deal with the positive side first: the expansion of the East India Company's activities from 1660 to 1688 was founded, first and foremost, on the Cromwellian charter. When Charles II became king constitutional propriety dictated that all laws passed and royal grants made during the interregnum be declared null and void and undergo reaffirmation in the new reign. The East India Company charter proved no exception. On 3 April 1661 the king granted the same strong privileges to the Company as Cromwell had done, including the forbidding clauses with regard to protection of the trade monopoly, which read: 'We do grant unto the said Governor and Company . . . full Power and Lawful Authority, to seize upon the Persons of all such English, or any other our Subjects, in the said East Indies . . . and send them to England.'[1] The Company, quite rightly, took such declarations as an immediate vote of confidence in its organization as a trading enterprise, and responded with a purge of all republicans from its committees and leadership. It was also wise enough to approve presents of £3,000 and £1,000 for the king and his brother, the Duke of York (the future James II) at the outset of the new reign. Over the next sixteen years, in fact, these presents would be supplemented with a further £170,000 in 'loans' (Hunter 1900, II: 162–3). In every sense of the word, these actions set the tone for a very profitable relationship to develop between the state and the Company over the next thirty years.

Thanks to the brilliant scholarship of Chaudhuri (1978; 1985) in this field, a detailed assessment of the particulars governing Company trading practices, its profits and ubiquitous relations with the state can be made. It is now known that the success of the Company in this period owed a great deal to the world trade upswing which, in turn, is linked by many scholars to the overwhelming influence of Dutch maritime enterprise. Just as northern Europeans suffered in the trade depression of the 1620s and 1630s, so they profited when trade boomed in the 1670s and 1680s. The Company itself also took a hand in ensuring its own prosperity through what would be seen in the late twentieth century as diversification of its product lines. In 1621, for example, pepper, indigo and other spices made up the bulk of East India Company cargoes; by 1677 calicoes, chintz, cotton-piece goods and raw and manufactured silks dominated. By the end of this period, in 1709, tea, obtained through a rapidly expanding China trade, then appeared as a prominent commodity in Company cargoes. The result of diversifying into these favourable markets, together with a buoyant oceanic trade structure, proved to be the amassing of immense profits over the whole period. In the first years of the Restoration the Company paid a dividend of 20 per cent to stockholders; by 1665 this figure rose to 40 per cent, and from 1685 to 1689 it actually reached 50 per cent. Annual Company profits after dividends were paid varied somewhat in these years, but most scholarly estimates put them in the region of £130,000. This figure represented wealth beyond compare for investors and it occurred in spite of the usual Stuart demands on the Company's treasury. Even the drain of £170,000 to the crown, which is acknowledged in official records, caused no liquidity problems whatsoever.

What could explain such bounty in the broader context of European rivalry in eastern waters? The least obvious, and yet most important, factor was the state and its support for the Company. It is frequently written that the East India Company's rise to power on the subcontinent represented a privatised imperial endeavour or empire-building by proxy – explained in part, no doubt, by the fact that no direct conquest by English forces took place. This image is certainly justified in light of the Company's control and later direction of Indian trade, but the meaning it carries should be treated with caution. There is an inference here of an absence of knowledge or interest on behalf of the state which is unsustainable. There was strong and decisive backing for the Company's monopoly privileges at Westminster, particularly in the House of Commons. In 1668–69 this support became public knowledge in the legal case of *Skinner v. The East India Company*. Skinner was an interloper in the eastern trade and had his ships confiscated by the Company, exercising its rights under the renewed charter. Skinner took his plea for redress first to the king and Council who then referred him to the House of Lords. The Lords, acting as a court of original jurisdiction, found for Skinner, awarding him damages at the Company's expense and, in effect, overriding charter rights granted by parliament. From this point on the case became a broader constitutional struggle between the executive and legislative branches of government with dire implications for the Company's monopoly should the former prevail (Kenyon 1986: 418–19). As it happened, the issue was resolved in the Commons' favour and, by implication, the Company's monopoly rights remained intact. The Lords could not deal with cases like Skinner's again. Redress for commoners in the future had to be sought on petition from the House of Commons. The whole affair proved something of a watershed for the East India Company. The outcome strengthened the Company's position at Westminster over the Restoration period and for the more serious struggles over the charter to come in the 1690s.

The late Stuart monarchy and its councillors also kept a very close watch on the development of all settlement and maritime enterprises abroad. An aggressive commercial policy overseas was, for Charles II and his brother, James II, the means to secure wealth and independence for the crown. The Company's trade expansion policies had, by financial necessity, to be encouraged and, where feasible, to be given practical support. These royal policy imperatives governing trade and foreign affairs not only make sense of Charles II's confirmation of the Company's exclusive charter rights but also the Navigation Acts passed in 1661, reaffirming the legislation introduced by the Rump Parliament a decade earlier. These Acts sought to exclude the Dutch from the carrying trade, ensuring that all imports from abroad arrived in English ports on English ships. Stuart conviction on this point was tested twice in two Anglo-Dutch wars in the 1660s and 1670s, and remained steadfast. The approach of the crown was logical, given the financial circumstances in which it had to discharge its responsibilities. Charles II and James II endorsed the Company's initiative in promoting eastern trade expansion as they saw the connection between its success and their own dynastic survival and prosperity.

To transform this aggressive intent into concrete accomplishment in the East required effective policies to safeguard Company interests. In the East India Company's case such policies emerged in the use of naval power in the Indian Ocean and on the coasts of India itself, combined with the building of fortified bases and enclaves in English factory ports. To modern eyes a strategy of this nature appears limited, if not mundane, but its success depended on the novelty of the concept for Asians that European navies could be used to expand the power of their home states. The land-based power-brokers of the Mogul Empire had nothing in their past or present experience of foreign traders to deal with an incursion from the seas such as that mounted by the Europeans (Chaudhuri 1985). By the late seventeenth century the English had overcome earlier logistical problems of replenishing water supplies and careening the ships' hulls by securing bases like St Helena in the South Atlantic, and friendly ports of call in East Africa *en route* to voyages into the Persian Gulf, India or the East Indian islands. The English Company's bases to which these ships sailed reflected the pattern of trade evolving over the first hundred years or so of operations. By 1709 there were permanent factories in the Gulf at Gombroon and Basra; major settlements at three centres, or presidencies, as they became known, on the Indian mainland – Bombay, Madras and Calcutta – and a further large base at Bantam or Java to oversee the spice trade.

Of these bases the most important were undoubtedly the three presidencies on the Indian mainland, and they are worthy of note as an illustration of how quickly Company priorities changed and policy evolved over the seventeenth century. In 1600 a strategy for eastern trade revolving around land bases in India would have been dismissed as nonsense, and yet by 1688 it provided the blueprint for all Company activity in the East. In part these changes transpired because of Dutch supremacy in the spice trade, but it would also be fair to say that the English crown and the East India Company responded to the prospect of fortified mainland bases with real initiative. Charles II led the way in 1661 by accepting the island settlement of Bombay in the dowry of his bride, Catherine of Braganza, from the Portuguese crown. Bombay proved too expensive for Charles to govern and develop, so in 1668 he handed the island with its inhabitants over to the Company for an annual rental fee of £10. Bombay's growth over the next fifty years was certainly impressive, considering its reputation as the bleakest and least appealing posting for Company employees who feared its climate and diseases. Furthermore, its geographical location on the west coast between warring Mogul and Maratha forces, determined that for much of this period the town was forever being attacked, besieged or overrun. Nevertheless, its natural features of a very good harbour and fortification, in tandem with the inspired leadership of Gerald Aungier, ensured that Bombay soon eclipsed Surat as the trading centre for the west coast. In 1687 the presidency, with its governor and council, moved from Surat to Bombay: a town which now consisted of some 60,000 inhabitants of mixed British, Portuguese and Indian origin.

Aungier was a remarkable man with a vision of what constituted successful English governance on foreign soil. His achievements included the setting up of courts of judicature in Bombay; the establishment of a stable currency; and the formation of a militia, together with the bare bones of a naval defence force (later called the Bombay Marine). He insisted on religious toleration for Catholics, Hindus and Muslims; local taxation was set by a general assembly of landowners on an equitable basis, and petty disputes were settled by elected magistrates in accordance with local community tradition and practice. Accountability of this sort, along with the ideal of representation and acknowledgement of local custom, represented innovative rule of the highest order. Aungier's actions provided precedents for later imperial policy not only in India but in eighteenth-century Quebec and beyond. Furber summed up Aungier's career well in his comment that here was a man 'far ahead of his time' (Furber 1976: 93).

The development of the presidencies on the east coast at Madras and Calcutta did not match the rapidity of Bombay's growth, as they followed a more steady and solid path to pre-eminence. Madras enjoyed the greater development of the two in this period because English activity on the Coromandel coast predated interest in the Bay of Bengal by some forty years. The emergence of the Madras presidency again owed much to the direction that Cromwell's charter had given to exploiting this site. It boasted the first purpose-built fort, named St George, and the first Anglican church, St Mary's, built by the English in India. By 1670 the population numbered in the region of 40,000 souls who were subject to English laws and courts of judicature within the confines of Madras itself. The day-to-day rule in Madras, however, was not as clearly defined as in Bombay, for powerful local rulers exercised claims of jurisdiction over their subjects living in Madras and its environs. The growth of the Calcutta presidency as the wealthiest and most influential centre of Company activity was very much an eighteenth-century phenomenon. By 1709 the English had staked out their trading goals in the region, nonetheless, and no one doubted their permanence in the Ganges delta. The English espoused a real commitment to operate in Bengal, for the trade goods involved were in increasing demand in European markets – saltpetre for armaments production; raw and wrought silks; sugar and cotton yarn. Even in the early eighteenth century this trade totalled £150,000 per annum for the English Company. It is little wonder that this site too witnessed the building of a large and intimidating fort, Fort William, to underline the permanence of English interests in this region.

These three presidencies would be the focus of Company trade and then territorial expansion over the next century and a half. Yet it should be stressed that in the period 1660–1709 they represented nothing more than English trade enclaves on a distant shore. No Mogul dignitary paid homage to their governors, and the Company's writ ran only in Bombay, Madras and Calcutta on the Emperor's sufferance expressed in his *firman*. (The *firman* or *farman* was the emperor's edict allowing particular foreign nationals, and/or their companies, the right to trade in the imperial domain.) The presidency system functioned at this time because of the efficient and effective administration of Company employees in London and the East. These Indian bases, along with those in the Persian Gulf and on Java were locked into an exchange network with a common currency and system of values that actually delivered the goods on time and to the right place. The key to this success lay in the fleets sailing East from London every year. After the 1657 charter grant, the Company decided to abandon shipbuilding and ownership, replacing its involvement in this industry with a policy of hiring 'East Indiamen' to do their business. This way of proceeding cut costs and incidentally gave rise to an insurance market and powerful shipping interest in the Company and the City. The eastern voyaging in the years 1660–88 proved very rewarding indeed as a result, and something like 404 return trips were complete with at least twenty East Indiamen being afloat, either homeward or outward bound, at any one time. Such figures indicate an enormous investment and concomitant confidence in the Company's performance.

This confidence was never entirely altruistic. The Company's voyages frequently enjoyed armed escort vessels as further insurance against failure and financial disaster. The naval guns of the English Company were by no means powerful enough to change whole trading patterns in the Indian oceans as the Dutch had, but they could exert influence over local rulers who sought to undermine or disrupt English trade in established markets (Parry 1981: 200). In practical terms the Company employed a policy which might be described as the moral economy of English naval gunnery in these local markets. It seems probable that this policy is what Aungier had in mind when he wrote to London in 1677 suggesting that 'the times require you to manage your general commerce with your sword in your hands' (Hunter 1899–1900, II: 227). A great deal has been read into this statement in the past apropos the march of British imperialism in the East; however, it is a mistake to read too much into it in this context. Aungier saw English naval guns for what they were: a means of reacting and protecting against predators in the immediate vicinity. They could be nothing more and did not need to be then because such limited arms met the Company's existing trade requirements. Again, as Chaudhuri rightly says, the Company's trade was always considered in the last resort to be an armed trade.

The speed of the Company's economic advance over the Restoration period was something to marvel at, but this hard-won prize very nearly evaporated in a short three-year span from 1688 to 1691. During these years the Company lost sight of its corporate purpose, declared war on the Mogul Empire and threw its whole presidency system into doubt. Analyses of these events in general texts covering this period have usually erred on the side of caution when explaining this aberrant English aggression. The Mogul emperor, Aurangzeb, was involved in wars of expansion and pacification throughout India in the late seventeenth century, many of which encroached on areas of English activity such as Surat and Bombay in the West and the Bay of Bengal in the East. This imperial activity tended to destabilize relations between local Hindu rulers and their Mogul overlords, resulting in a subsequent disruption of European trade patterns. In this deteriorating situation the English determined upon a policy of armed defensive actions as the best means of protecting their trade and economic interests in the three presidencies.

In both Bombay and Bengal this strategic decision proved disastrous because of the diplomatic naivety of Company commanders, particularly Sir John Child in Bombay, and also the chronic English indecision and confusion in the face of complex Mogul military alliances. In the end the Company was forced to go on bended knee to Aurangzeb and ask his indulgence with respect to continuing Company trade in India. Fortunately, as far as the Company's future was concerned, Aurangzeb took the view that the English were nothing more than an irritant in the greater imperial scheme of things, and he issued a new *firman* confirming their old privileges in the three presidencies. In return the Company had to issue abject apologies and pay the Emperor £15,000 in compensation (Dodwell 1929: 96–108). After a brief period of readjustment these unfortunate incidents were forgotten and trade relations returned to normal.

Of late this standard interpretation has come under scrutiny and been found wanting on certain points. To view the Company's actions as moving from passive to defensive in the 1680s ignores the evidence of real aggressive intent on the Company's part to exploit a distracted Mogul power for commercial gain. This new strategy arose in response to a reconfiguration of political alliances and goals between the Company and the late Stuart regime. In the 1680s, in particular, the belligerent leadership of the East India Company under Sir Josiah Child became identified with a Stuart monarchy pursuing an equally bold and authoritarian imperial policy around the globe. Rather than react to the disturbances in India caused by Aurangzeb's expansionist campaigns, Child sought to seize the initiative. To fulfil this design he intended to utilize the arms and naval guns under the command of his protégé and namesake, Sir John Child, at Bombay, and a fleet supported by infantrymen in the Bay of Bengal. The fact that these missions were hopelessly equipped for the task assigned and ended in ignominious defeat or surrender does not detract from the aggressive intent of the English Company and state. The essential motive behind Child's strategy was identical to that which brought success to Robert Clive's territorial wars in the 1750s; the only difference between the two campaigns lay in execution and the resources available. In the seventeenth century the armaments employed by Company forces were more or less equal in effect to those used by the Mogul Empire. By the 1750s, however, the Europeans had gained a decided technological edge which completely changed the nature of the Company's military role in India (Lenman 1968; 1987).

TO THE BRINK AGAIN: 1688–1709

Such revisions to the traditional picture of East India Company expansion as being an eighteenth-century phenomenon not only help in understanding the Stuarts' approach to overseas expansion and the Company's role in their ambitious imperial plans but also make sense of the hostile reaction to these policies and the Company itself after the fall of James II in 1688–89. While it is true to say that failure of the aggressive policies towards the Mogul Empire had not ended in expulsion from India, it did become clear that the old relationship between the Company and the crown was shattered. The denigration of the Company's long-standing mandate to trade peacefully in the East by Child and his cohorts, coupled with the advent of the new monarchy with a more Eurocentric view of the world, set off an internal political struggle for control of the eastern trade that again threatened the very existence of the East India Company. To some extent these troubles transpired because the Company became a victim of its own economic successes. In the years from 1689 to 1709 competing economic and political forces in English society fought over gaining access to the massive profits to be had from trade in the Orient. Viewed from the Company's perspective, a crisis ensued after James II's fall, but not, as before, from the fact of Dutch hostility or natural calamities in India. This crisis concerned a struggle for control of the Company's assets, emanating from a simple desire to divide the rich cake of eastern trade more equitably amongst England's commercial élites.

Difficulties for the Company in this context began with the very close relations Sir Josiah Child built up with the Stuart monarchy. The vision shared over the 1670s and 1680s of expanding English enterprise was fortified with liberal amounts of Company moneys flowing into the pockets of courtiers and MPs. Child simply took the old policy of keeping in step with the wishes of the state to its logical conclusion. However, after James II had been replaced with the joint sovereigns, William and Mary, in 1689, Child's policy of aggression and state imperialism by proxy collapsed. The Company's armaments had failed in India and its leadership faced a new monarchy without a vision or the influence at court to keep the organization's critics at bay. To make matters worse, the charter came up for renewal in 1690. In Child's warped view of the political world, damage control in India, in concert with bribes at home might, he believed, yet save the Company's privileged position with the state. It represented a desperate strategy on Child's part but one born out of necessity and lack of alternatives. In 1690, for example, it was reported that the king's closest advisers, led by the Duke of Portland, received some £50,000 in bribes and presents to persuade William that the Company's charter privileges should remain intact. Even the Speaker of the House of Commons became implicated in a bribe scandal aimed at persuading MPs to vote for the renewal – an implication which later brought about his removal.

This underhand way of proceeding was extremely risky, to say the least. Its ultimate success depended solely on the emollients dispensed by the Company treasury and the short-sighted view that every man had his price. At best this represented a strategy for the immediate future, and it perished in the 1690s when it became clear that greater forces in the English body politic were at work against the Company's monopoly and privileges: forces that could not be staunched by a few well-placed bribes. The national political debate splintered into what Plumb called 'the rage of party', expressed in a struggle between competing constitutional ideologies of Whigs and Tories or court and country groupings (Plumb 1967). This development was portentous for the East India Company for under Child's leadership the organization had become identified with the Tories and their view of a strong monarchical presence in the constitution. Now, in the new reign, the Tories suddenly found themselves out of favour with William and Mary. This fact did not mean the new sovereigns were antipathetic to the East India Company *per se* – like their Stuart predecessors William and Mary saw the advantage of a healthy Company in terms of tax revenue from its trade operations. It is true to say, however, that Whig party politicians were the most trusted by the new monarchy and within their ranks resided individuals and factions resentful of the East India Company's power and privileges in the City, at court and in the eastern trade structure.

How did this animosity manifest itself? In the 1690s and early 1700s attacks on the Company were launched on two closely linked fronts: one through parliament and the other through the City's financial network. It would be easy to present this conflict as one of Whig versus Tory or even, to take the teleological view, one of the forces of progress and development – the Whigs – taking on the bastions of conservatism and state-vested interests in the post-Glorious Revolution world – the Tories. The Whigs, after all, took responsibility for setting up the Bank of England in 1694; endorsing the move of the House of Commons to seize control of initiating money bills in parliament, and controlling the succession in the 1701 Act of Settlement to ensure that no further Catholic monarchs ascended the English throne.

All these events have traditionally been seen in a very positive light by historians to the deliberate detriment of Tory ideology and political conduct. This sort of interpretation is too simplistic, however, for, to coin a phrase from Colley's masterful study of this period, not all Tories subscribed to the East India Company or supported its monopoly, while not all Whigs opposed Company privileges or endorsed the attacks on its charter rights (Colley 1982). What occurred in the political turmoil over the renewal of the Company charter in the 1690s was a collision of opinion about who should control the future development of eastern trade, and what vehicles should be employed to achieve this goal. Caught on the middle ground of this debate, more often than not, was the crown which recognized the intention of all parties concerned to make trade in the East even more profitable than before, but found it difficult to mediate a consistent policy line between the competing visions of the future.

The dilemma faced by William and Mary in the 1690s over the Company can certainly be appreciated in the context of the numerous efforts made to change state policy governing the eastern trade after their accession. In 1689, for example, a Commons committee was formed to investigate the East India Company's conduct and make recommendations about future management of the eastern trade. In January 1690 its report came down firmly against the renewal of an exclusive charter due to be enacted in 1693, proposing in its stead a much more open joint-stock company with less restrictive membership regulations or sweeping monopoly powers. Two years later the committee pushed for enactment of these recommendations by resolving to petition the crown on the matter of the old Company's charter.[2]

It can be seen from this sort of activity that the ever-present, anti-monopoly feeling evident since the Jacobean period had not faded away during the course of the seventeenth century. And it took three hard years of counter-lobbying, present-giving and parliamentary argument on the Company's part to secure the charter renewal in 1693. Yet the renewal did not put an end to the activities of the Company's critics. In January 1694 forces opposed to the East India Company in the House of Commons passed a resolution declaring that 'all subjects of *England* have equal right to trade to the *East-Indies*, unless prohibited by Act of Parliament'.[3] The wording of this resolution was ominous for the crown and its chartered Company because parliament now appeared to be inching towards the constitutional claim that in the first instance it (parliament) rather than the crown should decree who was to receive particular trading privileges.

The initial effort at putting this intent into action came in 1695 when the English merchants opposed to the East India Company, supported by their political allies at Westminster, helped to finance the formation of a Scottish East India Company. In a clever constitutional manoeuvre the Company received its patents for operation from the Scottish parliament, as a means of avoiding the question of challenging English privileges and rights from the English crown. The key to the success of this Scottish Company nevertheless lay in its backing from England and, more specifically, those moneyed interests excluded from the English East India Company. In the early stages of the enterprise the risk seemed to pay off, as the very large sum of £300,000 was subscribed in the Scottish Company, a great deal of which came from Whig financiers controlling the Bank of England. This well-backed endeavour represented a real threat to the old East India Company, and the English organization had to use all means available, fair and foul, to undermine this rival body. Intense pressure, fuelled by the Company's treasury, was exerted on both Houses of Parliament and at court to bring about the Scottish Company's demise; and in December 1695 the crown responded by forbidding all English investment in the Scottish East India Company as well as any assistance overseas with its trade. This prohibition proved to be a death sentence to the Scottish Company and, to add insult to injury, the prohibitory order was postulated on the very dubious principle that English investment and involvement had given succour to a foreign power!

Holding opponents of the Company's privileged position at bay in these years certainly bore witness to the immense resources and expertise available to the organization. But in the end, not even this considerable power could annihilate its very rich and powerful enemies. The Company's ability to resist depended in the last resort on the crown's proclivity to stick with the traditional approach to eastern trade. Just how steadfast this royal commitment would be in a future conflict over the East no one in the Company knew, but by the late 1690s the omens were unpromising.

Three factors were uppermost: from 1696 onwards parliamentary revelations of East India Company bribery practices began to scandalize even the most cynical MPs; the Whig Junto government sought to force the issue of rescinding Company privileges by blocking approval for its loans to the monarchy in parliament; as a result of this action and William's war with France, the crown found itself desperately short of money. To cut a long story short, William's nerve cracked in 1698 under this duress and he gave consideration to ending the East India Company's century-old monopoly. It proved a remarkable procedure for there was nothing less than an auction of the right to lend money to the crown through the grant of a new monopoly charter to trade in the East. In this exercise a new organization emerged led by the Whig magnates thwarted in the Scottish East India Company endeavour. They possessed vast capital resources, sufficient to challenge the old Company's pre-eminence. In the bidding for the crown's favours the East India Company offered a £700,000 loan to the government at 4 per cent interest; the new organization meanwhile offered £2 million at 8 per cent interest. It came as no surprise that the cash-starved king took the latter offer in spite of the higher interest rate, condemning the old Company to another operating crisis of the worst kind.

As in every other dire circumstance affecting the old Company over the seventeenth century, its demise was forestalled at the last minute by some clever politicking. On 5 September 1698 the new and impressive English East India Company Trading to the East Indies was incorporated and granted the monopoly of eastern trade. But this organization, well financed and organized as it was, exhibited a fundamental flaw in that it was not constituted as a joint-stock body pure and simple. The new Company remained a 'General Society' founded, without apology, and with a broad membership, in order to secure the subscription of the £2 million loan to the government. William and his ministers held no preference how the 'Society' traded as long as they received the promised loan so, in practice, the new organization became a mishmash of old-fashioned regulated ventures, private voyages and some pooled risk. There existed a great deal of money and enthusiasm, but little direction or experience when it came to the eastern trade patterns and markets. This basic fault in the structure of the new Company played right into the hands of the old Company, and the latter seized the initiative with alacrity, using all the accumulated knowledge of a century's trading practices. First of all in 1699 the old Company lobbied successfully for a law permitting the organization to continue operations as a corporation beyond the statutory three-year winding-down period.[4] The old Company then had the legitimate right, and confidence, to subscribe £380,000 worth of the £2 million in stocks floated by the new Company, thus becoming its largest shareholder. From this position the old Company operated within the new as it always had, using its own contacts and factories in the East to exclude its rival and control products, markets and profits.

This strategy proved a master-stroke, for it undermined the new Company from within and opened the way for the only real option to resolve this problem – a merger. Between 1701 and 1709, therefore, detailed negotiations about the financial and administrative structure of a united company were brought to fruition. In 1709 a United Company of Merchants Trading to the East Indies emerged from the union, to the relief of the government and all subscribers previously concerned in the ruinous competition between the two bodies. The United Company certainly represented something bigger and better able to exploit eastern markets than what had existed before. In theory it offered an opportunity for all merchants interested in the East to participate in the trade, including those in London, the outports and, after the Union of 1707, those in Scotland too. In practice, however, it must be said that complaints of exclusionism by merchants outside London's financial markets illustrated the stranglehold that the City's moneyed élite still held over the trade. Nevertheless, it cannot be denied that the United Company did have access to greater capital funds and a new management structure that refined the streamlined executive structure of the old Company. At its heart was still the General Court of proprietors who now elected a Court of Directors, or Directorate as it became known, which, in turn, oversaw the activities of the Committees and governance of the presidencies in India. More important, the merger entailed a reaffirmation of the East India Company's original mandate, as an organization committed to peaceful trade. The collective view of the United Company at its inception was that the errant policies of aggression pursued in India of the 1680s and early 1690s could not bear repetition. The dispatches from London to East India Company employees over the next fifty years or so cautioned against any interference in Mogul politics or local disputes as inconsistent with the aims of a business enterprise based in Europe. This eirenic mission and ethos refined the eastern enterprise to its original purpose and ushered in a period of stability in which the United Company's interests and performance flourished.

This political conflict leading to union not only proved a watershed in the eastern enterprise but also showed how important the trade to the East had become in England, and, after 1707, the whole of Britain itself. Company politics had become interwoven with national political debates and philosophies about the exercise of power within the state. And in relation to eastern trade rights no one doubted that parliament had wrested control of the grant of these privileges from the crown. The union of the two Companies had been engineered by parliamentary politicians through statute endorsed by the monarch; a complete reversal of initiative and procedure from the pre-Glorious Revolution years. The intensity of the exchanges in the struggle for the trade can be understood if the stakes are taken into consideration: that is by 1709 the East India Company had become a financial institution of the first rank, lending huge sums of money to the state; dispensing lucrative contracts to London merchants and their counterparts around the country, and becoming an integral part of the engine that drove what Dickson described as the financial revolution unfolding in Britain between 1688 and 1756 (Dickson 1967). It is little wonder that the struggle over the Company's destiny became so intense or that it overlapped other debates in the national political arena riven with party conflicts.

THE EAST INDIA COMPANY AS PUBLIC DOMAIN

In his speech at the opening of parliament on 23 November 1695, William III asked the House of Commons directly to 'consider such laws as may be proper for the advancement of trade; and will have a particular regard to that of *The East Indies*, lest it should be lost to the nation'.[5] On the surface there appeared nothing untoward in such concern, and yet in the wording of this simple but urgent plea it is possible to see that the East India Company had assumed an importance to the state beyond a simple trading enterprise.

By the late 1690s the viability of the eastern enterprise warranted national concern. East India Company affairs received increasing public attention in the press and debate at Westminster after the fall of James II, and a greater awareness emerged of the Company's place in the fabric of English social, economic and political life. This process of self-education about the organization is not difficult to understand, given the immense increase in eastern trade over the previous generation and the consequent enlargement of the tax revenue base it produced. Expanding public revenues proved to be the lifeblood for a nation fighting incessant wars in Europe and beyond over the next century. They enabled loans to be arranged and credit extended; by definition, the success of overseas trade proved crucial to nourishing the sinews of state power (Brewer 1989). There was, however, more to this increasing awareness of the East India Company's activities than a one-dimensional obsession with money and taxes. England's involvement in trade to the East had ensured that the Company's development became a thing of the senses for a great many people at the time whether or not they were interested or involved with the eastern trade.

In a historical sense the simplest measure of this growing awareness of Company activities can be found in the parliamentary records of the 1690s and first decade of the eighteenth century. Numerous debates, committees, resolutions, statutes and petitions testify to a recognition that the Company and its trade could only be ignored at the nation's peril. This material is fascinating, for it illustrates how the dissenting themes such as opposition to monopoly and special charter privileges endured, while also highlighting new concerns that arose out of English success in its trade expansion. It appears, in fact, that each generation over the next 120 years had to go through this learning process, only for the lessons to be forgotten. Of particular importance in this discourse was the idea of encouraging commercial competition in the East and elsewhere as a legitimate means of increasing wealth at home by means of statutory regulations or, as it might be termed today, government involvement. Leading scholar–politicians of the time such as John Pollexfen (1697), Charles Davenant (1696) and Daniel Defoe (1719) wrote and published on this question which had obvious links to the monopoly question but also breached the concept of what was England's role in the wider trading world. In brief, should English commercial interests develop through a free-for-all, in which all citizens could take part, or be controlled by restrictive parliamentary statutes which sought to avoid the reckless and criminal potential of English merchant marines given free rein in foreign seas?

Historians have been tempted to interpret these debates as embryonic pleas for free trade, predating similar ideas put forward by Adam Smith seventy-five years later. Such conclusions are too modern; those arguing against regulation and for broader access to the expanding overseas trade structure wanted less exclusive rights for London merchants in the main, especially those connected to the court. To say a movement sprang up to rid England of government-imposed trade regulation posits ideas that never really crossed late-seventeenth-century minds (Cherry 1953). The East India Company's trade could not exist without the involvement of the state, and everyone recognized this fact, in spite of the argument about the nature of the relationship.

Another facet of the East India Company's enhanced profile in the political and economic debates of the day was the growing amount of published material given over to describing or analysing the East and England's activity there. The full scope of this material still requires historical analysis, but it is safe to say that it fell into several different categories, informing and educating various audiences as it went along

(Lawson 1989). One huge genre that conveyed an image of the East usually of both fiction and fact was the travelogue, or historical account of eastern climes. This material mixed amateur anthropological, scientific and cultural research with good old-fashioned story-telling for as broad a market as possible. Some of these publications were French translations, like the work of François Legaut (1708) and François Catron (1708/9). Others represented the labours of authors who had travelled to the East, such as John Ovington (1696) or John Fryer (1698). The impact of such writing must have been as unpredictable as the readership, but it cannot be denied that it created an image both attractive and repugnant to English readers. On the one hand, the mystery of the Orient found expression in the extravagant prose of these works and played its part in luring many an adventurer to the East in the hope of securing some of the treasure and luxury described therein. On the other, the deep-seated prejudices against alien forms of government, which in the East were seen as autocratic and corrupt, coupled with basic philosophical and spiritual objections to Muslim and Hindu religious practices, can be found in the pages of these contemporary works. Such themes in the later period of Anglo-Indian history have been examined successfully in the twentieth-century scholarship of Marshall and Williams (1982) and Said (1978). However, it is worth stressing here that the East India Company brought forth these experiences and emotions in the seventeenth century. This early contact foreshadowed the more violent debates in the modern era and occurred because the East had already assumed such an important role in England's trade expansion after 1660. For those readers and observers more interested in the immediate impact of the Company's activities in national politics there existed a good sized body of literature referring exclusively to the rights and debates over control and direction of the eastern trade in this period. Much of this type of published material reflected the points made in speeches or petitions to parliament because debates at that time were not systematically recounted or publicized. Arguments put forward by critics of the Company's monopoly privileges, such as Pollexfen, found their way into tracts like *A letter concerning the* ***East India*** *trade to a Gentleman* (1698) which echoed with Pollexfen's diatribes against the East India Company's special rights which he called 'the worst foundation of any trade'.[6] Common to all the published work on the Company at this time, however, was an acceptance that the eastern trade represented a worthy endeavour. Criticism of its means was one thing, a desire to make its profitable ends endure quite another. Contemporary writers acknowledged that the Company increased the country's wealth and raised England's profile on the European diplomatic scene at the expense of the country's competitors, especially the Dutch. Indeed, a great deal of space was allotted to musings over why the Dutch had been so successful in overseas trade during the seventeenth century, and how the English might emulate this performance. Sir Josiah Child himself produced one of the most influential tracts on English trade in this and the next century, reaching the sensible conclusion that Dutch primacy lay not in a magic formula but revolved around the more mundane subject of low interest and freight rates combined with reasonable insurance costs (1693). In this manner of anthology and immediacy did the process of educating and informing about eastern trade, Company policy and state involvement take place.

To talk solely of printed sources as the vehicle to spread knowledge about the East India Company's activities, however, gives the mistaken impression that only the élites within English society appreciated the changes expansion of the eastern trade brought in its wake. At all levels of society and day-to-day life the English came to know of the Company's influence on their diets, clothing and, for Londoners in particular, architecture and workplaces around them. The arrival of spices like pepper, mace, cinnamon and cloves at the beginning of the seventeenth century had been an expensive novelty. By 1700 it was no longer so for the market had been flooded with these products and the price for commodities such as pepper collapsed to the point where the majority of the population had access to the spice. If meats tasted more palatable in the winter and spring months, the East India Company and its monopoly gladly took responsibility for this welcome change. Perhaps the most stupendous change in English dietary habits that took place in the seventeenth century as a result of Company activity concerned the consumption of tea, and to a lesser extent coffee and chocolate. Tea was only introduced as a beverage for English tastes in the 1680s and 1690s and did not become an article of mass consumption until the next century. Nevertheless, tea complemented sugar – the primary import to England from the West Indies – and by 1709 few people had not heard of or experienced the sensation of this combination of cane and leaf. Indeed in the first decade of the eighteenth century many had already become hooked on the caffeine charge that resulted from drinking huge amounts of tea. Up to fifty cups a day was common because it was often recommended as a health-giving elixir by doctors and commentators of the time (Clark 1969: 203). Companies such as Twinings emerged in this decade to meet the demand, and the domestic brewing industry which provided the ales for domestic consumption of liquids atrophied within a generation.

Another aspect of the general public awareness of the East India Company's trading practices concerned textiles. After the great surge of spice imports in the early seventeenth century, calicoes, cotton piece goods, such as Madras prints, and silks took over as the most profitable trade products for the Company. This development had a consequent impact on fashion and taste, first among the top reaches of society, where the desire for silks, then as now, seemed insatiable. A domestic industry of working raw silk suddenly found itself under threat in the 1690s, as more wrought silks were imported from the East to meet burgeoning demand from the home market. High import duties and petitions to parliament saved the industry in this instance. But these workers required constant protection over the next century too as finished silks became the status symbol of the age, and, in this volatile market, the London silk-weavers were sometimes in touch with fashion tastes, sometimes they were not. If they were not, buyers looked to foreign markets for the latest styles and the home weavers suffered accordingly. At the lower end of the social scale, the sale of textiles met the needs of the household and everyday clothing. And, as with the introduction of silk, cotton imports became popular at the expense of an established domestic trade – in this case, wool. Once introduced, however, nothing could stop the advance of lightweight cotton goods with fast, bright colours that are still evident today in chintz, muslin and Madras prints. There was nothing short of a revolution in dress design as heavy coarse woollen goods were abandoned for the fashionable lighter cottons in both formal and leisure garments (Douglas 1969; Appleby 1978: 169).

Like all East India Company imports, tea and textiles were stored after 1660 in ever-expanding bonded warehouses, where the goods were later auctioned to wholesalers under strict regulations laid down in the *Laws and Standing Orders*. The procedure became known to contemporaries as sale 'by inch candle', that is each sale would last the time it took a one-inch candle to burn out. The auction often took place at East India Company House itself where ships' cargoes would be brought up in carts and stored in warehouses in the garden at the back of the House. In the sale of 21 September 1675, for example, auction sessions were spread over a seven-day period, each session devoted to a commodity such as spices or cotton goods and each subject to the 'inch candle' rule (Thieme 1982). It had the appearance of a modern auction people would recognize today, down to the regulation that if goods were not paid for in full within a specified period the Company would reclaim them for auction at a later date. The whole business was publicized in advance and open to any interested person or party to attend. The government liked the system too because bond goods released to wholesalers meant very little effort in collecting duties and doing the requisite book-keeping. It was a system, in short, that satisfied all needs, from tax man to consumer.

As a concluding point, it is worth noting that in addition to being able to read about, taste, smell and wear the products of England's eastern enterprise there was also visible evidence of the experience. London, in particular, underwent a transformation as the physical plant needed to enable the Company to thrive went up in the old City and along the Thames. To a contemporary observer the most striking change would be the number of East Indiamen with the distinctive Company flag of red and white stripes with the Union Jack, added later, in the corner. These ships could be seen on the water or berthed in the magnificent Howland Great Dock near Deptford, waiting for repair or passage to the Company's dockyard and offices at Blackwall. The complex at Blackwall itself grew during the seventeenth century from the original buildings erected in 1612–14 to include a chapel, almshouses and warehouses. This activity was down-river from East India House in Leadenhall Street, but no one could mistake the connection between the two. The three-storied House boasted a distinctive façade decorated with sailing ships, the Company's coat of arms and a statue of a mariner flanked by two dolphins: a fitting tribute to a Company brought into being by an expansionist and exhibitionist Tudor monarchy. By the eighteenth century such triviality was abandoned as the Company's vision of its purpose in the East became more focused and deterministic. And in a telling reflection of the United Company's ambition, the old façade was torn down in the 1720s and replaced with a classical frontage which bespoke a new-found confidence in its corporate power at home and abroad. In the shadow of such architecture the restoration of the Company's fortunes since 1660 could not be doubted.

NOTES

1. Madden and Fieldhouse, *Select Documents*, I, 415.
2. *Journals of the House of Commons*, X, 834.
3. Ibid., XI, 64.
4. *Journals of the House of Lords*, XVI, 525, 578.

5. Ibid., xv, 599.
6. *Historical Manuscripts Commission: Lords MSS*, 14th Report Appendix, Part vi, II.

CHAPTER FOUR

The Company's Expanding Universe: 1709–48

Over the forty years or so after the union of the two East India Companies in 1709, growth, development and consolidation became the watchwords of the eastern enterprise. In modern terms, the performance of the united Company in the first half of the eighteenth century represented a shareholders' bonanza of constant dividends, unshakeable investor confidence and stocks of gilt-edged security. In the previous century the Company had triumphed over formidable critics in securing its monopoly privileges in the eastern trade, and the lessons learned during these struggles enabled its administrators to plot an ambitious course of trade expansion and increased wealth. Thanks to the splendid work of Lucy Sutherland (1952) that part of the story relating to the Company's experience in British history during this period is well known and has been assimilated by scholars presenting surveys of the age. Yet it would be wrong to say that the picture of the Company's history is by any means complete. A great deal of work has been done since the 1950s on other aspects of the East India Company's activities, both at home and abroad, that had previously been overlooked. And it is this output that needs to be incorporated not only into the retelling of the Company's particular story but also to the broader dynamic of British trade and territorial expansion overseas in the eighteenth century.

A primary focus of this chapter will therefore be on what might be termed the Asian end of the East India Company's operations. In taking this route it is intended to reveal those events and causations in the Anglo-Indian past that have given rise to some very lively historiographical debates about the Company over the last generation.

At the core of these debates lies an overarching problem of historical interpretation regarding the decline of Mogul rule, and the emergence of European power on the sub-continent. The traditional arguments on this matter were straightforward enough: one side believing that Mogul decline predated European advance; the other maintaining that European advance became the precursor to Mogul decline. Would that this matter could be explained so simply in the late twentieth century! For what has happened to this field of study can only be summarized as the disintegration of existing explanatory models and approaches. The present discussion about these issues of Mogul decline and European intrusion into India during the eighteenth century is, as a result, far more complex. Consensus on this topic now eludes historians, and for those engaged in recasting the debate what seems to be left is 'an ambiguous process' (Bayly 1988: 3).

It is not possible in this context to cover even the smallest range of issues raised in this current reassessment, but two facets of the overarching theme are still very pertinent to any history of the East India Company, and certainly warrant further discussion. First, just what did Company operations amount to in India during this period? How did its employees fulfil the Company's mandate and exercise their power over trading concerns in the East? (The concept behind these two questions is neatly summed up in Peter Marshall's phrase 'the view from Bengal' (1976: 29).) Second, and the obverse of the above, how did this view from India correspond to the aims and aspirations of the Company's administrators in London charged with controlling their employees (or servants, as they were known) in the East? In pursuing answers to these two questions, light can also be shed on a third issue that has tormented historians dealing with this period of the Company's history. Simply put, how did the East India Company become an imperial power in the Orient when its laws and standing orders forbade such an outcome?

THE PRESIDENCY SYSTEM: THEORY AND PRACTICE

To understand the nature of the East India Company's rising economic and political power in the East during this period, it might be helpful to construct a model of the contemporary trading systems in that region. A most accessible and suitable prototype for this purpose can be fashioned from the 'core-periphery' structure put forward by Immanuel Wallerstein (1980). This thesis proposes in part, that power and influence emanate from hubs of intense economic activity in a particular trading zone, and, in a rippling effect, control from these hubs then spreads over adjacent areas of commerce. During the course of world history since the decline of Rome around AD 600, various cores and their peripheries have risen and fallen. The range included land powers, such as the Mongols and Ottomans, and sea-borne powers, such as Venice, Spain and Holland. In the eighteenth century it can be argued that the expansion of the East India Company's interests in India followed the imperatives embodied in this model. In the period 1709–48, the Company became firmly established at three bases, or presidencies, on the sub-continent: Bombay, Madras and Calcutta. Each of these bases sought, with considerable success, to maximize profits for the Company in London; and, in doing so, had a profound impact on the existing trade systems in the vicinity. Indeed, success was such that it can be maintained that by the late eighteenth century the city of Calcutta, and the province of Bengal, became the core operation of all East India Company activity. The other presidencies and trade operations in the East became peripheral to this one centre. All recent statistical analyses support this fact (Bhattacharya 1954; Chaudhuri 1978), and the remarkable changes this development brought for the Company and India in its wake.

The beguiling question within this story, however, is how the Company could advance so quickly from its humble origins in the seventeenth century. From 1709 to 1748, economic progress did certainly not result from force of numbers. By mid-century, for example, the Calcutta presidency had no more than seventy employees in its civil service. In terms of military personnel, too, the position was not impressive. The Madras army comprised some 300 soldiers, that in Bengal about 500. A generous assessment by historians would characterize these units as a rag-bag collection of mixed races with little military capability in battle (Cohen 1971: 6–7). The foundation of the Company's success in the East during these years actually lay in the simple fact that it exploited all the opportunities offered to its traders. In terms of entrepreneurial skills, the East India Company responded to and then outperformed its rivals in India by a wide margin. Some of the advantages the Company enjoyed in this rise to prominence were fortuitous, such as the decline of Portuguese power and the changing structure of Mogul rule over India itself. Others flowed directly from the expertise and adaptable skills of Company traders and administrators on the spot. These individuals seized the initiative in establishing contacts with both the overland and sea-borne traders around their enclaves (e.g. Gill 1961). It was these servants of the Company who benefited from the ample monetary resources of the British financial networks being invested in establishing the trade in the East. The success of these enterprises would, in turn become visible in the balanced books of the Company's auditors in Leadenhall Street, London.

This is not to say that the experience of each presidency was similarly successful in these years – far from it. The striking trend revealed in the Company's operations over the eighteenth century was the decline of the west of India trade centred in Bombay, Surat and the Malabar coast. By 1750 either a Bombay posting for an East India Company employee or a 'Bombay voyage' for one of its captains were viewed as the least attractive option for personal advancement. Far more appealing were the richer presidencies of Madras and Bengal where economic activity was buoyant, and captains eagerly looked to use their privileges of private trade on what were known as the 'Coast and Bay' or 'Coast and China' voyages. The Company itself became aware of this transformation in the trade patterns centred on the presidencies through its separate dealings with each administration. Different London committees, such as Correspondence and Accounts, kept up a meticulous correspondence and book-keeping record with Bombay, Madras and Calcutta, making the task of analysing economic performance that much easier. The volume of trade and aggregate sales record computed in London from these records revealed the decline in the west of India and the rise of the eastern centres, especially Bengal. This variation did not concern the Company so much as the individuals being sent out to serve in one presidency or another. Corporate control in these years remained stable and profits grew steadily over the whole period.

It is such growth and profitability that illuminates and supports the core-periphery analysis of Company activity in the first half of the eighteenth century. The position of Bombay may have declined, for instance, but it still functioned as the centre of an ongoing, multi-layered, regional trade pattern. In Bombay itself the Company drew traders from the city and its environs who filled its warehouses with goods for the annual fleets. The Company also ran three small factories on the east coast to receive trade goods from overland routes to the interior and the sea-borne coastal exchanges. Expanding this peripheral area still further, ships from the Persian Gulf ports of Gombroon and Basra were also drawn to Bombay by dint of a trade in such products as coffee and spices. It could even be said that east African ports across the Arabian Sea also felt the touch of Bombay's influence on their economic livelihood, as East India Company ships worked and traded there before continuing on to the Gulf and west coast of India. The durability of this British influence on Bombay and its development can be discerned in practices of today. Budgeting arrangements, the legal holidays and even sailing seasons from the city reflect an agenda established in the eighteenth century under East India Company direction (Furber 1976: 191–201).

The experience of the west coast presidencies, Madras and Bengal, offers an even more impressive illustration of the growing influence exerted by British trade power over older patterns of exchange. By 1748 Madras had developed considerably under Company guidance into a trade entrepôt. Like Bombay, this presidency also enjoyed a multi-faceted growth of its economy. At the primary level, Madras drew merchants to its harbours and markets from the interior, as well as those involved in the coastal trade of the Bay of Bengal and the Coromandel coast. At the next level, Madras also played an important role in the more distant trade of fabrics to the East Indian islands (present-day Indonesia), in return for spices. At its greatest extent, the peripheral trade from Madras stretched to China, as the Coromandel coast became a vital staging point for the increasingly lucrative trade in tea. In China, the East India Company maintained supercargoes at Canton, during the 'in' trading season and Macau over the 'off' season. These bases were linked to the Bay trade and Madras itself through products such as copper, mercury, alum and sugar (Arasaratnam 1986). There were far more entrepreneurial opportunities in this trading world for Company and private profit than in the small, and declining, economic periphery in the Arabian Sea to the west. Thus it was Madras and its eastern trading zone that rose with the realization of this economic potential during the first half of the eighteenth century.

It is fitting to talk of Bengal last in this tripartite model because it became the most wealthy and influential presidency over the whole period. In fact, by the end of the eighteenth century, Bengal exerted an economic influence over all the East India Company's operations in the East. The growth of official Company activities during 1709–48 in the Bay area, and the city of Calcutta itself, proved phenomenal. But, as Peter Marshall so skilfully points out, judgement on the rapidity of this development should be tempered by the knowledge of earlier, unofficial involvement in the area (1976: 29). Long before Calcutta's meteoric expansion and the advent of Company control over the Bay trade, the East India Company had recognized the importance of

Bengal as the hub of a land and maritime exchange system in the region. Even in the early eighteenth century, when official Company activity in the Bay area appeared minuscule, 60 per cent of all Asian imports to Britain originated from Bengal. The formal drive by the East India Company to expand its operations in the region was based, therefore, on a sound business knowledge of the existing trade and its possibilities for enhancement.

How was the Company able to achieve its trade aspirations in Bengal by 1748? In practice, it was partly by luck but mainly by good management. Some factors that were beyond the Company's control did prove extremely beneficial in furthering its trading fortunes. Of particular importance in the local Indian context was the economic and political stability of Bengal under Mogul rule in the early eighteenth century. In contrast to the Bombay and Madras presidencies which existed in more volatile regions of the empire, Bengal enjoyed a structured governance under the hand of strong imperial rulers such as the nawab Murshid Kuli Khan, who died in 1727. This ordered polity encouraged a regularized and predictable relationship to emerge between the Company and the local rulers or country powers – an arrangement that proved to be mutually beneficial. Other factors aiding the Company's enterprises in Bengal owed more to the aggressive diplomacy of its employees. This was no more true than the winning of an imperial *firman* from the Mogul Emperor, Frauksiyar, in 1717, granting the Company the right to trade in Bengal without payment of customs. This grant was made in return for an annual, derisory payment of 3,000 rupees, and can only be described as a huge coup for the Company. Indeed, many observers then and since have referred to the *firman* as the Company's own Magna Carta. Hyperbole or not, most historians are agreed that the grant represented an unprecedented privilege for any European power operating under Mogul rule at the time. It is not easy to recreate the special trading status such a *firman* bestowed on the Company. The grant confirmed the unique place that British traders held in the Emperor's dominions, and the principle of this exemption from customs in Bengal remained intact until 1857. Such a prestigious position for the Company in Bengal did not eliminate the constant wrangling and bickering with local rulers over the detailed terms of operating the *firman*. Nevertheless, from this point onwards the Company found itself in a much stronger position than its European competitors, and, no less important, now had the ability to deal with the country powers from a much more powerful position.

In fact it is the degree to which Company operations became

integrated after 1717 into the local economy of Bengal that lies at the heart of its trading success over these years. Change came quickly to the core of the Company's profitable activities that built up around Calcutta, and the old patterns of exchange between London and the Bay involving spices, textiles and minerals faded away. More lucrative networks of trade, no longer reliant solely on British bullion being imported to Bengal, evolved in their place. The imperial *firman* granted access to an interior country trade in cotton piece goods, raw and wrought silks, along with agricultural products. None of those involved in this interior trade were concerned with exports at all, but survived and profited from a highly competitive cash-nexus economy in the region itself. The sophistication of India's banking and commercial systems drew the Company's employees into credit relations with Hindu and Muslim traders that can only be described as ones of mutual dependence. The purpose of such relations was to exploit the economic opportunities offered under Mogul overlordship, and it worked well. The relationship served both Indian and British economic relationships.

A good reason for this success was the flexibility evident in the dealings between merchants and traders. For example, the Company often sold its custom's exemption under the *firman* to Indian traders in return for credit or favours elsewhere. Such findings by scholars working in this field of study have given cause for serious revision to the traditional picture of European intrusions into India during the eighteenth century. It is now too simplistic to present the Company as a rapacious organization, exploiting a vulnerable populace under a declining imperial rule. New research on the structure of Anglo-Indian relations points firmly in the direction of an equilibrium. Indeed, in the latest authoritative analysis of this whole dynamic, Chris Bayly was prompted to write: 'The British were sucked into the Indian economy by the dynamic of its political economy as much as by their own relentless drive for profit' (1988: 46). The question of who was exploiting whom is, as a result of these fresh insights, far more complex and difficult to answer.

Beyond the core of Company activity in and around Calcutta, a periphery of profitable trade existed with ships carrying on an import–export trade to the supercargoes in Canton and bases in the East Indian islands. At the very limit of this sphere of activity there were, of course, the East Indiamen eventually sailing back to London with cargoes of indigo, cotton piece goods, raw silk, pottery, spices and tea. It was such products that filled the Company's warehouses on the Thames, to be sold later at auctions. The irony of this trade pattern established by the mid-eighteenth century is that the Company had, almost by oversight, fulfilled its original goal. In 1600 it had been hoped to build a lasting, profitable trade, based on the East Indian islands, in which India would play an incidental role. Quite the opposite had happened over the seventeenth century, and yet by 1748 something approaching the Company's initial aims had been achieved. East India Company interests had become firmly established on the Indian sub-continent, and the tentacles of its operations reached across adjacent seas to the whole trading world of Asia itself.

In describing the structure of the Company's trade in the East so far, there has been a clear emphasis on the ideal model. As with all cliometric models, however, variables exist, casting their dim shadow on this story of corporate success and creating hostages to fortune for the Company's leaders in London. The most debilitating aspect of any trade system in the eighteenth-century world was always unofficial or illicit trade. No matter how well-trained, conscientious or vigilant the Company's servants happened to be, smuggling, cheating and corruption eroded profit and rendered certain accounting procedures problematic. Much scholarly effort has been expended trying to produce a scientific measure of the impact smuggling had on the imperial and domestic economy of early modern Britain. Most of this effort has been directed to the Americas where illegal trade practices reached epidemic proportions after 1688, and government bodies under Privy Council guidance sought in vain to eradicate the problem. Less attention has been paid to the East, but there is no doubt that smuggling and cheating were just as widespread. Illegalities occurred wherever East Indiamen docked. In October 1721, for instance, the Privy Council issued instructions forbidding an illicit trade in Madagascar between East India Company merchants and American colonists. The Americans picked up Indian goods and slaves in Africa supplied by the Company which was not itself allowed to transport cargoes directly to the West Indies or the mainland colonies.[1] Cutting out the London stop for payment of duties, and the middle-man's share of the profit, obviously brought rich rewards for those willing to risk working on the wrong side of the law.

Throughout its history the Company always sought to put an end to smuggling and related transgressions, but failed to do so. Its campaigns to eradicate deception proved ineffective, in part, because the Company's own organization and terms of service invited fraudulent behaviour. Admittance to the Company's civil service in eighteenth-century India began with a nomination from one of the London Directors, together with securities worth £500. The human side of this process is nicely portrayed in Lord Egmont's diary entry for 14 January 1733:

> I visited Mr. Drummond, a director of the East India Company, to desire my cousin Percival, at the Fort St. George might enter the Company's service. He said there are so many noblemen's relations already in the service that it could not be, and that his going out on private account was what disabled him, for he would not have liberty even to stay there. But on my desiring that favour at least might be shown him, he said he would do what he could, and bid me give him a note of my request before Wednesday.[2]

Once accepted, the employee beginning a career in the Company on this route would then be sent to the East as a 'writer' or 'apprentice'. By the mid-eighteenth century most writers would be in their late teens (the minimum age being sixteen years), and have undergone some training in commercial or mathematical accounting. With some very notable exceptions for merit, rising through the Company's ranks depended on seniority and perseverance within the hierarchy. Five years service as a writer would be followed by promotion to the post of factor which would, in turn, lead after another three years to an appointment as junior merchant. After another three-year stint in this position, the Company employee could then attain the most elevated rank of senior merchant. These senior merchants became the members of the governing council in each presidency, and, sometimes, even gained the office of governor itself. It did, however, take a candidate with enormous fortitude and powers of persistence to endure this rigid and deliberate process. As a social group, the main body of Company servants in India during this period was drawn from mercantile families, very often Scottish in origin.[3] These men did not represent the type of wastrels or ne'er-do-wells of popular myth, but were instead eager and ambitious neophytes who knew exactly what economic purpose lay ahead of them when they sailed from London to take up their posts in the East.

What was this purpose? In short, it was two-fold: to make money for the Company and attempt to enrich oneself while doing so. The Company and its servants saw no contradiction in this at that time, for it seemed the two purposes could dovetail. Salaries paid to the lower ranks of Company employees proved sufficient to live on, though not in any grand style. To avoid penury, therefore, many supplemented the official wage by indulging in private trade with Indian merchants in the Company's existing orbit. In this way the Company employee ran two businesses: one account covering trade for the East India

Company and the other for himself. For some this system worked smoothly: their endeavours enriching both the Company and themselves. For others it proved a personal disaster. Often the lines between the two accounts became blurred. Bad investment decisions on private trade led to personal indebtedness to Indian bankers or creditors, who then petitioned the Company, as employer, for redress. The opportunity and, more sinister, temptation to cheat in such circumstances became manifest. In consequence, whole illicit networks of credit, debt and deceit evolved wherever Company interests overlapped with private trading enterprises (Watson 1980b). These networks, in turn, frequently formed the backdrop to more audacious ventures, such as smuggling, interloping and even piracy. In the first half of the eighteenth century it would be true to say that these networks proved nothing more than an irritant to the smooth operation of the Company's trade in the East. In the second half of the century, however, this delicate balance between legal and illegal activity evolved into a major problem, as Mogul rule retreated and militarism entered the equation. By the 1740s, Indo-European trading relations built up in the past on trust and experience, collapsed slowly but surely into armed struggles, defying all Company directives and intentions.

LONDON AND THE COMPANY'S SUCCESS

How did this economic promise and development in Asia appear to the Company's administrators in London? The overall judgement was success upon success. All the terms of measurement pointed to an excellent return for both the nation and the Company on investments in the East. In the years 1709–48 the Company only failed twice to pay dividends to its shareholders. In 1709 the total value of exports from Britain to Asia were £552,154, by 1748 that figure had risen to £1,105,845 – an increase in the region of 100 per cent (Chaudhuri 1978: 507). The investor confidence that such figures embody lay not only in the Company's trading performance but also the stability of its relations with government. Under Robert Walpole's long premiership from 1719–41, the Company established a rock-solid reputation for reliability and consistency. The Company became a major player in financing loans to the government, and a vehicle for large and small investors expecting safety and predictability of stock values, along with the requisite dividend payments. In fact a pattern revealed in the East India Company's history is that stable central governments coincided with profit and development over the first 200 years of operations. When the Company experienced its worst troubles, as in the 1680s–90s and 1760s, 1770s and 1780s, there was matching instability in national politics.

No such trouble occurred, however, under Walpole. The Company's enterprise in these years came to be seen as something of a national endeavour, in which the fortunes of the state, the Company and its shareholders were linked. This image is not difficult to understand in view of the involvement that many British citizens had in the Company's welfare. The connection began with the diversity of investors in this period that included all manner of people and social classes from maidservants, widows, journeymen and gentlemen on up to aristocrats of the royal blood. All these people, men and women alike, were entitled to vote in Company elections and did so.[4] This involvement can then be expanded to cover those connected with the secondary and tertiary economic sectors related to Company activities, especially in London. Tradesmen, wholesalers and suppliers employed by the organization, on contract or directly, may not have possessed Company stock but they were certainly affected by its performance. Moreover, there was the all-important and powerful shipping interest to be reckoned with. This group supplied 'bottoms' to the Company and exercised control over this contract through a tight web of family patronage. Each ship built for the East India Company attracted multiple investors in much the same way people invest in thoroughbred racehorses today to lessen risk. Once built, the ship would then be leased to the Company on very favourable terms for the investors. This procedure worked because the shipping interest controlled the number of ships built and the number of sailings each unit made to the East, usually for the investors the position could not have been more attractive. By the 1740s the fleet size was controlled by the suppliers and they had established the very twentieth-century concept of built-in obsolescence! Only greed got the better of the shipping interests; for by the 1780s the Company found it had too many ships and was forced to rectify the abuses within its leasing procedures.

A further instance of how quickly the Company embedded itself in the fiscal life of the state concerned money-lending. Since the union of 1709, the East India Company had been in an anomalous position with regard to its capital funding. As a condition of union and receiving a new monopoly charter, the Company had been obliged to lend the state £3,200,000. This sum represented the whole equity capital of the newly constituted Company, forcing the Directors to look elsewhere for immediate working capital. This action took the specific form of issuing short-term, fixed-interest East India Company bonds. These bonds became very solid investments indeed on the London money-market, and for good reason. The interest fluctuated only very mildly over the first half of the eighteenth century (between 3.5 and 6 per cent), and the amount of bond debt was determined by the government. Up to 1744 the limit was £6 million. As the century wore on, it was such bond issues, supplemented by Bank of England loans, that provided the liquidity for day-to-day operations. Investment in stocks alone could not produce the flow of funds required for the scale of Company operations, and financial crises, by mid-century.

The net effect of such activities, in any event, was to draw the City and its leading players more closely into the Company's financial networks. City politicians came to occupy important posts in East India House, and Company policy came to be debated in the capital's council chambers (Rogers 1989). Company magnates also came to advise the government on financial policy and to lend large amounts to the state through its system of 'closed subscription' (Sutherland 1952: 25). All in all, the national endeavour evolved because of the Company's importance to the finances of the state and its people. MPs speaking in parliamentary debates, as early as the 1720s, recognized that the Company required special attention and treatment. On the one hand its viability ensured the country large revenues through taxes on its trade. On the other, if the state became too demanding in its levies and careless of maintaining the climate for profitable trade, disaster might result. Sir Edward Knatchbull expressed these sentiments in his parliamentary diary after sitting through a debate on dividends on 26 February 1730. The dismantling of the Company's statutory privileges by the state, he wrote, could cause investors to 'lose all they have given above for their stock and would affect men, women, and children and take away people's property vested in them by Act of Parliament . . .'[5]

These were not idle words. The importance of the Company to state finances and its emergence as a national endeavour made its performance and stock values a matter for public debate. London Coffee Houses, for example, not only provided a rendezvous for those interested in Company news but also acted as a forum for the unofficial exchange of stocks and bonds. The tone of these debates across the tables can be followed in many contemporary accounts, all revealing the huge amounts of money involved and the importance attached to decisions taken affecting the Company's operations. Lord

Egmont's diary for Sunday, 22 February 1735 illustrates this point. After prayers at home, he proceeded to 'the Coffee House' where he fell into conversation with Sir Edward Knight (MP for Norfolk) on the problem for the East India Company of smuggled tea. Egmont wondered why the government did not do something sensible for a solution, such as removing the duty on tea, making it uneconomical for smugglers to 'run' that product. Knight knew the answer to this line of thinking: the government liked to seize the contraband tea because all profits from the seizure, via the Admiralty Courts, went straight into the Treasury's coffers. Accepting a Company compromise of removing the duty in return for compensation would require parliamentary approval, and Walpole preferred the deception of the status quo. To Knight this connivance was understandable, as the seizures brought in a staggering £200,000 per annum to the government. Egmont's view of this practice proved less pragmatic. In a fit of outrage he wrote,

> What a miserable thing is this! Rogues are permitted to destroy the fair trader, luxury to infect the lower class of people, the rogues when taken are transported, frequent murders fall out on making seizures, and it must go on because there is a benefit goes into the king's purse unaccountable to Parliament.[6]

The issue illuminated here is that Walpole never disturbed a revenue source, shady or not, that produced the desired results. Again, thanks to the superb research of Lucy Sutherland (1952) it is known exactly how valuable the Company became to the nation's fiscal planning, in particular, and the country's trading performance, in general. The legislation passed in the period 1709–48, aimed at providing the framework for the Company to prosper with minimal regulation of its day-to-day affairs. In practice this took two forms now familiar to anyone knowledgeable about the Company's past experience. First, the government had to ratify a charter providing the company with long-term security in its trading operations. The provision of long-term security was crucial to investor confidence, commitments by suppliers and those involved in maintaining the Company's infrastructure. Second, the charter grant had to contain cast-iron guarantees of the Company's monopoly privileges to trade in the East, for the very same reasons of confidence and stability. Interlopers, smugglers, pirates or rivals of any description had to be forbidden a share of the rich bounty to be made from the East India Company's trade networks.

An examination of the major East India Company legislation passed by parliament in these years reveals the government's sensitivity to these requirements. The United Company charter was granted for an initial period of eighteen years. There was a first renewal for another thirteen years in 1726, and then two major statements of confidence in 1733 and 1744 when the charter underwent further renewals until 1783. To protect the Company's trading privileges and immunities under the charter, parliament also passed legislation in 1712, 1733 and 1744, guaranteeing the practice of monopoly trade in the East. The Company won these privileges in return for financial favours to the government. In 1730 it paid £200,000 in hard cash for these rights. In fact these years, 1709–48, saw the Company in the strongest position it would ever enjoy with respect to negotiations with the state. Its profitability and surpluses enabled the organization to lend large sums of money to the government, and it reaped the statutory reward. Cultivating this relationship was always a priority for the Company because its very existence depended on the parliamentary charter and the goodwill of the government of the day that controlled the majority in the House of Commons and Lords.

Only when the Company's profitability started to falter after 1760 did this long-standing relationship break down. No one in the early years of the eighteenth century sensed the woes that would befall the Company's operations when writing the legislation to defend the monopoly of eastern trade. Quite the opposite: innocuous as it may seem at first sight, the wording of the Act of 1712 expressed the very essence of the unfolding national endeavour. The government's motives in granting all these privileges were a response, as it said in the Act, 'upon the said company's humble petition', so that 'the East India Company and their successors may be better encouraged to proceed in their trade, and to make such lasting settlements for the support and maintenance thereof for the benefit of the British nation'.[7]

In this overall picture of prosperity and success a word must be said about the Company's own conduct. After the Union of the old and new Companies came into effect, certain reforms to the administrative structure of the organization assisted the improved economic performance. A conscious effort was made to cleanse the Company of the Child legacy, viewed then as corrupt and demeaning to the best interests of the organization. In consequence, the executive was transformed from a self-perpetuating Governor and Court of Committee structure into a more responsive body with a Chairman, Deputy and Court of twenty-four Directors (Directorate). Each Director could only serve four consecutive years before having to step down, by 'rotation', for at least a year. To be eligible for a Director's seat a prospective candidate had to possess £2,000-worth of Company stock. This stipulation was specifically designed to give the impression that only major investors would have a sufficiently serious intent about management of the Company's affairs. The Court of Proprietors (general stockholders) was also enlarged to about 2,000 subscribers whose right to vote in Company elections rested on a £500 stockholding. One vote per stockholder became the rule no matter how many £500 blocks of shares a person held. The remarkable aspect of this body throughout this, and the later period, is the participatory levels of voting and stockholding. It was not uncommon for 1,000 people to vote at East India Company House in the annual elections of the Directorate or on dividend rates and relations with the government. This figure included an immense diversity of both rich and poor, men and women, from all backgrounds and age groups.

The existence of this type of broad-based stockholding in a national trade endeavour did not last long beyond mid-century. Concerted research in the Company's stock ledgers over the eighteenth century has determined that after 1760 a general trend towards larger and larger concentrations of stocks, in fewer hands, developed. Certain influential Directors and their cohorts, in particular, came to possess large blocks of stock, and this quickly undermined the impact of the Court of Proprietors on Company policy-making in the broader sense of trade development in the East (Bowen 1986a; 1989). It must be said, however, that the interest of the public in the Company's fate did not decline with the power of the Proprietors. Work done over the last decade by historians interested in drawing imperial concerns into the general discourse over Hanoverian Britain has uncovered a great deal of interest outside Westminster politics in the nation's enterprises overseas. Preliminary findings from the evidence provided by newspapers, magazines, songs, ballads, plays and poems testify to an interest not simply with glorifying the march of British power abroad, East or West, but also the impact that march had on the nation itself (Lawson and Phillips 1984; Wilson 1988). The East India Company's activities from 1760 on were public domain and did not escape this sort of attention. Thus even at the most qualified level, East India Company stockholders in the first half of the eighteenth century represented, in Huw Bowen's words, 'an indirect investment in empire' (1989: 193). Only further research in these records will shed more light on these matters.

In the final analysis what encouraged all this interest in the East India Company's operations was its overwhelming financial success.

Year after year it met all its obligations and still had money to spare to lend to the government. Few companies then or now could boast such a record over forty years or more of operation. The open accounting procedures practised by the Company certainly promoted public confidence in such prosperous times. The rising value of the stock in these years was reported in news journals and magazines, and the profitability of trade became a topic of general discussion and pride. Official Company figures for the years 1738–42 alone show that profit from trade transactions realized approximately £1.1 million annually. Only the Bank of England itself could claim a more important place in the national pecking order of joint-stock companies. It is little wonder that the new East India House built in Leadenhall Street from 1726 to 1729 displayed a grander, more confident style of decor than its predecessor. In 1732 six pictures were purchased to adorn the Court Room of the interior, and they spoke directly of the Company's vision and self-knowledge of its position in the trading world of that era. The paintings contained a series of ships and buildings that could be seen on the voyage from London to the East. This pictorial excursion began in St Helena, continued on to Cape Town, Bombay, Tellicherry and ended in Bengal (Foster 1924: 134). These simple depictions by George Lambert and Samuel Scott laid bare the *raison d'être* of the Company in the first half of the eighteenth century as poignantly as any tract, diary or ledger.

THE PRICE OF SUCCESS

This picture of success did have some irregularities that detracted from the overall impression of perfection. There appeared disturbing details relating to the Company's activities in both Britain and the East. One cause of these operational flaws lay with the structures of the organization in London. A close look at certain mechanisms of control over the day-to-day operation of Company business suggests that the old tinge of corruption from Child's day had not entirely been exorcized. It seems clear that the enlarged General Court of Proprietors offered ample opportunity for a two-fold conspiracy against the collective will of the Company's investors. First, especially after 1730, those holding vast blocks of stock were able to enjoy influencing Company elections by the practice of 'stock splitting'. For example, an investor holding £6,000 worth of stock could divide this sum into twelve £500 blocks and distribute it to friends, who, in return for a small fee, would vote as instructed by the patron. After the elections were over, the stock would be transferred back to the original owner. Second, and an extension of the first, such abuses very quickly led to the emergence of wealthy power-brokers in the Company's ranks. These were the sort of men, who, in turn, frequently rose to the rank of Director. Once in that position, the Directors tended to act as a united executive body, dictating policy and 'slates' of candidates to be elected to this or that Committee and even the Directorate itself. When these influential Directors were then obliged to stand down after four years service, 'by rotation', they would arrange for a compliant candidate to take their place for a year before returning on 'the slate' in the next annual election of Company officers.

The point to remember in this context, and that of the Company's future problems, is that such procedural abuses made the organization vulnerable to the most unscrupulous forces inside and outside its ranks. As stockholdings became increasingly concentrated in the hands of certain company magnates, or, as they would be known, nabobs, the scale of corrupt practices expanded accordingly. In view of the fact that the ultimate prize could be control of the Directorate and Company trade policy, ample incentive existed for long and bloody battles in the General Court. The mechanisms were in place for such contests, all they required were the catalysts of motive and opportunity. More ominous still, there was the political factor to consider. From the beginning, the Company had always enjoyed widespread investment from MPs in its operations. The pattern was set in the early seventeenth century when the proportion of MPs investing in all the different trading companies had reached 33 per cent of the Commons. By the 1760s this figure had probably not changed a great deal with respect to the East India Company, for it is calculated that just over 28 per cent of sitting Members now held Company stock (Russell 1971: 192; Bowen 1986a: 40). Indeed the significance of these figures up to 1748 is that they seem to have been insignificant to the Company's overall operations. During this early period of the Company's history, politicians had kept the organization at arm's length whenever possible. Statutory regulation had attracted parliamentary attention it is true, but most politicians viewed the prospect of direct interference in the complexities of eastern trade management with understandable reserve. Nevertheless, by the middle of the eighteenth century a reconfiguration of old patterns governing the Company's relationship with the state was in process. In the end, politicians were more or less forced to take an interest in the Company's operations because of war and the imperatives of directing the nation's foreign policy around the globe. Once involved at this level of Company diplomacy with the native powers in the East, it proved a short step to political involvement with the Company's organization in London.

This potential for diplomatic complications overseas leads naturally into the next stage of discussion about the price paid by the Company for its success. In particular the question arises how did the Company administrators in London view some of the less desirable activities of their employees in the East? The Directors knew well that abuses of private trade privileges were commonplace. They also recognized the increasing problems arising from these practices, such as the rising number of court cases in the presidencies and the fractious relations between the country powers, private traders and the Company. All these matters signalled the worsening of an inherent administrative problem relating to control. To address these problems proved, however, a daunting task for the Company's administration in London. The system of governance for Company servants in the presidencies, and elsewhere, demanded loyalty and integrity in large measures to make it run. Statutes and standing orders, sanctions against abusing trade privileges, and missives from London on correct procedures for dealing with Indian merchants relied on cooperation not force for their application. In the first 140 years of the Company's operation this cooperation and loyalty had been in sufficient supply, fuelling the success of the whole trading enterprise. By the fourth decade of the eighteenth century, however, the flaws that had appeared at the London end of the operation began to surface more regularly in the East, tarnishing the broader image of integrity and loyal service.

Before the 1740s it would be fair to say that London's approach to abuses by Company servants in India had been low-key. Profits and stability cautioned the Directors against upsetting the balance between private and Company enterprise on the part of its employees in the East. This complacency ended mid-century, however, under the duress of war with France and certain native powers in India. The background to this conflict, known in European history as the War of Austrian Succession (1740–48), has been interpreted several different ways. Some histories present the outbreak of hostilities on the sub-continent between Britain and France as the symptom of broader global contests for control over the expanding trading and colonial world. Others prefer to emphasize changes within the Mogul Empire as the precursor to European conflict in India. It is not, however, a simple historiographical debate. It used to be generally accepted, for instance, that a decline in Mogul rule over India created a political vacuum into which Europeans charged so they could dominate the subcontinent after the emperor's fall. Now this idea is considered too simplistic. More stress has been laid of late on the long drawn out changes in Indian society under Mogul rule and how they affected Europeans involved in trade there. Mogul power did not decline in a sudden and predictable way nor did Europeans always exert control over the conflicts into which they were drawn. Sometimes warring nations under declining Mogul power used Europeans to their advantage. On other occasions and in different locations this relationship was reversed. Anglo French activities and hostilities in India over this period frequently carried ramifications beyond their comprehension because of the complex forces at work in the decline of Mogul power.

Interpretations of this type are not mutually exclusive. A strong European angle to the Anglo-French rivalry that developed in India can be traced through the tortuous history of the Paris-based Compagnie des Indes. The French had been attempting to emulate the Dutch and English East India Companies since the early seventeenth century. Its promoters had formed and reformed various organizations until the breakthrough came in the 1720s with the establishment of a well-financed and organized trade to bases in India such as Mahé in the west and Pondicherry on the east coast. From 1725 to 1755 the Company prospered on its trade in the East (Furber 1976: 201–11). The Company relied on state funds for survival, being private only in name, but it did make profits in this period in the sale of its goods brought from the bases in India. In these circumstances of obvious rivalry between European trading Companies in India and the East Indies, it is easy to believe that conflict was somehow inevitable: that disagreements between London and Paris were bound to spill over into armed disputes in the East. Teleology of this sort requires severe qualification, however. These European powers were rivals, but it was not axiomatic that trade competition would lead to war. On the contrary, up to 1740 France and Britain came to a series of informal agreements in India to avoid that very outcome. These Europeans represented very minor players on a much larger imperial scale, and it had proved to be in everyone's interest to eschew conflict in return for the Mogul emperor's *firmans* and the trade profits that went with them.

These arrangements did not last, however, because by the 1740s two factors emerged to upset the settled conditions of inter-continental trade between Europe and India. First of all, nations such as Britain and France did become more aggressive in the strategic use of depredations against a rival's overseas trade and colonies, as a means of settling European quarrels. There was also the destabilization of Mogul power to contend with. Wherever its roots lay, the effect of this disruption could be seen clearly in warring native powers in India, especially along the Coromandel coast of the south-east. In the political and economic confusion emanating from these conflicts, Europeans suddenly found themselves being dragged, sometimes willingly, some times not, into local dynastic struggles whose outcome was often very uncertain.

With the benefit of hindsight it seems straightforward to lay the blame for these events on aggressive European tactics. The French, under the leadership of figures like Dupleix and de Bussy, had the resources and will to make France a power in the south-east of India. It was a position that France intended to seize at the expense of her rivals. For a while the French were unstoppable, with successes in the War of Austrian Succession at Madras in 1746 (which they captured from the British) and at Adyar in the same year (where they defeated British Indian allies). Adyar, in fact, signalled the rise of a new type of military force to be reckoned with on the sub-continent, for the French had achieved a superiority in this theatre by the uses of European artillery techniques and Indian manpower.

It is easy to get carried away with the illusion of Europeans taking all before them after such successes, but, as Geoffrey Parker points out, Adyar was a strategic/military turning point in India's history, not one that dictated the trade, politics and economy of the sub-continent over the next century (1988: 133). In essence, the Europeans were still weak. The British had no more than 2,000 troops under arms in the whole of India during the war, and the French success at Adyar was secured by 300 French fusiliers and 700 native sepoys (the word sepoy being derived from the Persian *sipahi*, meaning soldier). The French, for example, soon discovered that the maintenance of armies and aggression against rivals in trade demanded resources that neither the government in Paris nor the Compagnie des Indes could provide. The British were definitely mauled in the encounters of the 1740s, but in the long term they held a stronger position simply because their trade in the East brought in about four times more revenue than the French Company. When the English Company finally acquired good field-commanders, such as Lawrence, Eyre Coote and Clive, to match those of France, its deeper pockets of money proved to be the key to eventual defeat of the French threat.

It should also be noted that British weaknesses during the war in the south-east of India were compounded by the fact that the Company spread its resources thinly across the whole sub-continent. To defend trading positions linked to all three presidencies required dexterity at all times, especially in view of private trade and inter-European rivalries. Playing off one native prince with aspirations to grandeur against another with equally strong intentions of seizing the Mogul writ proved a dangerous game. Failure by Europeans to take sides in a local dispute, as the British discovered time and again, could be just as disastrous as offering their slender military resources to one of the combatants. The histories of Anglo-French and Indo-European hostilities in the years 1740–48 can be reduced to tales of France taking Madras and Clive relieving Arcot or the clauses affecting Indian possessions of Britain and France in the Peace of Aix-la-Chapelle. But this sort of Eurocentric account is nonsensical in the context of the complexities and true nature of Indian power struggles under Mogul rule in the first half of the eighteenth century. The Aix-la-Chapelle treaty of 1748 may look definitive in western textbooks, yet it solved nothing with respect to the profound problems afflicting the East India Company's trading viability in either the Carnatic or, as it turned out, Bengal.

The real importance of these hostilities and tripartite rivalries to the Company's history lay not in causation *per se* but the fact that administrators awakened to long-dormant problems with established trade practices. More trade, both official and private; more personnel, both honourable and disreputable; and more contact with native powers, both diplomatic and nefarious, had created a volatile administrative mixture for the London Company. Profits were high, but so too were the risks of allowing the Company to continue its practices under lax supervision. The potential for the ruination of the trade in the whole eastern sphere of operations became self-evident by 1748. Mastering the French threat to the Company's trade was by no means a foregone conclusion – not least, as Percival Spear's highly readable account puts it, because the French possessed 'more attractive manners' (1983: 68). The Company's position in London appeared to be strong, but promise of even better results could be undermined by tyrants from within. A combination of a powerful stockholder with an exaggerated ambition to control Company policy could spell as much trouble for trade and profit as Dupleix himself. In short, the next phase of the Company's history would be crucial to resolving the problems that arose in the aftermath of its own prosperity and economic progress. The price of success was escalating all the time.

NOTES

1. Madden and Fieldhouse, *Select Documents*, II, 301–2.
2, *Historical Manuscripts Commission: Egmont MSS* (3 vols. 1923), II, 6.
3. McGilvary, 'East India Patronage and the Political Management of Scotland 1720–1774' (unpublished Ph.D. thesis, 1989).
4. Bowen, 'British Politics and the East India Company, 1766–1773' (unpublished Ph.D. thesis, 1986), pp. 38–41.
5. Newman (ed.), *The Parliamentary Diary of Sir Edward Knatchbull 1722–1730* (1963), p. 109.
6. *Historical Manuscripts Commission: Egmont MSS* (3 vols, 1923), II, 236.
7. 10 Anne c. 35, *Statutes of the Realm*, IX, 704.

CHAPTER FIVE

From Trading Company To Political Power: 1748–63

> May we not feel tempted to exclaim that it was an evil hour for England when the daring genius of Clive turned a trading company into a political Power . . . ?[1]

This rhetorical sweep is how the great nineteenth-century scholar of England's expansion overseas, Sir John Seeley, viewed the experience of the East India Company in the years 1748–63. Success in war, the acquisition of territory and expansion of trade transformed the Company from just another enterprise in India to power-broker, and even kingmaker in Bengal. It proved a climactic period for the Company, and one that Seeley recognized, quite rightly, as carrying crucial, even sinister, implications for the final century of operations. Much scholarly effort has been expended, and many words printed, about the motive and causation behind the Company's transformation into a political and territorial power. And yet, the subject and context of this dynamic remain contentious to this day. In fact, the taxonomy of historical writing on this matter is worthy of a study in itself, for it would reveal not only the sheer mass of disparate theses but also how historians have changed their views about the Company's changed role in India since Seeley's brilliant and biting analysis. An explanation of why this diverse volume of literature exists cannot be attempted in this particular study. However, one elemental factor in all these accounts which illuminates the whole debate can certainly be explored, and that is the career of Robert Clive as Company administrator and soldier in this period. Through a look at Clive's adventures in India it is possible to glimpse the power of a personality who transformed both his own fortunes and those of the Company in one explosive decade of activity. In a unique and spontaneous manner the fate of the man and the Company became intertwined. The history of one part of this union cannot be understood without reference to the other.

In writing of Clive it is easy to be drawn into the heroic school of interpretation, portraying a figure who transcends the perfunctory concerns of a trading company in the East. Indeed, there is no end of effusive prose on library shelves following this pattern. The trend began in Clive's own lifetime with his own employee, Robert Orme, who dutifully recorded his master's shining exploits in India for posterity. This uncritical approach continued in the nineteenth century with authors such as Sir John Malcolm (1836), Lord Macaulay (1830) and Sir A.J. Arbuthnot (1888), and can be found in many twentieth-century publications, most persistently through popular histories of the Raj. Rather than dwell on the shortcomings of these historiographical developments, it is intended in what follows to place Clive firmly in his setting as an East India Company employee. By this means it can be appreciated why he rose to a position of unprecedented military authority, and why the Company lost control of its original economic purpose in the East, becoming a territorial, as well as trading, power on the Indian sub-continent. In this process three distinct themes will emerge: first, Clive's influence on the Company in wartime; second, the question of sovereign powers for the Company, and third, the impact that acquiring territory and political powers had on the Company's trading performance.

CLIVE AS COMPANY SERVANT

The remarkable thing about Robert Clive's early career in East India Company service is its conventionality. A wayward son of Shropshire gentry stock, without much money or prospect of improvement, Clive gained an apprenticeship to the East India Company, as a 'writer' or clerk in the Madras presidency. As he sailed for India in 1743, Clive's dreams and aspirations matched those of his contemporaries. The apprenticeship would lead in time to promotion through the ranks to merchant, and, should the opportunity arise, Clive fully intended to supplement his meagre salary with some private trade in and around Madras. However, the War of Austrian Succession and its repercussions in India dramatically changed this career plan. Clive transferred from the Company's civil to its military service, and found that his unrelenting and unforgiving drive, added to a genuine flair for leadership and strategy, perfectly suited the needs of the Company's desperate military position in the Carnatic at that time. After recounting the battlefield victories that followed this posting, it is common in traditional accounts of Clive's life to assume that his star continued to ascend until he reached the status of national hero; all the while providing material around which later mythologies grew up. This picture of Clive's exploits should not be taken seriously. Clive soon discovered that once hostilities ended, life for a Company servant resumed its normal, mundane routine. After the French threat disappeared in the Carnatic and around Madras in the early 1750s, Clive's need to be in uniform vanished too. His transfer was reversed, and, for a very brief period before his return to England in 1753, Clive found himself back in the Company's civil service. All excitement was at an end and his health failing.

This outcome did not really conform to what Clive had in mind to further his fortune and career. He soon discovered that returning to England with modest resources gleaned from the war left him vulnerable to rivals and creditors. In London the Company thanked Clive for his services and presented him with a diamond-studded sword as a mark of gratitude. Little went right for Clive, however, after this event. He had sufficient money to sustain a regular lifestyle for someone of his social position, and yet he chose a life of ostentation and extravagance much more in keeping with the unflattering eighteenth-century view of nabobs (a corruption of the Mogul term, *nawab*, meaning governor). Nabobs were Company servants who returned to Britain with wealth from the East and became notorious for their financial excesses (Lawson and Phillips 1984). Contemporaries viewed them as unpleasant parvenus without taste or sensibility, trying to buy their way into the upper social strata. Worse still, Clive became involved in an expensive and futile attempt to win election to the House of Commons by way of the volatile Mitchell constituency in Cornwall. It proved a bitter experience for Clive, whose election at the actual poll was rejected in the House of Commons for irregularities, and his opponent took the seat (Colley 1976). This defeat was not only a blow to his overarching ambition but also underlined his lack of connection to the powerful politicians at Westminster who could have secured his parliamentary seat. In short, he remained an outsider whose unattractive behaviour as a returned nabob appeared no different from, nor any more compelling than others of his ilk.

Thus, by 1754, blooded in politics and confronting severely depleted financial resources, it is not surprising that Clive's thoughts turned once more to India. What had been done before could surely be repeated. More important still to this calculation, the East India Company itself was not averse to accepting Clive back into its service, and, in this instance, neither was the state. Again, war, or at least the threat of it in 1755, came to the rescue of Clive's career simply because the position in India was adjudged to require the most resolute military commander available, if the French were to be subdued. Clive, in consequence, was appointed Governor of Fort St David, south of Madras, and, in addition, commissioned as a lieutenant-colonel in the British army – a more prestigious post by far than the equivalent Company rank. Unlike many other impoverished nabobs, Clive had now been given the opportunity by the Company to rescue his career and personal fortune in one fell swoop. And it is important to stress that nothing in Clive's correspondence or journals of the time indicates he had any other goals in mind. Nevertheless, the Company had inadvertently created a situation where it held a tiger by the tail. Clive's personal ambition in conjunction with the implicit encouragement of the Company and state to defend all of Britain's interests in India invited a perilous independence of thought and deed.

Clive did not disappoint. From his arrival in India at the outbreak of the Seven Years War in 1756 until his departure five years later, he led the Company from a position of vulnerability to complete dominance over its European rivals on the sub-continent. The chronology is straightforward. After securing the presidency at Madras and its satellite base, Fort St David, Clive was asked to respond to an emergency in Bengal where the new Nawab, Siraj-ud-Daula, had captured Calcutta on 20 June 1756. These events in Bengal were not part of the general conflict emanating from the European struggle of the Seven Years War but a problem of Mogul rivalry that spilled over into the British sphere of activity there. In this action the Nawab had imprisoned 146 Europeans in a crowded cell where, in one night, 123 met their deaths. The incident became known by the phrase, 'the black-hole of Calcutta', and later provided an emotive touchstone for moral outrage in Britain at the Nawab's behaviour just as powerful, if not more so, than the animosity a century before over the actions of the Dutch at Amboina. The revulsion at hearing the news of the episode undoubtedly spurred on the combined relief force sent from Madras under the leadership of Clive and Admiral Watson. In January 1757 they recaptured Calcutta, and on 23 June that year Clive experienced the greatest success of all in his military career, with the defeat of the Nawab's forces at Plassey. In the aftermath of this campaign, Clive became fabulously wealthy thanks to the enormous amount of plunder and presents put at his disposal. Moreover, the new Nawab of Bengal, Mir Jafar, became a puppet ruler beholden to the East India Company, through Clive, for his position and authority. In the end, therefore, the East India Company found itself with immense power over trade and political relations within the wealthiest kingdom under Mogul rule. In all but name, the Company had usurped imperial authority and sovereignty over the region (Lenman and Lawson 1983).

For a brief time between 1758 and 1761, a French counter-attack on British interests in the south-east threatened Clive's successes. Under the command of Lally, French forces captured Fort St David and moved from their base at Pondicherry to beseige Madras in 1758. But prompt action by Eyre Coote and the British forces at his command brought victory over the French at Wandiwash in January 1760, and final surrender at Pondicherry in 1761. In practical terms Wandiwash put an end to French pretensions for good, and should, in that sense, always be seen as no less important to the history of British advance in India than Plassey.

Dealing with the sequential aspect of Clive's career is a good deal easier than analysing the why and wherefore behind his actions. What has occurred in much British historical writing on this topic is a tendency to take the victor's view of affairs at face value. Clive, like his contemporary James Wolfe, became a national hero because of success at the very moment Britain appeared in peril in the global war against France from 1756 to 1763. Their martial achievements formed then, and have since, vital ingredients in the evolution of a national pride based on collective memory and consciousness of the special place these events held in the country's past. In this rarefied historical atmosphere more prosaic considerations in recounting this story are hardly addressed. In this particular case it is pertinent to ask: did Clive enact the wishes of his employers during this period, or did he merely engage in a massive exercise of personal aggrandizement in which Company interests played a minor part at best? Such questions spoil the heroic formulation of Clive's achievements in British history, but to ignore them is to gloss over the source of fundamental problems facing the East India Company over the next half century.

The initial point of historical dispute is what did the Company expect of Clive and his army in the circumstances of global war with France? It certainly did not change the standing orders or established ethos that determined the Company's mandate as a trading organization. Nor did the Directorate in London issue explicit instructions to Clive or any other commander to extend Company activities over additional territories and polities. The pervading assumption was that British interests in India, based on the East India Company's three presidencies, would be defended against French aggression by whatever means commanders in the field saw fit. In view of the political and military disruption caused by the European war, and the rising ambitions of certain Mogul rulers, such assumptions proved inappropriate to deal with the unfolding drama in Bengal after 1756. Clive's perception of the problem of security for Company and national interests in the field differed wildly from the perceptions of London administrators. The latter always had in mind cost-effective control and retrenchment when it came to strategic affairs. For Clive, in 1756, this type of policy would have meant the end of British trade in India and the East. As a result, he took action which he believed would secure the long-term position of the Company in the richest region of India. Bryant (1986) describes Clive's motivation for involvement in Bengal politics as that of the pacifier, rather than the opportunist in search of imperial grandeur. In the short term, this ideal required British troops and naval power to build a peaceful trade zone in that area of Mogul India; in the long term, however, profit and peaceful coexistence would result.

This policy is not representative of empire-building in its classical sense, though many historians of India's relationship with the East India Company have been keen to see it as such. True there existed an army of 20,000 Royal and Company troops in India during the war; but to accept that territorial expansion and imperial glory were the purposes of this body would, in the light of the evidence, be an invention – a leap of faith. Neither Clive nor the British officer class thought of themselves as the imperial vanguard in India. Such abstract notions cannot be discovered in the private records of these personnel. Rather, the more basic combative motive of wishing to engage the enemy, together with that of self-enrichment, claimed centre stage in their thoughts (Bryant 1978). Few Company servants, military or civil, ever pondered over the consequences of immediate actions or conflicts. Anxieties over surviving the heat and endemic diseases, followed closely by financial worries, remained the dominant concerns of all those serving in India (Marshall and Williams 1982).

These facts should surprise no one familiar with this period in the Company's history. With the benefit of hindsight, it is known that the British came to dominate the sub-continent over the next hundred years, yet it should be acknowledged that the initial advance lacked precise deliberation or forethought. On the contrary, the Company's expansion in the mid-eighteenth century most frequently arose from events dictated by the native powers in India, and without direction from London or the presidencies. In the words of Rees Davies, who has examined this dynamic in a different, but highly relevant, context: 'Domination is often most successfully asserted where it is unplanned and unconscious, where it arises (as it were) out of the natural weft of political relationships' (1990: 5).

THE EAST INDIA COMPANY AND CLIVE'S LEGACY

Planned or not, the results of Clive's handiwork in Bengal became the troublesome legacy inherited by the Company's Directors in London. It was an unenviable situation. Clive had exceeded his orders on several points, which resulted in the Company facing certain unpleasant repercussions. In Bengal alone, for example, military expenditures had risen from £375,000 in 1756 to £885,000 ten years later. Reductions in this expenditure would not be straightforward, as Clive had now dragged the Company into the tangled web of Mogul politics. Perhaps most disturbing of all for the Directors, however, was the fact that Clive's standing with the British people could not have been higher. If the Directorate wished to punish or even rein in its most famous employee, it would have to be done in the face of rising nationalist pride that saw Clive as that 'heaven born general', and the man who decided 'the fate of India' (Macaulay 1830). It doubtless came as a great relief to the Directors that Clive decided to leave India in 1761 and return to London. Removed from the scene of his great military triumphs, Clive, in the view of the Directorate, posed less of a threat to the financial well-being of the Company and its operations.

The most pressing problems for the Company lay in Bengal. The Bombay and Madras presidencies had, for the moment, been secured from harassment by other Europeans, and trade relations set on a firmer footing. The damaging involvement of the Company in the political rivalries of these Mogul domains would come later. In Bengal, the problems were more immediate, due to Clive; and involvement in local affairs became part-and-parcel of the Company's whole operation in north-east India. In practice this meant that the Company had to deal with several unprecedented problems at once, none of which could be solved by adapting practices of the pre-war years. And nothing better encapsulated the dilemmas facing the Company than the question of Clive's *jagir.*

A *jagir* in Mogul India was actually a military command rank with a stipend drawn from land-tax revenues. Mir Jafar granted Clive one such *jagir* in Bengal to an annual value of £28,000 which would be collected by the East India Company itself in lieu of the Mogul *zamindar* or revenue collector. The money would then be remitted to Clive annually through the Company's treasury. This prodigious and prestigious grant to Clive was not untoward in Mogul political culture, as a show of appreciation for services rendered. It certainly added up to very little in terms of what the new Nawab could expect to extract from his subjects in that region of India. Nevertheless, the existence of the *jagir* connected to one Company servant raised the most profound issues of legitimacy for the whole organization and its future in the East.

The obvious point confronting the Company's administrators on hearing this news concerned right. Did a trading organization have the authority to enter into a diplomatic agreement, to make and unmake Indian rulers, and then set itself up as a tax-gathering body supported, in the event of trouble, with force of arms? The exercise of these powers clearly belonged to an agency of the state not a trading company; though even here the constitutional case for Westminster to assume such powers appeared weak.[2] As it happened, the Company was not afforded the luxury of a debate on these topics, for the Directorate received the news of a *jagir* and related matters as a *fait accompli.* The Directorate had to adjust to the new reality in Bengal without warning or preparation. If this was not bad enough, there was also the question of whether or not Clive could be allowed to keep his *jagir.* In the first place he was not the only Company employee who had fought to defend British interests in Bengal during the Seven Years War. Others had a claim to such awards, if they were allowed at all. Second, it could be argued that Clive's heroism had now spilled over into simple audacity with his expectation that the Company itself would collect his 'present' from Mir Jafar and serve it up annually on top of his normal salary. Apart from the jealousy and distaste this caused among the Company's servants in general, accepting Clive's conditions set the sort of precedent that no corporate body would wish to live with. If Clive, why not every other Company employee who embarked on similarly ambitious schemes and experienced the same good fortune?

At first there was little the Company could do other than accept the enhanced role for its administrators and soldiers in India. Over the long haul, however, forces within the Directorate saw the potential for financial ruination in allowing Clive's expansionist policies to go unchecked. The Company therefore sought to reform the very managerial procedures that had allowed this situation to develop. These forces for reform were initially in the hands of Laurence Sulivan, whose career is brilliantly traced by Lucy Sutherland in her account of the Company during these years (1952: 49–80). Sulivan took an empirical view of the Company's administrative failings and, although he did not always practise what he preached, in the 1750s and early 1760s he did move against the most glaring structural abuses both at home and abroad. On the home front, he disliked the shady manner in which stock-splitting influenced Company elections, in which Sulivan himself had taken part, and was no more enthusiastic about the restrictive manner in which contracts were dispensed. In India, he sought remedies to the abuses prevalent in private trade between Company servants and native merchants. The Directorate dispatched stern missives to each presidency, warning against dishonest contracts, known euphemistically as 'the taking of presents'. Sulivan objected in principle to employees enriching themselves by threats, cheats and bribes, literally at the expense of Company profits and permanent trading interests in the East.

With such a man as Sulivan at the helm of the Company in the very period of Clive's greatest exploits and self-aggrandizement, a clash between the two always seemed imminent. The only question was on what grounds the conflict would occur. The answer came in 1759 in the debate over presents. Of all Clive's activities that Sulivan found reprehensible none offended him more than the acquisition of the *jagir*. Put simply, Clive had ignored all Sulivan's missives about integrity in Anglo-Indian relations. He had accepted the ultimate present and done so to the Company's cost. Clive's hero status did not concern Sulivan who believed that only by making an example of Clive would his leadership of the Company be upheld. Thus when Clive returned to England in 1760 boasting of fabulous personal wealth – to the tune of some £300,000 and the annual payment from the *jagir* of £28,000 – Sulivan felt obliged to act. His initial strategy was to keep Clive out of Company affairs by threatening to suspend the *jagir* payments. In theory, this cajolery imposed a neutrality on Clive, buying time, as it were, to allow Sulivan to continue his reform of certain procedures within the Company. But, in practice, the neutering caused an explosion of fury on Clive's part, and a determination in 1763 to put an end to Sulivan's interference in his affairs forever.

Clive was not a person prone to vacillation when challenged. As the diarist Horace Walpole put it, Clive was 'one of those extraordinary men, whose great soul broke out under all the disadvantages of an ugly and contemptible person'.[3] He intended to thwart Sulivan, whom he considered a self-interested hypocrite, by using his vast wealth and influence to initiate campaigns in parliament, the press and the Company itself, and seize control of his own destiny. Clive wished to create a Company with a Directorate that served and reflected his interests, especially the security of the *jagir*, and bring to an end Sulivan's reign and influence.[4] Thus, in early 1763 Sulivan found himself on the defensive and desperate for allies to counter the brute financial influence of Clive in the forthcoming elections. Sulivan knew of only one source of power that could match Clive – the state – and he appealed to the government for assistance in his struggle to complete the reforms and bring Clive to heel. This represented a momentous decision on the Company's part because its whole history had been devoted to keeping the state at arm's length. Now it had invited ministers to become involved in the very nuts and bolts of Company administration and governance. That the government accepted this invitation, under the aegis of Henry Fox and Lord Shelburne, proved no less remarkable, as the state had, almost in principle, avoided direct involvement in Company politics. The charter negotiations at renewal time were one thing, influencing the internal elections of the Company to defeat Clive quite another. Nothing between Company and state would be the same again after these decisions were taken.

What transpired from Sulivan's invitation was an unprecedented orgy of stocksplitting, polemical press campaigns and party-political blood-letting. The extremely well-funded supporters of Clive were pitted against the equally well-organized, and politically connected, forces of Sulivan; and, in the end, the hero of Plassey went down to ignominious defeat.

The ramifications of this struggle were two-fold. First, the government and its critics in parliament had played a part in East India Company affairs that could not easily be reversed. Sulivan may have calculated that he might use ministerial resources to further his own ends, but it did not quite work out this way. The politicians who had wielded power in these East India House elections saw no immediate reason to withdraw. Quite the opposite, the Company offered a ready pool of patronage and political networks that both government and opposition found irresistible. Over the next generation, in fact, the Company became, to use John Brewer's description, an alternative structure of politics to be exploited for public or parliamentary purposes by MPs and their respective followers (1976). The state and the Company had become involved in the initial stages of a relationship in which divorce ceased to be an option after 1763. Government had come to know of the Company's ample financial resources during the campaign against Clive, and this knowledge convinced successive administrations that some of this booty had to be yielded up to the state. The second result of Clive's defeat was instant suspension of the *jagir* payments. For a very brief period during the spring of 1763, Sulivan's reforming way triumphed over the greed and graft of the Company's most (in?)famous employee. The old trading mandate had been resurrected, and the penalties for transgressing instructions from the Directorate clearly laid out. It proved an illusion, of course, for only the first act in the drama of Clive's legacy had actually been played out.

TEA TOTAL: THE DOMINANCE OF THE TEA TRADE IN COMPANY OPERATIONS

The Company's trials and tribulations in the early 1760s seem somehow predictable in light of Clive and Sulivan's contrasting personalities and vision, vying for authority over the direction of policy. There is a subtext within this narrative, however, and it concerns the pertinent issue of what was at stake. Did the East India Company warrant such rancour and acrimony? After all, Clive's personal fortune and Sulivan's reforming zeal would be worthless if their conflict placed the Company's future in jeopardy. Fortunately for both protagonists this did not happen, and control of the Company proved worth fighting for. After hostilities ended in 1763 the East India Company began to enjoy a period of growth on all economic fronts. Its prosperity was a matter of national pride, and the government took special care during the peace negotiations with France (1761–63), to ensure that this situation endured (Sutherland 1947). The sophistication and accuracy of the Company's records for this period has allowed scholars to trace, down to finite details, the growth of trading activity in familiar products, such as raw silks, minerals, dyes and textiles. The confidence and capabilities of the committees charged with ordering, itemizing and financing specific quantities of trade goods before each sailing season were unequalled by any contemporary organization in Britain. The Company's books testify to a command system of exchange in which market conditions were fully understood and met (Chaudhuri 1978: 484–548).

One significant change did take place in Company trading practice by mid-century, however, and it involved tea. If the seventeenth century could be described as the era of spices, the eighteenth century undoubtedly proved to be the age of tea. This development had been foreshadowed after the union of the old and new Companies in 1708, when tea became an attractive and profitable import for those involved in the Bay and China trade. Yet nothing then really foretold the rapid acceleration in demand and supply that occurred in the 1740s, 1750s and 1760s. The trade did not represent something new or innovative for any of the Europeans trading in the East, but the scale upon which it developed for the English East India Company surely did. From a very minor role in Company activity in 1700, among much larger cargoes of textiles, spices and the like, tea came to dominate the shipping lanes from China to London in less than fifty years. Why this phenomenon happened at this time has yet to be adequately explained. Some parts of an answer might be gained, however, from a discussion of the history and practicalities of the supplying of tea to Britain and the existing market conditions.

Two remarkable facts stand out in any analysis of tea and the East India Company in these years: the elasticity of supply and the rapidity of market penetration. In the eighteenth century tea was supplied to the West from only one source – China. The Chinese themselves had drunk the beverage for hundreds of years before Europeans took up the habit. Two types of tea, green and black, were picked up by the Company ships in Canton for the home market at this time. The difference between the two lay with the process of withering and fermenting the leaves after picking rather than botanical factors. The tastes of the British, initially, favoured green tea but by the 1760s, some 60 per cent of imports were taken up with the black teas familiar to twentieth-century consumers (Mui and Mui 1984: 4–12). The volumes of tea being imported in this way were truly astounding. In the period 1711–17, approximately 200,000 lbs of tea per annum was landed in Britain by Company ships. By 1757 this figure had reached the staggering sum of 3,000,000 lbs per annum; making it the Company's dominant trade product. The ubiquitous tea chests in which the Company packed the leaves in China, evolved into the symbol of wealth and expanding trade influence for the whole enterprise in the East. Moreover, the teas were carried all over the world from the Company's London warehouses. Wherever the British traded, settled or colonized, tea would follow. Hard though it is to believe, for example, the 1.75 million American colonists actually consumed more tea by the mid-eighteenth century than the much larger population of the mother country.

To keep this explosive demand under control required an obvious flexibility on the part of the Chinese growers. Tea was grown in several Chinese centres without suffering from climatic difficulties, transportation or labour problems. Much to the Company's delight, supply from these centres could be increased by simple cultivation of extra bushes. Later in the century the East India Company, not happy with this single source of supply, appointed the great botanist, Joseph Banks, as an adviser on such matters. (It was under his direction that the idea of moving plants and vegetation from one area of British activity in the world to another came to pass. In one of the most notorious episodes of such initiatives, William Bligh moved breadfruit from the South Pacific to the West Indies. Less well known, but no less important, tea bushes were also transported to northern India and Ceylon, after its seizure in 1802, for production purposes.)

These policies help to explain the security and flexibility involved in tea supplies, but the market penetration of the leaf at the expense of other imports, such as coffee and chocolate, was quite a different story. To explain this, a whole range of factors, some tangible others less so, have to be considered. The first of these factors must be the nature of mass addiction to the chemicals occurring naturally in tea, especially caffeine and tannin. The addiction did not appear harmful and, moreover, it was cheap: one that could be met with a spoonful of leaves, a pan or kettle of boiling water, and a little sugar or milk. It used to be a popular joke that Hitler could have reduced Britain to its knees in the Second World War if he had been able to cut off tea supplies to the people. The same might be said of Napoleon in the late eighteenth and early nineteenth centuries, such was the scale of consumption and desire for the product. Since the Hanoverian period, the British addiction to tea has spread over the world and determined trade and agricultural patterns in large geographical areas of the East to this day.

Another aspect of this trade that encouraged a boom in consumption was the socialization of tea-drinking. The taking of tea by all classes of society in the eighteenth century, prompted changes in the nature and form of communal exchanges, including manners, dress and deportment. Consuming tea as a formal social activity in the mid-afternoon, for example, not only demanded hot water and tea leaves but a whole paraphernalia of tables, chairs, tongs, caddies and pottery. Conventions built around the holding of tea cups, the consumption of delicacies and organization of the social group made the supply of tea necessary to the ritual in itself. A further imperative by mid-century to ensuring supply were the secondary and tertiary economic activities linked to tea-drinking. Of the former, the most poignant example is the development of the pottery industry. The Chinaware that went along with tea consumption originally came entirely from the country which gave its name to the cups, saucers and dishes. The Company itself imported vast quantities of the merchandise on its tea ships. By the mid-eighteenth century, however, entrepreneurs like Josiah Wedgwood began to see a market developing for mass-produced ceramics to meet the requirements of tea-drinkers, and developed product lines accordingly.

A further instance of the Company's tea providing a fine catalyst for economic development concerns the distribution trades. After the tea was landed and stored in the Company's bonded warehouses, it fell into the hands of licensed distributors who bought huge amounts of the commodity at auction. Most, but not all, of the major distributors resided in London from which point they sought to control the national market. The means of doing this has a real aura of modernity, for the distributors used commercial travellers, sales catalogues and newspaper advertisements to attract wholesalers and shopkeepers to their wares (Mui and Mui 1989: 8–28). The distributors also worked out lines of credit or cash on delivery arrangements for their customers, predicated on records of solvency and dependability. The whole pattern of exchange from Company to shopkeepers' shelves involved brokers, commissions and extended capital investments of the type very familiar to commercial activity today. Like most other aspects of the Company's activities the business ran very efficiently: though it is a matter of regret that the tea ledgers belonging to the Company itself were destroyed by fire. Only for one or two years in the 1720s and 1730s had oversupply been a problem due to miscalculations by the purchasing committees.

The cumulative impact of tea-drinking on the British and their colonies should be viewed as profound in every sense. Tea brought knowledge of the East India Company and its activities to the rituals of daily life for the average citizen, enhancing the earlier familiarity with the Company's public face. Moreover, securing these supplies for future generations involved the Company and the state in political and economic decisions that bore directly on the development of a formal empire in the East. Robert Clive raised this very point in 1759 with William Pitt, the leader of the wartime coalition government in

London. In an ominous summary of the Company's rapid expansion in Bengal and future direction of policy there, Clive wrote:

> But so large a sovereignty may possibly be an object too expensive for a mercantile company; and it is feared they are not of themselves able, without the nation's assistance, to maintain so wide a dominion. I have therefore presumed, Sir, to represent this matter to you, and submit it to your consideration, whether the execution of a design, that may hereafter be still carried to greater lengths, be worthy of the Government's taking into hand. I flatter myself I have made it pretty clear to you, that there will be little or no difficulty in obtaining the absolute possession of these rich kingdoms . . .[5]

The Company Directors expressed horror at the sentiments expressed in Clive's letter; it merely reinforced their view that he was out of control and should be recalled. Nevertheless, Clive had struck at the heart of the Company's dilemma after the Seven Years War. The situation in India had changed, new responsibilities had been assumed and the clock could not be turned back. No one in London wanted to throw over the financial advantages arising from the Company's new role, especially in Bengal, and the booming tea trade from China. Indeed, in the circumstances of such expansion and success, the tea trade was viewed universally as a cash cow to be tendered with great care. From the Company's standpoint, tea represented the ideal trade commodity. Unlike textiles and wrought-silk imports, tea did not compete with domestic manufacturers. The product itself was easily transported and shared an excellent profit in ratio to its weight and bulk (Barber 1975: 65–72).

Two marginal factors did intrude on this excellent prospect. The first concerned the changing pattern of trade for Company ships in the East. In practice the focus of the tea trade was China rather than India. The tea clippers in this trade had to sail much further than the normal Coast and Bay voyage, with the added costs and wear and tear that this involved. As a result, a voyaging pattern evolved that missed out the Madras and Bengal portion of the return journey. This development, in turn, lessened the influence of the east coast presidencies on the tea trade and enhanced the position of the supercargoes in Canton in their stead. The second intrusion for the Company to address was the problem of smuggling. Those involved in the illicit tea trade not only included British subjects but also those of Dutch, French and even Portuguese origin. In certain years smuggling occurred on such a grand scale that it ruined Company accounting and purchasing procedures, deflating tea prices and disrupting wholesale and retail markets. Historians are faced with a vexed problem when assessing the impact of smuggled tea on the domestic economy because such activities always go unrecorded! Most scholars agree, however, that dealing in smuggled tea in these years was pervasive and the economic impact considerable: in any one year, for example, Britain and its American colonies could have been handling tea of which 50 per cent was landed illegally. These practices were simply an infuriating fact of life for the Company's administrators over which they exercised little control. The problem was out of the Company's hands and always would be.

The regulatory bodies that the Company relied upon to deal with malpractices like smuggling were controlled by the government, and good reasons existed for ministers to act on these abuses. Simply put, the national treasury drew large amounts of tax revenue from the Company's booming trade in tea. In the unfettered market that existed before 1784 and the passage of the Commutation Act, the *ad valorem* duty on tea reached 112 per cent. With the passage of the Act in 1784, this duty was reduced and fixed at an average of 20 per cent (the shortfall being made up or 'commuted' from a new window tax). This high rate of taxation became a two-edged sword in the 1750s and 1760s: it generated considerable revenue for the government but also provided a direct stimulus to smuggling. The huge duty made the risk of being caught with illicit tea worthwhile, and certainly damaged the Company's trade and profits. It would be wrong, nevertheless, to assume that everything the government did with respect to regulation of the Company's tea trade caused problems. In the 1750s, for instance, the old criticism against the Company's monopoly of trade in the East was revived. The trade to China, as William Beckford pointed out in the House of Commons in 1757, was not part of the original charter grant and should be thrown open so that everyone in Britain could enjoy this lucrative operation.[6] It was a strong argument in theory, but the government remained steadfast in support of the Company's monopoly privileges and its sole right to the profits from supplying tea. The government also took care in the 1740s to pass legislation ensuring that tea supplies as a whole were stabilized, and not artificially kept in dearth to raise prices.[7] These gestures represented small matters in the overall structure of state–Company relations, but they proved crucial to the Company's survival and profitability, and certainly helped to mitigate resentment at the scale of smuggling and related abuses.

In 1763 then, the Company found itself irritated by minor ailments of process and regulation, yet confident in its future. Annual profits exceeded £1 million per annum on all operations and looked set to rise further on present performance figures. The development of the tea trade nicely complemented the Company's other activities, and solidified its position as the great national endeavour in the East. Company affairs came before parliament and the press as a matter of routine, and the great mass of the population literally consumed the Company's products on a daily basis. By the mid-eighteenth century, Company stocks had become a most reliable long-term investment, and the whole trade operation had woven itself into the financial and social fabric of the country. Nothing could be guaranteed in trade and business, however, as the Company knew all too well from past experience. The final outcome of Clive's legacy had been postponed, not resolved. What appeared to be irritants in early 1763 would become chronic maladies for the Company and the state over the next twenty-five years, that not even the finest pekoe teas could cure.

NOTES

1. Seeley, *The Expansion of England*, p. 153.
2. Madden and Fieldhouse, *Select Documents*, II, 32.
3. *Horace Walpole: Memoirs of King George II*, II, 280.
4. Lawson, 'Faction in Politics: George Grenville and his Followers 1765–70' (unpublished Ph.D. thesis, 1980), pp. 233–51.
5. Malcolm, *Life of Lord Clive*, II, 122.
6. Cobbett, *Parliamentary History of England*, XIV, 1218.
7. 18 George 2 c.26, 10 Pickering, *Statutes at Large*, XVIII, 366–7.

CHAPTER SIX

The Fall From Grace: 1763–84

The view from Leadenhall Street of East India Company business between 1763 and 1784 defied comprehension. In every aspect of the Company's operations at home or abroad, confusion and consternation became the order of the day. The cause of this confused state lay with the sudden loss of direction within the Company's leadership. The trading mandate that had governed the Company's existence since the seventeenth century disintegrated. Where commerce had once reigned supreme there now appeared territorial and political power in India with all its vexed responsibilities for the Company. Indeed the East India Company became nothing less than the *de facto* ruler of the wealthiest area of the sub-continent – Bengal. In the context of the Company's traditional activities in India, the world had turned upside down. From being a client of the Mogul Empire, the Company became its principal agent and military power in north-east India. From this point on, the determining factor in decisions affecting British operations in India would be straightforward. In the words of the Bengal council in March 1765, action would result 'from such resolutions as might appear to us best-calculated for the Company's interest and the good of the country in general'.[1]

The order of priority here – Company first and India second – bespoke a new way of thinking about Britain's role in the East. It was a revision that flowed directly from Clive's legacy of territorial conquest and acquisition during the Seven Years War. And although it would be true to say that the Company Directorate in London neither designed nor promoted this changed role, the fact remains that it represented nothing less than a 'revolution' in Anglo-Indian relations

(Marshall 1987a: 78). In 1763 few observers in London realized the implications of the changes wrought by Clive and the Company in India or that such a revolution in responsibilities would have to be confronted down the road. When the realization dawned in the later 1760s and 1770s, and attempts were made to deal with these new problems, grief ensued because the Company structures proved unequal to the task. It was bad enough that in the period up to 1763 the traditional independence of the Company from the meddling hands of Westminster politicians had been abandoned. But matters worsened considerably when this ignominy was followed by horrendous diplomatic problems for the Company in India, leading to war and near bankruptcy. Whether it liked it or not, the Company lost control of its own destiny in these years and jeopardized British interests and investments both at home and abroad. In this process the Company also lost its most favoured position in the eyes of the government and the nation at large. Pride certainly came before the fall in the history of the Company over the years 1763–84. What had previously been unthinkable became standard practice: that is the state had to intervene several times in the Company's affairs to prevent the demise of what had previously been held so dear. It was a fall as painful as it was sudden for all concerned.

THE PERCEPTION FROM ENGLAND

To explain the reversal of fortunes for the Company after 1763 requires some recapitulation of the Clive (now Baron Clive of Plassey) legacy as seen by the Directorate in London. In the Seven Years War Clive succeeded in bringing to the Company some military glory, a potential for expanded trade and a whole host of administrative problems. Transforming the East India Company into a territorial power caught Leadenhall Street by surprise and complicated immeasurably the internal reforms then being enacted by Laurence Sulivan.

The struggle over the *jagir* proved to be just one act in an unfolding drama. Clive had returned to England in 1761 amid a great deal of personal acclaim, but few in London at the time understood that he had left behind a volatile political situation in Bengal reliant on his presence in India. After his departure for London, the treaty with the Mogul rulers in north-east India collapsed into war and by 1763 the conflict was offering a direct threat to British interests there. This turn for the worse placed the Directors in a very awkward situation indeed. While they recognized Clive as a troublesome employee who should be brought to heel, there was also a body of opinion at Leadenhall Street who saw him as the only commander capable of restoring Company fortunes in Bengal. It proved an agonizing time for the Directors because the choices being offered were the sensible long-term reforms of Sulivan or the short-term remedies implicit in armed aggression. In the event, military necessity took precedence over all other considerations. After some heavy pressure from within the Company, and also from the prime minister, George Grenville, it was decided in the fall of 1763 to use Clive as saviour. In the strangest way, therefore, Clive found himself transformed in higher Company circles from *persona non grata* to Good Samaritan, coming to the rescue of British interests in India.

In taking this decision there is no doubt that the Directorate erred in its judgement of where the Company's best interests lay. In the first place, Clive was permitted to leave London in 1764 with no clear delineation of what should be done in Bengal. Quite the opposite, in fact, because the Company Proclamation, declaring Clive Commander-in-Chief on 1 June 1764, granted the sort of sweeping civil and military powers that invited trouble. Past experience seemed to have taught the Directors nothing in this context. The Council in Bengal was told that Clive's reappearance on the Indian scene arose from the simple intent 'that by His Lordship's character and influence, peace and tranquillity might be the easier restored and established in that subahship'.[2] Such innocuous phrasing hardly concealed to anyone familiar with Clive's ambition and strategic thought that herein lay an explicit sanction of further military adventures at the expense of local Mogul rulers.

Indeed, within a year of his landing in Calcutta, Clive had raised a force of Company and native troops, destroyed the power of the incumbent Nawab, Mir Kasim, and replaced him with Mir Jafar, who was replaced by Nazim-ud-Daula in early 1765 after Mir Jafar died. The new Nawab was an old ally of Clive and someone far more receptive to the desires of the Company in north-east India. Clive did not stop at this point of success, however, for he wanted to restructure the future balance of power between the Company and Mogul rule. He aimed, in the most calculating manner, to ensure that no further destabilization of British interests occurred. How was this done? By a simple clinical exploitation of the Company's military might is the answer. Clive decided that in the future the Company would collect the territorial revenues due to the Nawab and then dispense sums from this account to support the administration in Bengal. The lowliest tax-gatherer to the Nawab's court itself would be funded by this means.

To all intents and purposes this policy rendered the independence of the old imperial government null and void. The Mogul rulers' 'acquiescence' had, as Malcolm put it euphemistically in his memoir of this period, been gained, and it was not to be given up at any price.[3] This action represented a complete reversal of the old relationship between the Company and the Mogul empire. Yet it proved to be one that the imperial rulers in and around Bengal had little option but to accept. In a very grand and ostentatious ceremony on 12 August 1765 at Allahabad, the transfer of effective authority was confirmed when the Mogul emperor, Shah Alam II, granted the Company the post of *diwan* (revenue collector) of the imperial provinces of Bengal, Bihar and Orissa.

The Company's administrators in London received this news with understandable enthusiasm because they had no conception of the broader implications of Clive's policy. They believed the old order had been restored and did not immediately comprehend that, as one contemporary observed: 'This Empire has been acquired by a Company of Merchants; and they retained the character of exclusive trader after they had assumed that of sovereign . . . Sovereign and trader, are characters incompatible.'[4]

It is easy to blame the Directorate for failing to perceive what might be the outcome of entrusting ultimate power in India to a man like Clive, but that would misrepresent the context in which Company decisions were taken. In the eyes of those in London observing the news of events in India after the Seven Years War, many factors came into play which made it imperative that something be done to salvage the desperate situation in Bengal. First of all there was the unique position that the Company occupied in the nation's financial and political structures. As Huw Bowen has explained so well in his study of these years, the Company was a source of taxation for the state; a haven for investors of long- and short-term stocks and bonds, and its affairs became a matter of national political debate (1991: 39–41). Such an important component of the fiscal and commercial state could not be neglected. And this fact was underlined in the fall of 1763 when not only was the news from India bad but a general European credit crisis threatened to ruin international trade. It was in this atmosphere that the Company and government became convinced that Bengal's troubles had to be rectified or they would have a dire impact on the national economy, its credit and trading performance. In these circumstances it is not difficult to sympathize with those who believed that desperate times demanded desperate measures, and Clive became the man of the moment.

What happened after Clive's pacification of Bengal had been seen to succeed by 1766? The brutal truth of the matter was that Company policy failed to keep pace with events. The approach of the Company's Directors in London became irrelevant, in most cases, to the behaviour of its servants in India. The reasons for this breakdown of communication were straightforward. It had always been the intention of the Directorate to support and nurture native rulers in India who offered the best opportunities for peaceful trade and increased profits. Now that Clive had taken over the local administration and made the Company the real power in Bengal, the Directorate found itself bereft of an essential purpose in its dealings with the Mogul rulers. Over the next two decades a pattern very quickly emerged in which policy became determined by local emergencies and realities rather than London directives. As the ever-vigilant diarist Horace Walpole pointed out at the time, the Company was attempting to govern 'nations to which it takes a year to send orders'.[5] It proved a vain attempt once the Company in London began reacting to, instead of directing, the deeds of its employees in the East. What made matters worse, as recent research has shown, is that party politics began to spill over from Westminster into the dealings of the General Court and the election of Directors. This development surprised few at the time in the light of the fact that East India Company business was still seen by the majority of interested observers as a domestic issue (Bowen 1991: 43–4). Nevertheless, party politics did little to help the Company resolve its difficulties at home or abroad. Internecine strife, coupled with a lack of initiative in responding to events across two oceans, handicapped the Company's policy-makers to the point of confusion and indecision.

Added to all these difficulties was the fundamental issue of war and conquest. The consequences of Clive's military adventures in 1765–66 were played out over the following two decades and, for the most part, the Company stood by helplessly as aggression increased and profits fell. The problem lay in the fact that to onlookers and investors in Britain, Clive's exploits appeared to have succeeded, bringing the country and the Company untold wealth in the process. Clive himself boasted that the *diwani* or tax revenues from Bengal, Bihar and Orissa would enhance Company revenues by some £4 million. Such fabulous wealth inspired pride and expectations at home that simply could not be met. East India Company stock exploded in value and dividend payments more than doubled by early 1767 to 12.5 per cent. However, this bull market arose from speculation not performance. The £4 million was not profit but a wild estimate of the Company's whole revenue from its expanded responsibilities before other costs had been calculated.

Most important of all, the policy of military pacification by the Company in India cost a vast amount of money which was not covered by normal operating capital. As Peter Marshall points out by way of example, the war waged by the Company in Bihar alone from 1763–64 cost more than the £600,000 raised annually from land then under its control (1987a: 88–9). The shortfall had to be made up by exhorting the collectors under the Company's influence to extract more, or by borrowing on the open market in London. In the best circumstances such policies would be viewed as somewhat risky, in the twenty years of unsteady leadership after the Seven Years War they proved to be the Company's undoing.

To explain this dynamic it might be helpful to truncate what turned out to be a very convoluted process. In the beginning the loss of control in London over trade policy created an administrative hiatus in India, permitting the private traders and military adventurers to flourish. The difficulty for the Directorate in London was to exert control over the situation. On the one hand, it forbad further conquest after Clive for good economic reasons. Yet, on the other, it could also recognize that in certain cases the use of force to support legitimate trading ends was justified. Unresolved as it was, the tragedy of this dichotomy soon became apparent to the Company after Clive's departure from India. No matter how many missives left London promoting peaceful trade, it always transpired that commanders on the ground took the decisions about the use of force. The results were predictable – some decisions were good, others proved disastrous to the Company's best interests. Each local commander, whether in Bombay, Madras or Calcutta, had his own view of where pacification ended and outright aggression began. These Company soldiers were not civil administrators and often proved insensible to the imperatives governing Indian alliances. Decisions made on the spot for what seemed perfectly justifiable strategic reasons frequently ended in bloody and expensive encounters with local rulers, which were seriously detrimental to the Company's position and performance.

The history of this period from the London perspective, therefore, is characterized by war and expansion in defiance of orders from

London. The Company's administrators found themselves trapped: they could neither turn the clock back to the halcyon days before Clive's appearance on the scene nor reassert control over the future direction of policy in his wake. Wars in the Mysore region around Madras in 1768–9 and 1780, and armed conflict with the Marathas in north central India in 1779, all testified to the failure and inadequacy of the Company's leadership in England. The experience of these years represented what Sir John Malcolm aptly described as a scene of 'disasters and mismanagement' from which the Company would never fully recover.[6]

THE REALITY IN INDIA

What made the scene in London far worse than imagined for those trying to control Company affairs from afar was the extent to which British and Mogul interests became enmeshed. The Directorate never really comprehended the full scope of the revolution occurring in the Company's activities around its three presidencies. It was one thing to receive a letter from Calcutta describing the office of the *diwan*, it was quite another to grasp the true meaning of its influence on the lives of those subject to the Company's new status. Indeed, just reading over the published volumes of correspondence between Fort William and Leadenhall Street offers a glimpse of how perplexing it must have been for the Directors from 1763 to 1784. In the main, Company letters from India were marvels of concision, revealing the essentials about the Company's operations without the incriminating contexts. These sources have certainly been useful to historians in reconstructing the eighteenth-century British advance in India, but whether the information which they contained was fully understood by Company administrators at the time seems less certain.

The letters were usually read by people who had no first-hand experience of India or its social and economic structures. Such ignorance was unavoidable for most Company administrators in London, and yet they were charged with responding to the concerns raised by their servants in India. It proved an onerous responsibility and brings to the fore the obvious question: what did all this information from India mean if it could not be properly understood? Not a great deal is the conclusion to be reached from an examination of the actions taken in London during this period. The fact of the matter was that no one could convey how rapidly the scene in India, especially in the north-east, changed after 1765. In every aspect of Mogul political, social, economic and military affairs, the Company's presence left its indelible mark of change. Some of those changes were deliberate, others were not, but hardly any letter travelling from India to London carried the true meaning and reality of what had transpired after 1763.

The most obvious example of a region that witnessed and endured the Company's new way of governing in India is the well-documented case of Bengal. When the Company took over the responsibility for tax-gathering here it became drawn into the warp and weft of Indian economic relations in a quite unpredictable manner. It had to oversee the traditional practice of transferring annual agricultural surpluses into tribute for the Mogul court, and this proved no simple matter. To make the system work required a deep knowledge of relations not only between Hindus of different castes but also Hindus and their Muslim overlords whom the British wished to replace. After the assumption of the *diwani* in 1765, the Company supervised native administrators who assessed the tax burden on each producer (*ryot*), enforced the fiscal laws in revenue (*zamandari*) courts, and arranged for the collection of all moneys through the Office of Revenue (*khalsa*). Any flaw in appreciating the subtleties of this system meant a reduction in revenue, as the Company soon came to realize. Despite consulting Muslim lawyers and Hindu middlemen, it failed almost immediately to meet its monetary goals from the *diwani*. In response, the Company sought early reforms to traditional procedures. It first did away with the annual tribute ceremony (*punyah*) in 1772, where the money collected in Bengal had been given to the Emperor or his representative in person. In its place, the familiar European practice of tax-farming with European collectors was initiated. Five-year leases on fixed returns were granted at auction by the Company, and many of the leases ended up in the hands of the old *zamindars* originally usurped by the Company (Bowen 1991: 113–15). This proved a profoundly important change in process with a subsequently wide-ranging impact on Indian life. The reforms surprised none of the East India Company's servants in India at the time, however, because the intricacies of the tax system had simply overwhelmed the English administrators. They did not master but adapted to the established Mogul system as they saw fit. It was therefore a painful transition and one that proved extremely difficult to convey in letters to London. If Company servants in India could barely comprehend the economic changes occurring around them, then how on earth could the Directors in London who supposedly made policy on these matters do so?

Comprehending the structure and purpose of diplomatic alliances between the Company and Mogul rulers proved no less problematical for the Directorate. The example of Madras is particularly relevant in this context because the disputes over troubles in this presidency found their way back to London for settlement in the 1780s (Phillips 1985). Company policy in southern India had always been to cultivate the imperial ruler, the Nawab of Arcot, in return for trading privileges and exclusion of European rivals. Matters got out of hand, however, after the Company had supported the Nawab in military campaigns against his rivals in the First Mysore War (1767–69); and later in wars in the vassal State of Tanjore (1771 and 1773). The more unscrupulous Company servants negotiating with the Nawab demanded presents, rights and privileges, which quickly drove the Nawab into debt, and titular subservience to the East India Company. The only means the Mogul ruler had of keeping up with payments due to the Company and its servants was to exploit state revenues and those of vassal kingdoms, such as Tanjore, to the point of exhaustion.

The insensitivities manifest in the Company's dealings with the Nawab were epitomized by the short career of Sir Thomas Rumbold as Governor of Madras (1778–80). In less than two years in office, Rumbold had acquired a personal fortune of £750,000, at least a third of which came in the form of bribes and pay-offs from the Nawab himself. Yet at the same time Rumbold had done nothing to stabilize relations with the native powers in the area. On the contrary, after his departure war broke out when Haidar Ali, the Nawab's rival in the Carnatic, took control of much of the hinterland around Madras. On his return to London, Rumbold suffered the embarrassment of inquiries by parliament and the General Court of the East India Company into his conduct (Phillips 1988). He did not, however, suffer too much, as all efforts at exerting some punitive sanction on Rumbold's behaviour came to naught.

The point to be made is that Rumbold and others caught in this web argued that, given the situation in India in which the Company found itself, such behaviour was legitimate. In their eyes, the directives about diplomacy from London displayed neither an understanding of the fluid state of Mogul politics nor a deep awareness of operating on these economic frontiers with their alien values and cultures. Success in trade demanded compromises and connivances in the structure of local alliances. All Europeans operating in and around Madras understood these demands but Company servants failed to persuade

London of the benefits of this way of proceeding. In consequence many orders from the Directorate went unheeded. For example, even though Company policy forbade contact with the French and Dutch traders both country's fleets were part of everyday Company activity because the situation demanded it. A shortage of cargo space in English vessels could be met by Dutch carriers; a surplus of raw silk could be carried back to Europe by the French. These actions defied the Company line from London but made sense in the context of operating in this polyglot trading world. As will be seen in the next section, it took near bankruptcy, several parliamentary inquiries and state regulation for the Company in London to appreciate these facts fully.

To be fair it was not always the Company's rapacious habits that initiated a deeper involvement in Mogul affairs. What Clive had envisaged from his experience of dealing with the Mogul empire was a limited diplomatic and military role for the Company around its three presidencies. The complexity of Mogul alliances had, however, confounded this diktat. At the moment of East India Company intervention in Bengal affairs during the early 1760s, for example, the neighbouring province of Awadh had been attempting to establish itself as an autonomous region under Mogul rule. Its ambitious leader, Wazir Shujah-ud-Daulah, expanded Awadh's territory and power base around Faizabad by 1761, and plans were afoot for further advances. Political and economic relations with Bengal were good at this point because Awadh's economy depended on the land- and river-borne trade in the Ganges delta. To the East India Company such developments caused little concern, as its interests were seen to lie firmly within the orbit of Fort William, the centre of all Bengal operations.

Nevertheless, trouble ensued for both Company and Awadh when the Wazir and the Emperor Shah Alam II took the side of Mir Kasim in 1763 against British interests. In the famous battle of Baksar in 1764, the Company defeated the combined forces of Mir Kasim and Shujah-ud-Daulah, ending peaceful coexistence between British interests in Bengal and those of the Wazir. Even though the Company had not desired such an outcome in its dealings with the Wazir, relations deteriorated incrementally over the next generation as British influence – both official and unofficial – expanded into Awadh (Marshall 1975b). The Company believed that it could never again trust the ruling élite in Awadh, nor could it ignore the province, for the economy of Bengal had such close links with its neighbours. Awadh was eventually annexed by the Company in 1801, but only after a rancorous and at times destructive history of contact since 1763. Like many other problems they confronted in this period, Company servants reacted as they saw fit in the local circumstances. When the time came to explain their actions in dispatches to London, in terms that made sense of the context, the task proved to be excruciating. Nothing that was related about the Bengal–Awadh situation offered hope for peaceful coexistence in the future or proof that the Directorate could control events through its servants in India.

As a last instance of how difficult it could be for the Company's leaders in London to grasp the realities of service in India, it might be helpful to look at the career of Warren Hastings, Governor-General during 1774–85. A great deal has been said and written over the last two centuries on Hastings' contribution to the Company's history. Yet no consensus has been reached on an assessment of his role in India in this period, and aspects of his career are still hotly debated in scholarly publications. Disputes on this matter are understandable in the light of Hastings' own personality and the state of Company relations with the Mogul empire that he inherited as Governor-General in 1774. On the one hand there are Hastings' well-documented military campaigns against the Marathas and Benares. The daring march across the breadth of India from Calcutta to save Bombay from Maratha invaders became the stuff of legends. When the situation demanded it, Hastings could be as ruthless as Clive, brutally raising extra taxes to fight his wars; and unforgiving with opponents such as the Brahman Nandakumar, whom Hastings had executed for challenging his rule in 1776. The 1770s found the British at war all over the globe because of the American revolution and Hastings exploited this conflict at every opportunity to further Company interests. He possessed a vision of strong rule by the presidencies supported by English laws and justice. Each presidency was to be surrounded by friendly Mogul powers, providing a buffer against those hostile to Company operations. It proved an ambitious vision and yet Hastings more or less achieved the military and diplomatic goals that he had set out to accomplish. The bare bones of this strategic model of the Company's place in India endured until its demise in 1857 (Misra 1959: 23–7).

Did such actions represent a classic case of British imperial expansion at sword-point? For some historians the answer is an obvious affirmative. Hastings had a plan and the force to put it into effect. Any benefits that accrued to the Company later were acquired at the expense of the indigenous peoples and their governments. On the other hand, others view this explanatory model as too trite. There is a great deal more to Hastings and his thoughts on the British role in

India than straightforward campaigns of slash and burn against Mogul rulers. In Hastings the Company had appointed someone to high office who showed pride in his knowledge and regard for oriental government, society and culture. He understood, as few of his contemporaries did, that the Mogul empire was no monolith that could be reduced in one fell swoop to the benefit of the Company. Throughout his career Hastings strove to reproduce that peaceful coexistence with native powers around the presidencies so dear to the Directors' hearts in London. He wished to have Company servants respect the rule of law in the presidencies and recognize the laws and customs of the territories now under British influence. He sought to preserve local institutions and traditional practices wherever possible, and under his auspices Hindu and Muslim laws were translated into English for use by English judges in India. He patronized scholars interested in recording Indian art and literature; and founded the Calcutta Muslim College to train young men for state service. In 1784 he helped to establish the Asiatic Society for Bengal, and in 1780 he supervised the setting up of the first printing press in Calcutta, which published the *Bengal Gazette and Calcutta General Advertiser.* Under Hastings' leadership the great orientalist Sir William Jones, a judge in the Bengal Supreme Court, prospered, and he was positively encouraged to bring a deeper understanding of India and its cultures to a British readership (Bayly 1990: 114–15). Artists and writers from Britain roamed freely on the sub-continent during this period, capturing and recording for posterity the eighteenth-century British experience in India.

Thus it would be inaccurate to say that Hastings' career matched the classical pattern of the brutal, insensitive adventurer out to make a fortune for himself and the Company. In fact Hastings returned to England in 1785 with a very modest sum for his retirement and without the fanfare that had, for instance, greeted Clive. He did, however, prove to be a huge problem for Company administrators in London. The existence of Hastings' sympathy and respect for Indian ways and customs provided no help at all for a Directorate attempting to control the evolution of Company policy. The tender and terrible facets of Hastings' character complicated matters for London because the Directors were generally ignorant of India, its institutions and culture, and not well disposed to Hastings' military policies which proved ruinous to the Company exchequer and share dividends. The trouble that Hastings took to consider British responsibilities as the *diwan* and predominant military power in three large areas of the sub-continent escaped the comprehension of the Directorate.

At times these uneasy feelings at home turned to outright resentment at what Company servants did in India. In part this happened because of an increasing awareness that control had slipped away from London but also because the Company had attempted to reform itself and failed. In consequence the Company left the door open for government intervention. In the 1760s and 1770s the areas of Company concern ranged, not unnaturally, over the gamut of Indian operations: from the problems of setting up courts of law in each presidency, collecting revenue more efficiently to recruiting and training a viable army of European conscripts (Bowen 1986b). In each of these areas the Company gathered information from experts and began a methodical analysis of the problems to be addressed. On the issue of judicial and institutional reform some progress was made in the early 1770s for instituting proper procedures for hearing trials and dispatching Company business with native traders. On the large issue of revenue collection, however, one disaster followed another, thwarting all the Directors' efforts at coming to terms with the Company's enhanced responsibilities in India after 1765.

This failure was a particularly savage blow to the Company's fortunes because it tried so hard to reform its revenue and accounting practices. After the assumption of the *diwani* the Company had devised a three-fold purpose in reforming the revenue side of its operations. First it wished to keep expenditures on administration to a minimum and to maximize profits from all trade surpluses, especially from Bengal. Second, there was a great effort to improve the transfer of profits and hard cash from the Company's operation in India to the London treasury. Third a valiant attempt was made at computing the real worth of the Company's trade and profit. It turned into an unedifying experience for the Directorate. Documenting the Company's performance was a simple matter because the records were so good, revealing, for instance, that by the 1770s Bengal cargoes had overtaken tea in terms of value. Reforming the Company's procedures, on the other hand, proved quite another problem. Arguments broke out over long-term economic policy and development in Bengal between Indian administrators and the Company in London. Figures in London indicated that assumption of the *diwani* had actually incurred a loss to the Company in costs and profit, and the Directorate sought a short-term solution to the problem by exploiting profits on popular trade goods (Bowen 1991: 112–13).

If this strife was not bad enough, the Directors' hopes for reform in Bengal were completely undermined by war, famine and the harmful private business activities of Company servants. War and famine in the late 1760s and early 1770s, especially in north-east India, decimated the local populations, wrecking everyday trading relations and Company revenues. These concerns were then exacerbated by the devious and often corrupt behaviour of Company servants involved in private trade with local merchants. The major problem for the Company lay in the manner private Indian fortunes made by its employees were remitted back to Britain. The rule of thumb was that the Company issued bills of exchange in Calcutta, Madras or Bombay to the value of that person's goods or treasure in India. These bills could, in turn, be cashed in or drawn at East India House in London by the employee. Restrictions on the issue of these bills were laxly enforced and often ignored by Company administrators in the presidencies. The reality of the situation made it easier to give in to intimidating Company grandees, such as Clive, who demanded bills in very large amounts and cared little for the needs of others. Such capitulations in India, however, simply removed the accounting difficulty to London where it became a chronic problem. The summer of 1771 proved particularly painful because the Company found itself overdrawn on these bills and without the cash reserves to meet its obligations.

The Directors found no solace in any remedy they offered to the economic crises of these years. Everything they attempted seemed to end in disaster. Even its own three-man Supervisory Commission under Vansittart's leadership came to a sticky end. Dispatched to India in 1769 to observe first-hand and act as the Directors' nominees, the Commission sank with all hands on the *Aurora*, leaving Cape Town for India. The incident was symbolic of all the London initiatives about reform. The Company leadership had lost control of its servants in the 1760s after the full implications of Clive's legacy in India became apparent. There was no longer firm control from the centre of operations but a business and administration driven by local demands and emergencies. To restore some order to these affairs required an agency with more power and reserves than the Company could now muster.

THE STATE RESPONDS

The history of state interference in East India Company affairs up to the 1760s had been unprepossessing and limited to certain legal and constitutional requirements over the course of the Company's development. In particular, the Company's existence depended on the charter granted and renewed by parliament under the Royal seal. In this process throughout the first half of the eighteenth century, successive governments had seen fit to protect the monopoly privileges so valued by the Directors and believed to be so vital to the Company's financial survival. The argument that the Company had to possess sole control of the flow of goods from the East found its detractors from the beginning, but the anti-monopolists had made little headway by the 1760s in the face of this highly profitable and well-connected organization. This arrangement had benefited both Company and state over the first half of the eighteenth century. Profits and taxes rose while competitors were excluded by statute from any share in Company wealth. As the Company grew in size and stature, however, many observers began to question this limited role for the state in its affairs. In the light of the fact that East India Company's armies and traders had begun to assume the proxy power of a nation-state in India, critics demanded stiffer regulation and definition of where Company responsibilities ended and those of the British government began.

On the surface this critique did not appear a difficult matter for the government and its supporters in 1763. Yet to address the questions raised above would require examination of the very underlying factors that had inhibited government interference in Company affairs over the last century and a half. It proved an unpleasant experience for the politicians and Company servants concerned. The first objection to interfering in Company matters had always been the philosophical one, relating to the abrogation of charter rights. Most politicians in Hanoverian Britain viewed charters as property rights whose terms of sole possession and independence of operation were written in stone. The most common rhetoric used in this context stated quite simply that if governments could override chartered Company rights at will, what could stop evil ministers moving against the real property of individuals? A second perennial consideration for any government contemplating direct action on East India Company affairs was the existence of free debate in parliament. It spelt trouble for any ministry that sought to attack charters whether or not they covered domestic or overseas trade. Politicians would debate the matter furiously, raising the spectre of Stuart despotism more often than not; and pamphlets, polemics and newspaper articles would appear soon after to lend weight to those opposing government intervention. It became a rule of thumb that governments stayed well away from this subject, if at all possible, because it struck right at the heart of assumptions about liberty in the world of Hanoverian politics. In an era of developing party politics, the East India Company's troubles always had the potential to become a *cause célèbre* in opposition onslaughts about constitutional improprieties by the government of the day. The last, but by no means least, handicap for any administration planning direct involvement in East India Company affairs was ignorance. At the highest levels of government there existed a very shallow pool of knowledge about the Company's operations at home and abroad. Rapid education on the subject of the Company's activities would be required by any ministry contemplating deeper involvement in its affairs. Keeping the East India Company at arm's length had not only resulted in the state having a limited role in its day-to-day affairs but also little appreciation of the drama that had unfolded in India by the 1760s.

What changed this pattern of external control, and forced the government into direct involvement in the Company's internal affairs? In short, it proved to be the sheer magnitude of the crises faced by the Company in India and at home. Try as it might, from 1763 to 1784 the government simply could not galvanize the Directorate into putting Company affairs in order. The ineptitude of Company leadership in London and the wayward behaviour of many of its servants in India began to unravel the original purpose of British enterprise in the East. What started as an administrative problem for the Company became a cause for national concern after 1763, for the clear reason that the affairs of Company and state were so entwined. The immense value of the Company's activities to British tax and custom revenues could not be jeopardized, in the last resort, by a failure of will in Leadenhall Street. Clive's expansionist policies, and the new administrative responsibilities assumed in India in 1765, had opened a Pandora's Box of financial and diplomatic problems, defying Company-inspired solutions.

The government had to respond, therefore, because ministers could not bear to see the pillars of the old relationship dissolving into sand. First, the finances of the Company became highly volatile after 1765. What had been a rock-solid investment, suddenly became the prey of voracious speculators. East India Company stock lost its gilt-edged reputation and exploded in value over the late 1760s, bringing back memories of the South Sea Bubble for many observers. This type of speculation did not impress ministers used to a Company which lent money to government and stood by the names of reliability and stability over the previous fifty years. Second, there was the problem of what to do about the Company's military policies in India.

On a practical level, concern was expressed over territorial expansion, war parties, fortified settlements and the like because such practices cost a great deal of money. And such moneys could only be furnished from the profits on trade, lessening, in turn, the value of the Company's whole operation to the state. On a more theoretical level, the government found the idea of a Company making and breaking alliances with various Indian rulers very disturbing. Such prerogatives belonged to sovereign states not trading Companies, and, if not controlled, the Company could conceivably lead the nation into a ruinous war with the Mogul empire. Third, the government could not stand idly by, watching the demise of Company trade policy. So much of the nation's financial health was caught up in the eastern trade, and whole domestic industries depended on the regular supply of such commodities as tea.

A further set of adverse factors assisted the government in its intervention in Company business over the years, and these concerned the increasingly hostile public atmosphere within which the organization found itself operating. Any survey of the popular press over the third quarter of the eighteenth century reveals a distinctly frosty commentary on the Company and the activities of its servants. There was familiar disquiet at the monopoly being allowed to continue, together with a great deal of vicious and sarcastic comment on the wealthy Company servants (nabobs), with their tastes for the vulgar and ostentatious, who returned to Britain. There was also revulsion against the behaviour of what contemporaries referred to derisively as stock-jobbers, and the practice of making money by abject speculation or peculation.

Underlying all these concerns, however, was a public and parliamentary critique of the moral issues surrounding East India Company activity at home and abroad. The targets aimed at by the great speakers, such as Edmund Burke, and writers, such as William Cowper, were two-fold. One was the corruption of Indian civilization itself by the awful behaviour of the Company's servants – a practice Burke considered a breach of the most sacred trust one powerful nation held towards another.[7] The other was the impact this dubious means of enrichment had had on Britain itself. To many observers, those responsible for territorial expansion in India were inclined to import their brand of baseless adventurism. It was in their eyes a bad trend with dire implications and consequences for British liberties if allowed to continue. Indeed much ink was spilled and energy expended over this period to make sure this trend was reversed. In the words of Lord Chatham, great issues were at stake:

> The riches of Asia have been poured in upon us, and have brought with them not only Asiatic Luxury, but, I fear, Asiatic principles of government. Without connections, without any natural interest in the soil, the importers of foreign gold have forced their way into Parliament by such a torrent of private corruption as no hereditary fortune could resist.[8]

The sum of such hostility was to create a chilling climate for the Company's operations, allowing the government to deal more directly with its obvious shortcomings after 1763. It did not matter that such outbursts were impressionistic, lacking any factual or statistical proof. These hostile perceptions caught the mood of anti-Company feeling in the 1760s and 1770s, making state intervention that much easier.

The story of intervention is now well-documented and consisted of three legislative assaults, in 1767, 1773 and 1784, on the Company's procedures and operating mandate (Lawson 1982; Bowen 1991; Marshall 1968). These government initiatives were accompanied by an enormous effort of will on the part of parliament and the British public to come to terms with Clive's legacy and the wider implications of territorial expansion in India. There were hotly contested pamphlet debates, newspaper wars, parliamentary battles and in 1783 a full-blown constitutional crisis over East India Company legislation. And the one factor bedevilling government strategy over these years was a basic division of purpose in the regulation of Company operations. In 1766–67, for example, the Chatham ministry sought to establish the fundamental principle that the state not the Company owned the territory in India from which taxes were extracted. The legal basis for the government's claim lay in the decision of 24 December 1757, known as the Pratt-Yorke opinion. It ruled that sovereignty in settled and ceded colonies remained with the crown, but property rights in land could be vested in the Company.[9] By the mid-1760s this ruling was seen to be ambiguous when applied to Chatham's sweeping claim of total sovereignty over all Company operations and possessions. Members of his own cabinet even doubted the case for total sovereignty (Bowen 1988). In consequence, the essential question was avoided by a compromise: the East India Company agreed to pay the state £400,000 per annum and in return parliament limited itself to regulating voting qualifications and the dividend on stocks. Small-scale though it was, this preliminary state intervention into Company affairs did reveal differing visions of what regulatory role the government and parliament should adopt. All agreed it would be hopelessly impractical for the government to assume control of all Indian operations at this stage, but no consensus existed on any other aspect of dealing with these alien problems.

One positive outcome of the parliamentary inquiry in 1766–67, however, was a growing awareness of what East India Company business – good and bad – amounted to in Britain and India. Moreover, the precedent for parliamentary interference and legislative action had been established. When the next crisis developed over the disastrous wars and near bankruptcy of the Company in 1772, the government could draw on previous experience before intervening. Two parliamentary committees of inquiry (select and secret) studied the problem and came forward in 1773 with recommendations for the government of the day led by Lord North. North was a pragmatist when it came to dealing with the East India Company. He certainly believed in the sanctity of charters, viewing state intervention as a last resort to solve any problems and an open invitation to trouble at Westminster! Nevertheless, the financial and military situation had deteriorated so badly in London and India that government action on the Company's behalf became a necessity. Lord North's India Bill of 1773 or Regulating Act, does reflect the reticence with which his ministers proceeded on such matters, no matter how favourable the conditions for intervention. The immediate goal of North's legislation of 1773 can be characterized as doing only what was required to restore confidence in the Company's financial position and resolve the diplomatic impasse in India.

To achieve this end, the legislation focused on certain areas of Company administrative practices for reform and rescue. In terms of executive reform, the Regulating Act of 1773 appointed a Governor-General, based in Bengal, for the whole of India. The Governor would rule with a council of four others from outside the Company and approved by both the Directors and the cabinet. Warren Hastings was appointed as the first Governor-General in this reformed executive. To deal with the financial crisis, North arranged for the state to lend the Company £1,400,000 to help it avoid bankruptcy. Dividend payments on stock were limited to 6 per cent until all debts were cleared, and the bond dividend fixed at 7 per cent on the same conditions. Internal reforms were also initiated to the Directorate. It still consisted of twenty-four Directors, in total, but only six could stand for re-election every year. Voting in the General Court of Proprietors now required a £1,000 holding to qualify and the vote could only be exercised if the £1,000 had been held for a calendar year. The main legal adjustment to Company practices in India took the form of the establishment of a Supreme Court in Bengal for the whole of British operations on the sub-continent. The judges in this court would be appointed in Britain by the crown, and they could hear pleas and appeals from both Europeans and Indians. It was in this court that the great figures of Anglo-Indian history, such as Elijah Impey and William Jones, emerged.

With this package of specific remedies North intended to eradicate the immediate problems of Company indebtedness and administrative dysfunction. And in that sense he had some success. North's ministry survived the usual political agony over charter rights by pitching the debate in non-partisan terms, emphasizing the necessity of intervention in the affairs of this troubled national body, and also making the legislation temporary. The Regulating Act would be reviewed and renewed in 1780 but until that time all parties concerned were requested to give the legislation a chance to work. In all this activity North had proved himself to be the master of parliament and the legislative process, for, in hindsight it can be seen that the Regulating Act invoked an irrevocable change to state–Company relations. Despite all appearances to the contrary, North had in fact overridden or abrogated the clauses of the charter by parliamentary statute. In less than a decade, the defences of the Company's constitutional position had been broken and the state now had the right to interfere in all aspects of the most powerful commercial enterprise in the realm. All that remained was for the state to assert its right over all territorial revenues.

It was some time before contemporaries realized the full significance of North's initiative because short-term anxieties about the Company's performance still dominated debate in the 1770s. North's legislation did not resolve the undercurrent of concern at the continuing crises afflicting the Company after 1773. Military adventurers under Hastings and financial woes visited on the Company in London seemed unaffected by the Regulating Act. The belief that here was an organization out of the control of its Directors endured. The Act only partially allayed the fears of the Company's most ardent critics and proponents of reform. Over the next six years, therefore, attacks on the Company's conduct in India increased. Articles in the press and parliamentary orators, like Edmund Burke, refused to let the matter of more fundamental reform to the Company rest. Politicians and public alike came to know more of the heroes and villains working for the East India Company abroad, and the belief that the state should exert yet more control in India became commonplace. By 1780, however, North had no more enthusiasm for restructuring the relationship between state and Company than he exhibited in 1773. Furthermore the general political situation looked far more difficult when it came to the question of reforming this international trading enterprise. For a start the Regulating Act had clearly failed on two significant fronts: the Council in Bengal and the Directorate in London still lacked backbone when faced with corrupt servants abusing their offices and, worse still, war and territorial expansion had not ceased. Contrary to all hopes and expectations, these failures had by 1780 brought the Company to the verge of bankruptcy again. To those in London observing this unwelcome outcome of the Regulating Act no comfort could be found. The Company seemed unaware that there was now a global war in process, arising from the American War of Independence. In this struggle Britain was pitted against the major colonial powers of Europe and stood to lose most of its overseas possessions if matters did not improve in the near future.

In such circumstances no one at Westminster or Leadenhall Street doubted that a long-term solution to the problem of state–Company relations was required. Yet how could it be achieved against a backdrop of colonial crises and political instability at the highest levels of government? Between April 1782 and April 1784 no less than four ministries with four different prime ministers took power. Each had its own vision of how to proceed on the East India Company issue, and at one time or another each presented its own India legislation to parliament. Put crudely, the debate in these years came to centre on two visions of how to reform the relationship between state and Company. The first favoured placing power in the hands of parliamentary commissioners in London who would superintend all Company operations and appointments from Britain. The second supported the notion of strengthening royal control over the Company in India itself by enhancing the power of crown appointments on the sub-continent. The vehicles for this debate were initially two parliamentary committees of inquiry – one select and the other secret. The former became the mouthpiece of Edmund Burke, Charles James Fox and Lord North who believed in exercising parliamentary control over India from London. The latter, secret committee, fell under the spell of Henry Dundas, Lord Shelburne and William Pitt, the younger, who wished to reinforce the power of the crown in India, exerting control over Company operations *in situ*.

In the fall of 1783 these two visions of regulating and reforming East India Company operations collided in a parliamentary struggle of epic proportions. The king himself became involved in the various machinations that led to the fall of the Fox–North coalition over its India Bill in December 1783 (Cannon 1969: 7). In this process, the question of which vision of reform for the Company should prevail could not have been more clearly stated. Fox and North became the black hearts in this debate determined to put the 'King in chains' and control the East India Company through parliamentary majorities for their own personal, and nefarious, ends. Pitt and others ranged against them appeared as the white knights coming to the defence of disinterested royal prerogative and preserving the Company's wealth for the whole nation. In the end royal power won out. Supported by an enthusiastic public and press, Pitt emerged victorious in this struggle with his vision of reforming the Company intact. From the Company's perspective this whole constitutional crisis over Indian legislation had a hollow ring to it. Both visions of reform represented stiff medicine for the Company's ills and implied certain elimination of its old independence and buccaneering ways.

Such niceties were of no concern to the new ministry when Pitt presented his India Bill to parliament in the summer of 1784, as the final act in this saga. It became law in August of that year. To all intents and purposes the bill was the work of Henry Dundas and his secret committee. The clauses that mattered concerned the desire of government to oversee the political and diplomatic functions of the Company. A strong Board of Control under royal direction was established in London, therefore, to oversee and approve all dispatches between the Company and native powers. The power of war and peace, in other words, became the province of the state. In India itself, deadlock over decisions in the Bengal council was remedied by the appointment of a strong Governor-General in Bengal with the right of veto over decisions in all three presidencies. This office was tied directly to the crown and, by necessity, the prime minister of the day. The Company was still involved in revenue collection and the transfer mechanism. Yet the message sent by these clauses to the Company was that in the future its servants should concentrate more on the trading aspect of the operation. The government had now assumed control of the political and diplomatic powers previously held by the Company. The Directorate and General Court of Proprietors had indeed been right to fear further state intervention, for their respective influence over Company affairs had been reduced significantly. The Act, in fact, governed the basic outline of Company development and responsibilities until it was abolished in 1858.

Pitt's India Bill brought a disastrous period in the Company's history to a close. Every aspect of the East India Company's institutional probity and business acumen appeared to be heading towards inexorable decline. The original trading mandate of the Company had been ruined and then grudgingly rescued by state intervention. Its public reputation was severely tarnished, if not dulled beyond repair. By 1784 the Company had lost its favoured status in the country's eyes. When Clive and his imitators had delivered territory and tax revenues to the Company and the state, there seemed every reason to celebrate at the expense of Britain's rivals. After the full measure of Clive's legacy became apparent, however, the Company's iron will to succeed collapsed. As a result, the state had to intervene to salvage its own taxation sources and the Company's overall finances. In this outcome the Company found itself without allies to defend its old powers and privileges which fell away like discarded clothes. By January 1784 the position of the Directorate proved so weak and desperate that it prompted a motion to be sent to the government, declaring that 'on the subject of the civil or military government, or revenues of India, the Company was bound to conform to his Majesty's pleasure'. Self-knowledge of this sort embodied the fall from grace. The Company's loss of control over its own trading policies and dalliance with territorial expansion had ruined its finances and left it exposed to the whims of politicians. The Company's integrity had been compromised beyond redemption. Clive's legacy proved an indulgence that the Company could ill-afford. It had resulted in political intervention and that, in turn, changed the whole nature of the Company's role within Britain and the trading community at large.

NOTES

1. *Fort William–India House Correspondence*, IV, 314.
2. Ibid., p. 55.
3. Malcolm, *Life of Lord Clive*, II, 340.
4. Nicholls, *Recollections and Reflections*, II, 244–50.
5. Walpole, *Letters*, V, 30, 18 March 1764.
6. Malcolm, *Life of Lord Clive*, II, 264.
7. Marshall, *The Writings and Speeches of Edmund Burke*, V, 140–1.
8. Taylor and Pringle, *Chatham Correspondence*, III, 405.
9. Madden and Fieldhouse, *Select Documents*, II, 194–5.

CHAPTER SEVEN

The Company Set Adrift: 1784–1813

It is one of those perverse historiographical ironies that at the very moment of its remorseless decline, the East India Company's history could not have received more attention by scholars. Any student looking at this period in the Company's past will be struck, overwhelmed even, by the proliferation of narratives, accounts and analyses of every description and hue. Contemporary writers recognized this phenomenon themselves. Peter Auber, Secretary to the East India Company in the 1820s, prepared a massive two-volume history of the Company's constitution and development. In the introduction he lamented: 'It is rather a redundancy, than paucity of information, which is generally complained of.'[1] Indeed, between 1784 and 1813 public knowledge of Company affairs and British activities in India generally increased markedly. Every aspect of the Company's operation was openly debated in parliament and the press. Maps of India, the Near East and south-east Asia appeared in official and popular literature, revealing territorial possessions on the sub-continent and far-flung factories from Baghdad in the west to Penang in the east. Material was being gathered then for the splendid histories that are still with us today by authors such as Sir John Malcolm and James Mill.[2] Petitions arrived at Westminster protesting, declaiming and promoting all aspects of eastern trade, usually to the detriment of the Company's best interests. Auber was thus correct in his assessment of the volume of information available on India and the Company in this period. Not recognized so readily at the time, however, was an ominous sub-text to this debate on the Company's fortunes. Whereas there existed a great deal of enthusiasm for Britain's continued role in the East, less and less comment appeared on the failing fortunes of the East India Company in that same theatre.

In retrospect it is not so surprising that this obsession with the East developed in the 1780s and 1790s. The great war for America had been lost, changing the mood of the nation into one of patriotic excess. The virtues of the royal family and George III, in particular, were extolled and great pride expressed in the remaining imperial interests of the country (Colley 1984). It used to be said that a 'swing to the east' took place in this period, as the nation looked for compensation for America's loss. Most historians now believe this explanation to be too simplistic, crediting the government with more direct purpose than it ever possessed on these matters. Nevertheless, the swing does carry the germ of a convincing explanation for an exceptional popular interest in the East after 1784. The nation's wounded pride required succour and it could be found in the preservation of the eastern trade empire under a reformed central administration in London and Company rule in India.

There is no doubt that the British government attached immense importance to the reform of the Company and defence of India and the eastern trade at this time. Moreover, there was no lack of opportunity to launch investigations and reforming initiatives. Between 1784 and 1813, there were two charter renewals, accompanied by several parliamentary committees of inquiry, each one publishing witnesses' testimonies and recommendations for changing Company operations. To heighten interest further, all this activity took place with the French revolutionary and Napoleonic wars in the background. In the darkest days of these hostilities, British trade fell into a deep crisis, and the fear that France would invade India was openly discussed. To cap it all, the Company's monopoly came under the most concerted attacks from merchants and politicians out to put an end to its trade privileges. In previous attacks of this sort the Company had stood fast, but that did not prove the case in this campaign. In 1813 the Company's monopoly on all but the China trade disappeared. These were, to put it mildly, momentous times for the Company, and to understand the forces that drove its mandate into the ground over these years, three major themes will be examined: administrative paralysis, militarism and the gradual destruction of the Company's trading privileges.

COMPANY ADMINISTRATION AND FRUSTRATION

Pitt's India Act raised expectations in Britain that the East India Company would rediscover its original purpose and prosper. The judicial, political and diplomatic reforms in India, coupled with the establishment of the Board of Control in London, aimed to redirect the Company towards trade and the pursuit of profit. Clive's legacy had shattered many illusions about Company power in India and every effort would be made to avoid a repetition of these events. Those responsible for the legislation of 1784 went so far as to insert the following definitive statement about territorial expansion: 'that to pursue schemes of conquest and extension of dominion in India, are measures repugnant to the wish, the honour, and the policy of this nation'.[3] Nothing could be clearer than such declarations. They seemed designed specifically to meet the criticisms of commentators like Edmund Burke who would spend much of the 1780s and early 1790s forcing the impeachment of Warren Hastings for his conduct in India (Marshall 1965). To Burke, impeachment involved no personal animus. Hastings simply represented the face of the evil conqueror who had usurped all the legal and moral duties due to the Indian people. Pitt's Act, seen in this light, therefore, was an attempt to prevent a reoccurrence of these conditions, even though it did not save the old Governor-General himself. Thus, as Burke and other moralists pursued Hastings, the state and the Company had to devise a working relationship capable of producing the reformed government in India now prescribed as beneficial.

It proved a daunting task and one in which the Company played the role of junior partner. The reasons for the Company's weak position stemmed directly from the political imperatives behind Pitt's India Act. This legislation sought to revive royal power at home through the Presidents of the Board of Control and in India by means of an all-powerful Governor and Captain-General appointed by the crown. The Governor in India would have right of veto over the Bengal Council and decisions of the other presidencies. Modern scholarship has come to view such designs as inherently authoritarian. The government, with the Company's compliance, created in India the preconditions for a type of enlightened despotism familiar to continental Europeans in the late eighteenth century. This model of government had no precedence in the English-speaking world and the whole debate about its necessity adopted, what Peter Marshall calls, 'a highly doctrinaire tone' (1987b: 117). Reform in India might be discussed using terms like benevolent, improving or even progressive, but such verbiage signified a belief that the British had to take an authoritarian approach in order to secure the benefits of the East for the nation. In practice, this benevolent despotism took on a peculiar characteristic of sullen over-protection. Sir John Seeley expressed this notion perfectly when he described this period in Anglo-Indian history as being '*brahmanised*'.[4] The attempt was made to keep India as a kind of inviolate paradise into which no European culture, and especially the missionary variety, should be allowed to penetrate.

The person chosen by the crown, Board of Control and Directorate to institute these desired reforms was General Charles Cornwallis, the losing commander at Yorktown in 1781. Cornwallis had, despite his most recent unfortunate military past, a good reputation with politicians of all stripes in Britain. He possessed political, administrative and military experience in abundance and was known for moving decisively on a grand organizational scale. Such talents would be at a premium if the government in India was to be renewed. Cornwallis served as Governor-General from 1785 to 1793 and attempted increasingly throughout his time in office to achieve the reforms insisted upon in London. He had his successes too. No diplomatic or territorial adventures proceeded from his directives. Cornwallis defended the ruler of Travancore, a Company ally, against Tipu Sultan in the third Mysore War (1789–92), but no deliberate campaigns of expansion were undertaken. The Company's debt load was reduced significantly in this period and important restructuring of the judicial system took place.

Most important of all, Cornwallis introduced a professional ethos into the Company's bureaucracy. The motives for this reform have a modern ring. To induce Company servants to relinquish their involvement in and need for private trade, along with the unsavoury behaviour associated with such transactions, Cornwallis approved appointments based on merit with fixed, attractive salary scales. The injection of pride and incorruptibility as ideals in service to the Company proved a novel and welcome reform. It has been said, in fact, that such ideals in the Indian service assisted in the development of a professional bureaucracy in Britain, imbued with a similar ethos of civic virtue (Marshall 1981). Training for service in the Company's bureaucracy eventually became focused on a special college, Haileybury, established for this purpose in 1809. The curriculum was strictly controlled and included obligatory courses in Asian languages, laws and customs along with a smattering of political economy and accounting. In theory, no Company servant could sail to India after

1809 without first spending two years at the college (Misra 1959: 397–402).

The purpose of all these reforms, in Cornwallis's view, was to create that benevolent rule in India untouched by malevolent Europeans, as described in chapter six above. The crowning glory of this process came in 1793 with the great land reform known as the Permanent Settlement. It began in Bengal and lasted, in title at least, until 1947. The Settlement initially concerned revenues from land and production assessments in the wealthiest area of Company rule. These revenues were fixed in perpetuity and sought to raise annually the sum of £3 million. The agency by which collections would be made developed in the old imperial office of *zamindar*. It seems fair to say that Cornwallis and his circle viewed this group of people in much the same way as country gentlemen in England, collecting the taxes due from their tenant farmers (Guha, 1983). If the *zamindars* looked after their estates well and paid taxes on time, they would be left alone by the British and have total security of the land under their control. If, on the other hand, the *zamindar* in a particular area became delinquent, the land would be repossessed by the British and given to someone else who could fulfil the stipulations of the Permanent Settlement.

Much commentary has appeared over the years on this Permanent Settlement and many differing views have been put forward on its efficiency and impact. Certain historical schools posit the argument that it changed Indian society in Bengal irrevocably; others maintain quite a different view, arguing that the Permanent Settlement sought to turn the clock back, ossify the revenue system and kill any reform at all. There is a grain of truth in both these positions. Many Indian cultivators were indeed hurt by Company assessments which often proved unrealistic and severe. *Zamindar* agents were often tyrannical too, operating without checks on their behaviour. Yet some producers did benefit from the Settlement, as they consolidated land holdings and emerged wealthier by the early 1800s than before (Marshall 1987a: 122–7). What is clear, however, is that the Company had confessed its inability to bring about change itself, through its own officials. The active part of this Settlement lay in the hands of the *zamindars* who, in turn, were locked into an unchanging rural tax system. The titular overlord of this system, the East India Company, hardly sought progressive rates of taxation from this system, simply consistent supply. In consequence, many observers soon came to believe this rigid Settlement inhibited innovation, industriousness and progress. To so-called liberal thinkers of the early nineteenth century, the creation of this rustic abomination in India signalled the decline and corruption of a once-great Company. In the words of James Mill, the point is made clearly:

> It is the interest of permanent governments to promote the prosperity of their people, because the prosperity of the people is the prosperity of government. But the prosperity of the people depends entirely upon their freedom. What governments, in this account, have even promoted freedom? The propensity of the Zemindars was, to regard themselves as petty sovereigns.[5]

Whatever the results of the Permanent Settlement, and these are still hotly contested by scholars from Asia and the West, the Company had allowed itself to be used in the remodelling of the administration in north-east India. It had to follow now rather than lead. This turn-round occurred because the Governor-General and Board of Control, headed by Henry Dundas, were in accord on the question of '*brahmanizing*' government of the territories in India under British control. Much the same pattern emerged with Cornwallis's successor, Sir John Shore. He was highly thought of by Dundas and the prime minister, Pitt, and became acceptable to the Directorate by way of his career as a Company servant and his extensive administrative experience in India. Shore's talents, in fact, lay in economic affairs, and who better to oversee the Permanent Settlement in its formative years than a person with such a background? It would be a gross exaggeration to say that Shore was a man of vision who could restore the Company's energy and status in India and at home. As one of the leading scholars in this field put it, Shore's 'Lifetime habit was obedience' (Phillips 1961: 70). In truth, Dundas proved the dominant force behind the Governorships of both Cornwallis and Shore from 1785 to 1798. The desire to tie the Company's administrative hands worked because Dundas had the political power in London to get his own way. The judicial system, revenue collection and administrative procedures were restructured in that benevolent fashion designed to keep Company affairs static and predictable. In 1793 this 'project of imperial state-building' (Bayly 1989: 119) looked set fair, as £500,000 per annum was going into the exchequer in London from land revenues in Bengal. This success proved illusory, however, for one vital facet of the Company's institutional power had been neglected. In creating their inviolable Indian world within which the British could operate, Dundas and his advisers failed to remodel the army – with dire consequences for all concerned.

MILITARISM AND MISCHIEF

The East India Company's army in India formed a unique body, with three main limbs. By 1784 each presidency provided for its own defence with a mixed force of troops, including a small cavalry, artillery units and regular infantry (in Bombay a small fleet – 'the marine' – existed too). On the whole the majority of these forces consisted of sepoys officered by Europeans, mainly, but not always, British in origin. The conditions of service were particular to the Company's army. The officers could not purchase commissions as in the British army proper, for example, and promotion was based on seniority. The status of officers and men in the Indian army was seen to be inferior to those serving in the royal forces, and in war-time, when the two came together, regular British army officers always took precedence. These differences were further accentuated by the social make-up of the forces themselves. The British army had a much higher percentage of aristocrats and gentry in its ranks – 53 per cent – while the Indian army had only 23 per cent. The bulk of the officers in the Indian service came from the middling sorts out to improve their lot. The impact of such differentiations appeared as a tendency on the part of the Indian army to be very defensive about its privileges and unique character. It quickly developed a strident militaristic ethos and tradition, and an equally strong determination to protect its independence in the different presidencies.

In view of the strong centralizing efforts and authoritarian reforms being canvassed by Dundas, Cornwallis and Shore, it might seem that such independence would be shortlived. It was particularly dear to the hearts of both Dundas and Cornwallis that the Indian army should be made royal, and a clear division, along British lines, be drawn between civil and military power within the Company's jurisdictions in India. Nevertheless, the attempt at army reform with these aims in mind failed. All the energy and political influence from George III through Pitt and Dundas to Cornwallis and Shore, could not force the enactment of the desired institutional changes to the Indian army. In name and deed this force remained independent until 1857 (Callahan 1972). This failure is remarkable in itself when the forces for reform looked so much more powerful than the body of resistance. More important, however, are the broader implications of this miscarriage, for they do point directly to the fragile condition of Company rule by the 1790s in India. In fact the Indian army was no longer controlled by the Company at all. Indeed, many historians have argued of late that the actual picture of command was quite the reverse (Peers 1990: 287). Clive's legacy had rendered the defence of Company interests impossible without armed force. Awareness of this crucial fact had encouraged the army to seize the initiative in the Company's expanding territorial power of these years, making it indispensable to effective government by the British in India. Thus, some fifty years after Clive, the Indian army had exploited its fire-power to the full and come to dictate both trade and military policy.

Nothing could have been more disastrous for either the state or the Company's long-term interests than this outcome. Yet neither the Company in India nor the Board at home could halt this progression to militarism in the rule of the presidencies. The reasons for this impotence in the face of the army's advance are in dispute to this day, but several primary factors are common to all recent explanations of this dynamic. First of all the enfeeblement of Company rule from London since 1763 had allowed the strong and the armed to take the lead in controlling territory and revenue gathering in India. The numbers in armed service speak for themselves. In 1763 troops in the Company's employ totalled approximately 18,000 men, the division being: Bengal 6,580; Madras 9,000 and Bombay 2,550. By 1805 these figures had changed drastically to read: Bengal 64,000; Madras 64,000 and Bombay 26,500. Such expansion bespoke the principal occupation of the Company's defence forces – war. By 1800 these armies had long ago ceased to play the role of simply defending factories and fortifications. These forces ruled and controlled the areas under direct Company jurisdiction, and held in thrall those other areas within the Company's orbit. Despite the best efforts of Dundas, Cornwallis and Shore to bring the growth of military expenditure to a standstill, it continued apace.

Thus, a second factor needs to be considered by way of explanation, and this concerns the practical imperatives driving men and officers in the Indian army to want more control and influence over Company decisions. The obvious impetus in this context was financial gain and security. Most serving in the Indian army did so because of impoverishment in Britain. Some sought to make personal or family fortunes; others wished to restore them. A few, like Clive and Rumbold, succeeded, and it was the stories of such successes that drove the others on to private trade by force of arms, dubious deals with Mogul potentates and surrogate territorial conquests under Company colours. That the Indian army was serious about defending its position and privileges there is no doubt. The study of the officers in this force from 1765 to 1805, for example, reveals a distinctive view of the relationship between their employers, the Company, and ultimate overlord, the crown. The guiding principle of this officer class was to preserve the Indian army's independence from royal authority and protect its privileges from Company interference. If either was threatened, the army officers mutinied, and, quite remarkably, this weapon succeeded in exempting the force from reform to its procedures and prerequisites. On more than three well-publicized occasions between 1766 and 1809, the officers used the mutiny weapon with clinical precision to achieve their selfish ends. In effect, the Board of Control in London and Company administration in India admitted defeat on the issue of soldiers supplementing their regular pay through private enterprise. And it was a submission taken in the full knowledge that these practices frequently led to mischief and conflict.

How such independence from state and Company authority could be rationalized at the time, opens up a third area of debate, relating to the prevailing political mood in Britain. The advance of the Indian army over the Company's civil administration coincided with long periods of war in Europe against France and Napoleon. The distractions of these hostilities played into the hands of the militarists in India, as they were able to use the French threat to conceal adventures of their own. The French presence in the East was often trumped up to secure support for some private gain or strategic goal, and found expression in the particular campaigns against Awadh and the Carnatic in the 1790s. The Board of Control and its ministerial backers became victims of their own authoritarian policies in these years. They created the benign dictatorial Governors, Cornwallis and Shore, who followed instructions seeking to limit and retrench British interests in India as desired by Dundas and Pitt. In the actions of their successor, Marquess Wellesley (previously Lord Mornington), however, the authoritarian policy came home to roost.

Wellesley was Governor-General from 1798 to 1805: dispatched at a time when Dundas was very distracted by domestic and European affairs. Wellesley came from an Irish military family on the make. Two brothers were already serving in India: Henry was a Company administrator of some repute and Arthur (the future Duke of Wellington) a soldier in the Indian army. Wellesley's appointment was a compromise, and a dangerous one at that. He had no love for those involved in trade or any mercantile activity at all. The East India Company, on the other side, had no respect for his slender talents as an administrator. The Company's fears that here was a man simply bent on militaristic adventures to enrich his family and its prospects in Britain proved well-founded. Wellesley's governorship involved one expensive military excursion after another – made without any regard to cost or the Company's financial or trading interests. By 1805 Wellesley had covered himself and the Indian army in glory and sunk the Company deep in debt. There seems little doubt that in his own egotistical view of his role in these affairs, Wellesley used the Indian army quite cynically to achieve his own ends. He feigned belief that British interests in India were under external threat in the north and south-west, and acted accordingly. It is not surprising, therefore, that the Company came to believe that Wellesley held the wrong post and was fighting in the wrong force. He never possessed the mandate to undertake aggressive campaigns in Hyderabad, Mysore and Awadh, and completely twisted Dundas's idea of defensive operations in the East. As Edward Ingram aptly suggests, Wellesley needed fame to make his family reputation and fortune (1981: 121). In the India of militaristic belief and crumbling Mogul polities, Wellesley was provided with the ripest opportunity to achieve his ends. It proved too late by 1805 to undo the damage he inflicted on the Company. By this time it had succumbed to chronic debt and was ready to be dismembered.

Wellesley's role in this drama would not have been possible without a fourth factor coming into play; and that was support in Britain for an aggressive posture in India. In the 1790s there occurred an outpouring of patriotic royal fervour and nationalist celebration. This phenomenon can be categorized as a simple reflex action in response to the events in America and France. There were, however, more complex forces at work here than a conservative backlash to republicanism (Colley 1986). A revolt was under way in the attitude of the public and politicians to the established traditions in the conduct of national policy. In Britain the old oligarchic forms of government came under attack; bureaucratic reforms to the civil service were inaugurated and evangelicals preached against moral abuses such as slavery and Catholic exclusionism. The authoritarian figures identified with this renewed patriotic and royal fervour in the domestic political setting were Pitt and William Wilberforce. But also included in this pantheon were the imperial heroes whose stars had risen on far-flung battlefields and oceans. Men such as Rodney, Nelson and Wellesley fell into this group.

The East India Company could only have been dismayed at Wellesley's elevation to popular hero, and yet it was understandable in view of the war with France and the prevailing national mood. There existed a dark side to the atmosphere of ultra-loyalism, revealing itself in the denigration of those associated with any resistance to British authority. During the wars in India from the 1790s onwards, therefore, not only did France appear the antagonist but its allies too, particularly Tipu Sultan of Mysore. Tipu was killed at Seringapatam in 1799 during the Second Mysore War by Wellesley's forces, and the British celebrated this victory over French and Islamic 'tyranny' without reserve. A mystique built up around these warriors in the East and can still be found in the military art from the period and the artifacts displayed in regimental museums. There also appeared a disturbing racial and cultural overtone in the popular literature and ideologies associated with the march of white men over dark foes in hot and tropical climes (Bayly 1989: 113–14). Tipu became one figure in a long line of black-skinned villains, later found haunting the pages of imperialistic yarns by the likes of Henty, Haggard, and the stories in *Boy's Own* comics. The prevailing political and social climate of Britain in the 1790s protected and enhanced Wellesley's hero image, therefore, while encouraging the complete abandonment of the Company's best trading interests.

A final factor to be considered in the setting adrift of the Company in this period relates to the bureaucratic mind-set emerging in the wake of these events. Much to the Directors' dismay, a new class of administrators in both Britain and India expressed sympathy, by word and deed, with the militarism behind Wellesley's rule. Outside Wellesley's family circle, whose support was guaranteed, there were influential figures such as Thomas Munro, a settlement officer in the Madras presidency in the 1790s, who endorsed the revolutionary empire that the Governor had initiated. A younger generation of Anglo-Indian bureaucrats had no time for the old caution of Laurence Sulivan or Sir George Colebroke. They wanted a rule in India that did not simply respond to events in the localities but created opportunity for advancement. Masking their militarism in words of benevolent nationalism, very able Indian administrators would appear in the early nineteenth century to articulate the vision of a distinctive type of British army rule to be found nowhere else in the empire. In words and printed pages of active propagandists like John Malcolm and Charles Metcalf of the Bengal service, and Mountstuart Elphinstone in Bombay, the Company's trading mandate fell apart, as private interests were given full rein under the guise of a national military endeavour. The implicit pattern of military expansion and control that emerged from this period made it imperative that more money and resources be sucked into the support mechanisms for the army and its bureaucrats. Trade profits proved quite incapable of meeting this monetary demand and, apart from borrowing, that left only Indian allies, formed and coerced into subsidiary alliances, to fill the paymaster's void. Such policies were the thin end of the wedge for a Company on the brink of ruin.

MERCHANTS TO PROFESSIONAL ADMINISTRATORS

In the period 1784–1813 the original structure of the East India Company's trade to India and the East changed beyond recognition. Pitt's India Act sought to establish a clear delineation of the differing roles each group involved in the eastern trade would play. Politics, diplomacy and the law belonged to government in London, overseen by the Board of Control, while trade and administration remained a Company preserve. The overriding aims of this policy soon came to naught, however, because the vision in London where this legislative solution was conceived, failed to appreciate the complexity of the overlapping nature of trade, politics and warfare in India. In addition, economic pressures in Britain, together with a divided purpose at Leadenhall Street, led to a decline in profitability, exacerbating all the problems being experienced in India. This woeful story did not unfold suddenly, as in the period after Clive. When the East India Company charter came up for renewal in 1793, in fact, a great deal of self-congratulatory rhetoric appeared, pointing to the benefits provided to both Britain and India by the Company's 'vigilance and control'.[6] Yet by 1813 this confidence had evaporated. In its stead the Company found itself awaiting its fate at the hands of a hostile government. Its bargaining position by this time looked hopeless, being mired in debt and begging for parliamentary funds to rescue the Company's finances. In response the government delivered a most savage blow to this or any Company of deep-sea traders. All trading privileges and monopolies were removed, excepting those relating to the tea trade with Canton. As a result, the Company was left with the least glamorous function of all, providing bureaucrats as agents of royal power in India.

In the analysis of this drastic transformation in the Company's position no single causation theory appears viable. Many factors worked relentlessly to destroy the special trading privileges granted in the various charters up to 1813. And many of these, in the end, proved to be beyond the Company's control. In particular there was a revival of the anti-monopoly campaign in Britain over the 1780s and 1790s. The best-known and most-cited example from this campaign against the Company's monopoly is Adam Smith's *The Wealth of Nations* (1776). Critics of the Company then, and many scholars since, used Smith to explain and justify the movement leading to the end of its monopoly over the India trade. Many sections in Smith's long treatise can indeed be employed to support a damaging case against the exclusive rights enjoyed by the Company. Perpetual monopolies, in Smith's view, were harmful to the long-term trading interests of any nation. They raised prices artificially, encouraged waste, fraud and abuse and, in India, had interfered with the sovereign interests of the British government. The underlying message of the book was that open and competitive trade would be beneficial to all involved.

Smith did not, however, entirely dismiss the necessity for monopoly in the early period of any trade enterprise. Exclusion provided security for the risk and investment at the outset. In Smith's opinion, while the East India Company had been a trading endeavour, it had provided great service to the state and its people, justifying the monopoly privileges and helping its stockholders' dividends to grow. After territorial expansion occurred, this role and its privileges required revision, for Company interests were at cross purposes with those of the state. In other words there is no consistent line in Smith's work on the question of the Company's monopoly. His readers then and now, however, have certainly had no difficulty in seeing one.

Why the one interpretation that all monopolies were bad from start to finish held sway is perhaps best explained by the fact that the whole debate on the East India Company happened at the same time as the dislocations of war. The Napoleonic Wars, above all else, gave immense impetus to the anti-monopoly cause in the first dozen years of the nineteenth century. The Orders in Council issued to counteract Napoleon's trade blockade of Britain after 1805, caused severe hardship to domestic manufacturers, especially in the Midlands and the North. Employment and production in industries such as iron and textiles suffered badly through these lean years and one solution to the problem was seen to be the opening of eastern trade to all comers. In a stroke, ridding the Company of its monopoly would create new markets for these depressed areas and their products (Moss 1976). There was no way of knowing whether or not this remedy would work – it was an act of faith. But the desperation of the times with war in Europe and then the American Republic, brought the necessity of a radical solution in the East to the fore.

Support for these attacks on the monopoly also came from those in

India itself. Wellesley had no liking for the Company's monopoly and sought constantly to undermine its exclusive trading rights. A particularly contentious argument arose, for example, over shipping rights and private trade in India. The point at issue concerned the insistence of the Company's shipping interest in London on providing all 'the bottoms' for British trade activity in India. Wellesley and his circle thought this stipulation far too restrictive and expensive. Company rates for shipping always appeared higher, in their view, than private contractors' and there never seemed to be an adequate supply. The Governor fought hard to have the restriction removed, and scored something of a tactical and psychological victory during his time in office by having the private shipping allowance enlarged considerably. Whether it liked it or not, the Company was losing the battle with private and unlicensed traders because support for the monopoly was being eroded from within. External critics and divided purpose at Leadenhall Street proved a deadly combination when the time came for the Company to defend its privileges. Profits suffered and debt soared, undermining any stand the Company made against its enemies. Between 1802 and 1808 the Indian debt alone rose from £18 to £32 million – figures that tell their own story (Phillips 1961: 124).

At one level this growth in private trade resulted from the Company's own economic success in the East and its inability to maintain political control from London over its servants. Company activity and general British trading in the East became increasingly difficult to separate from one another by 1800. Where did one start and the other leave off? Whose ships, for instance, carried the otter skins from Vancouver Island to the Philippines and China, ostensibly an East India Company operation? Whose interests were really at stake in the expensive expeditions against the French Islands and Java in the late 1790s by Wellesley and his Company forces? It became more and more difficult for contemporary observers to determine the origin and direction of policy on such matters, for trade expansion in the East had clearly lost its exclusive character. To many of those same observers, in fact, the Company no longer existed to make profits for its shareholders, it simply provided a conduit for private men and adventurers to enrich themselves or gain honours of one sort or another while serving in India (Ingram 1981: 116–17).

Why could no one in London stop this expansion of private interests at the Company's expense? At a different level from the dynamic discussed above, the problem lay in the structure of political control over the Company after 1784. The Board of Control did not exert the direction over trade policy expected of it. The long tenure of Henry Dundas as president brought stability in the 1780s but after the outbreak of war with France his grip and attention on trade policy in the East slipped away. Matters deteriorated further after Dundas resigned in 1801, for there were no less than nine different presidents of the Board up to the Charter renewal in 1813. This instability at the top rendered consistent policy decisions on the Company's trade problematical. Many of the appointments made, furthermore, were inappropriate and even harmful to the Company's interests. Lewisham, president from 1801 to 1802, knew nothing about India at all and relied heavily on the advice of his cronies who just happened to be anti-monopolists. Castlereagh, president during 1802–06, accepted the post as a stepping-stone to something more prestigious in government service. He held the office after 1805 in conjunction with the Secretaryship for War and Colonies and found it impossible to give anything but superficial attention to India and trade policy there. The most notorious figure of all appeared in 1812 with the Earl of Buckinghamshire's appointment as president of the Board. This ex-governor of Madras had proved himself a headstrong bully in his past dealings with the Directorate and quite at odds with the Company's wish to restrict private trade. Those determined to end the monopoly gloried in the appointment and lobbied hard to persuade the Board and the government to break with the past. Buckinghamshire remained sympathetic to these pleas and played a great part in engineering parliamentary approval for the 1813 charter, ending the India trade monopoly. With friends like these at the Board of Control, the Company needed no other enemies!

The structure of the Board and its influence over government policy is not, however, the last aspect of the Company's difficulties over trade policy. In the final analysis the main reason that it lost the struggle to keep control of its trading privileges can be found, yet again, in militarism and debt. From 1805 on, the Company had to face the simple fact that it was no longer a viable profit-making entity. Two factors had undermined its performance over the long-term. The first related to decisions taken by the Company in the 1790s to invest more in official trade operations in India. These investments were not to be drawn from surpluses or profits on the India trade but borrowed on the money markets. In theory, the decision appeared sensible; as trade increased, especially in Bengal, more products would be carried back to Britain and sold or re-exported. This model fell down on two counts however: agricultural production completely failed to respond to British stimulation (Marshall 1987a: 154–5), and the administrators in London had no more success in curbing military spending than their predecessors. Thus, though the economic picture projected in the 1790s looked rosy, misconceptions about India and military spending sucked all the investments and profits in trade dry. Only borrowing and deficit-financing, as it is known today, could fund the demands of the Company's needs in India, driven, as they were, by militaristic endeavour and unregulated private trade.

To say that the Company appeared vulnerable to its predators by 1810, therefore, would be an understatement of major proportions. In the three years of parliamentary inquiries and public debate that led up to the 1813 charter renewal, the Company merely sought compromise as a means to survival. It did not have strong cards to play on the trade front and its bank balances were in tatters. To outsiders these worries aroused little interest. Reading over the material presented to the Committees of Inquiry, it is evident that a change had taken place in the perception of India's relationship to Britain.[7] At some juncture in the 1790s, the East India Company had ceased to be accepted as the power over Indian affairs. The state and armed force had replaced the old trading mission as the driving force on the sub-continent. The works of authors such as Mill carry this message quite openly. The Company had served its purpose and now a new phase of state power had begun. Such arguments, in fact, merely confirmed changes that had already taken place in the trading world of the East. British interests no longer revolved solely around the three presidencies, and the East India Company, in tandem with private traders, could be found operating in ports of the Red Sea in the west to bases in Indonesia in the south-east and then points north to Hong Kong and Canton. As these diverse trade interests waxed, Company control waned. When Peter Auber prepared his reports on the Company in 1826, he suffered no doubts about what had occurred in the history of this organization. The order of his chapters stated the obvious: a short Chapter One was entitled 'A Brief History of the East India Company', ending in 1813; a much longer Chapter Two appeared as, 'Of the Rise and Progress of British Power in India'. The latter told of the military and expansionist story right up to the time of publication.

As a last word on British territorial expansion in India, it must be said that a great deal of new light has been shed on this matter over the last twenty-five years or so. The old assumptions that the Company and state agreed on this policy, or that trade always followed the flag, have been effectively challenged. It is very difficult now to present a convincing case that the rise of industrialization in Britain in the second half of the eighteenth century caused a demand for raw products throughout the empire which, in turn, initiated aggressive expansionist policies to secure that supply and eliminate prospective industrial competitors. Research on India in this period has revealed no hard and fast rules about territorial expansion. In Awadh, for example, British private traders in the 1790s definitely resisted Wellesley's military advance because it would have undermined their operations and profits. Furthermore, the East India Company did not desire the expansion because the raw materials from Awadh offered direct competition with producers and manufacturers in Bengal under its jurisdiction (Marshall 1975b; Marshall and Mukherjee 1985; Mukherjee 1982). In north-western India, on the other hand, the annexation of Surat and Broach by the Bombay presidency did find its impetus from economic considerations. In this case, the cotton and manufactured piece goods trade could be monopolized by the British for the foreseeable future. The monopoly would also be of benefit to Company and private traders alike (Nightingale 1969: 174–7).

Such analyses prove the complexity of forces at work in India as Company influence over day-to-day events declined. The recent work on British history and the advent of industrialization has also shown just how loosely related British needs and Indian expansion happened to be (Bayly 1988: 105). The British who operated in trades like cotton, indigo and opium had little reason to think of home, as they drew their profits from trading patterns in the East. Opium went to China and cotton piece goods were carried all over Indonesia and the Near East, meeting more lucrative local demands. The tragedy of the situation from the Company's point of view lay not in British concerns at all but the fact that trade policy had succumbed to the demands of militarism over which it had no control.

Faced with these odds, it is little wonder the Company found itself unable to fend off the anti-monopolists. After the 1813 charter was renewed only fragments remained of the original mandate. The Company had begun to take on the identity of a bureaucratic shell. Haileybury remained as a training ground for the administrators sent to India to superintend the lands brought under British control. Their primary purpose was not, however, to support the enterprise of Company factors and agents. The military machine dictated the location and function of the bureaucracy after 1813 and it was private traders that ran fast and loose over the sub-continent now. It proved an ironic twist of fate that the one trade monopoly retained by the Company was that to China in tea. The tea trade had been something of an addendum to the East India Company's main trading interest in India, and yet after 1813 it was all the Company possessed.

Furthermore, the reasons for allowing the Company to keep this monopoly had more to do with the strict control over tea supplies of the Hong merchants in Canton than any sympathy for its business interests. The government recognized in 1813 that the Company ran this business efficiently and profitably, keeping good relations with the Chinese suppliers to the benefit of all concerned in the trade. Unfortunately, this fact simply made private traders more anxious than ever to break this last remnant of the Company's privileges over the next twenty years. Nor was there any reason to believe that they would not be successful. The East India Company remained in existence after 1813 adrift – a pale shadow of the vibrant trading enterprise so familiar to seventeenth- and eighteenth-century eyes. Economic advances gained over the preceding two centuries had now given way to the transient and ruinous military glories of Wellesley and his successors.

NOTES

1. Auber, *An Analysis of the Constitution of the East India Company: Supplement*, p. 19.
2. *Life of Lord Clive* and *The History of British India.*
3. 14 George III c. 83, published in full in *The Law Relating to India and the East India Company.*
4. *The Expansion of England*, p. 211
5. *The History of British India*, pp. 492–3.
6. Auber, *An Analysis of the Constitution of the East India Company*, p. xiv.
7. *Parliamentary Papers*: in particular see Reports 1–5, 1808–12, East India Company Select Committee of House of Commons; and Minutes of evidence before the House of Lords on East India Company affairs, 1813.

CHAPTER EIGHT

The Lull and the Storm: 1813–57

> The danger to India is not, in the present day, *external*, but *internal*; and, so long as we promote the well-being of the nations of British India, preserve their social and religious institutions, and do not interfere with their laws of inheritance and adoption, which are part and parcel of their religion, we shall have nothing to fear internally. Education is the stepping-stone to all knowledge.[1]

These words of retired Major William Hough of the Indian army (Bengal) encapsulate the mass of contradictions that made up the East India Company's history from 1813 to 1857. Written in 1852, only five years before the Great Rebellion in India, Hough sensed, like many of his contemporaries, that something had gone sadly wrong with Company rule of British territorial and trading interests in the East. It is not difficult to see why. In the forty years or so after the charter renewal of 1813, the Company had been forced to reinvent a role for its servants in the East. During this period the Company was stripped of all its monopoly privileges in trade and had no mandate to play politics or diplomatist with native governments. In effect, the Company became a department of state, ruled over by an all-powerful Governor-General based in Calcutta. As a consequence, the nature of Company supervision changed markedly. The executive power derived from the crown granted the Governors of India the status of proconsuls, running an eastern empire with an army of soldiers and bureaucrats whole and complete in itself. The flaw in this structure lay in the lack of a unified purpose by all those involved in its operations. Everyone wanted to make the eastern empire profitable but hardly any group in the civil and military administration possessed a unitary vision of how to achieve this goal.

The evidence of confusion and anxiety on these issues of profit and future viability had a familiar ring. In the first instance, the Company's administrators in London wanted to run a low-cost, lean and efficient bureaucracy after 1813; yet the military continued to expand British territory, absorbing all trade surpluses and more besides. Second, the Company wanted to keep a consistent line on its fiscal and social polices in those areas under its direct control; yet in the late 1820s the traditional hands-off approach to the people and institutions in the Company's territories was abandoned for a full-blown policy of Anglicism. In this process, missionary activity, English language, education and culture would be introduced to the people of India as a collective means to improvement. Third, the desires of the Directorate and General Court of Proprietors to retain some independence of action and identity collapsed in the aftermath of lost trading privileges and continual militaristic ventures of its Indian army. In writing of the Company in these years it is not easy to discern a separate role from the state for this old trading organization. It is not for nothing that Hough referred in the 1850s to 'British India' and not the East India Company's territories. That distinction had long ceased to be a reality in the day-to-day affairs of the eastern trading empire. Fourth, and last, the price paid for these contradictions in word and deed was the one most feared and dreaded by state and Company alike – large-scale rebellion by the people of India in 1857–58.

THE INDIAN ARMY FIRST AND LAST

The charter renewal of 1813 changed many aspects of British activity in the East but it did not touch the army in India or its activities in the territories under Company control. The function of the army in the presidencies and satellite states continued to be one of pacification and the preservation of administrative unity. In the brute terms of military strategy and measurement, it could be said the army succeeded in this role of pacifier. By the mid-nineteenth century the Indian land empire became a solid mass of princely states and Company territory guarded by an army that kept the enemy at bay on the ragged edges of its domain. The costs of such a policy proved, as ever, prohibitive. In its own logic, pacification required constant military action to deal with home-grown insurgents and external threats. In practice this policy entailed further wars and annexations, usually justified on a point of security. The list of wars and expeditions for the years 1813–56 represents an unrelenting advance of military interests under the guise of Company trade and revenue needs. In India itself, for example, there was the destruction of the Marathas in 1817–18; the conquest of the Gurkhas in the north (1814–16); in 1843 the area of modern Pakistan, known as the Sind, was occupied, followed by the annexation of the Punjab after the Sikh wars of 1848–49. Most belligerent of all was the ideology of expansion developed under Governor-General Dalhousie, (1848–56). In a nutshell, Dalhousie believed that any threat to British power in India and the East, either overt or covert, should be met with military force. His views of what constituted a threat certainly covered a wide spectrum too. Considerations such as disputes over succession in kingdoms neighbouring Company territory ('doctrine of lapse') or gross mismanagement, as he saw it, of native kingdoms impinging on British activities, warranted immediate intervention. The result was, as the territories of Nagpur, Satara and Awadh discovered to their cost, incorporation into the British land empire. Whatever his motive, Dalhousie certainly gave new meaning to the word pacification throughout his term in office.

To say that such thinking represented something novel would be in error because there was more continuity than change in military policy. One of the Company's grandees, Sir Charles Metcalfe, summed up the prevailing imperatives behind the army's activities when he wrote in 1820 from Calcutta: 'I abhor making wars, and meddling with other states for the sake of our aggrandizement – but war thrust upon us, or unavoidably entered into, should, if practicable, be turned to profit by the acquisition of new resources, to pay additional forces to defend what we have, and extend our possessions in future unavoidable wars.'[2] An ethos of this nature, however gratuitous, also had ramifications beyond the boundaries of India and the Company's territorial domain. The unique status of the Indian army and its expertise in dealing with eastern warriors and hostile native forces meant that the British government could employ Company regiments all over South-East Asia and the China seas to buttress and protect national interests. The Indian army became known as 'the fire brigade', putting out military fires in the East wherever they threatened British trading concerns. It is in this broader context, in fact, that the motives behind the wars against Burma (1824 and 1852), and those against China (1839 and 1856 – the Opium Wars), along with expeditions in Malaya and Afghanistan, can be appreciated more fully. In essence India became the core operation of new trading peripheries in the East (Porter 1984: 22). Sometimes movements within this structure coincided with the wishes of the authorities in London, while at other times, government in India served its own needs – more often than not however, the latter situation prevailed.

In assessing this historical phenomenon of the military government in India commanded by a British proconsul, it is easy to criticize and condemn. The resources that this military machine consumed ensured that the Company could never be profitable. In 1835, under Lord Bentinck's governorship, the Company boasted a £1–2 million surplus, but this was very quickly consumed by army budgets. In other years the picture was less rosy. Debt mounted and the Company made no profits on its operations in India, even though many of its servants profited from personal involvement in eastern trade. At the time of the charter renewal in 1833, the Company's accumulated debt was so large it was simply charged indefinitely to future revenues and possible surpluses. Yet the role of the army cannot be dismissed in this simple manner, for its impact on the Company's role in governing India proved far more crucial in this period than was understood at the time.

The work of historians such as Daniel Headrick (1981) on technology and British expansion overseas reveals a subplot in the story of the Company's development of immense interest and significance. It is now known from such research that the Company's military demands encouraged investment in, and the application of, what were then new technologies, especially steam engines, in the Eastern theatre. Steamships for passage to India and South-East Asia, gunboats driven by steam engines to patrol inland waterways and estuaries and paddle-steamers towing wooden battleships all played their part in enforcing British strategic needs in the East. The account of the First Opium War in China (1839–41), by those involved is one of awe at the sheer fire-power and destructive capability of the steam-driven vessels. One, in particular, the *Nemesis*, operating in the waters off Canton in 1841, single-handedly broke the fortifications and resistance of the Chinese defenders, prompting one eyewitness to comment: 'They are more afraid of her [the *Nemesis*] than all the line of battleships put together' (cited in Headrick 1981: 50). Technological innovation and the defence of British interests frequently went hand-in-hand therefore; although not always in such brute fashion. A great many public works and civil engineering projects on the sub-continent, for instance, were undertaken by the

Indian army's corps of engineers, who both serviced the military machine and put out fires effectively. Canals were dug in Bengal, roads laid in Madras and surveying and mapping done in Bombay to ensure, in part, that the military could patrol and move more quickly around its theatre of operations. If the civilian population benefited from the investment in these activities, it could be viewed as a bonus to the primary aim of security and pacification.

Thus it can be seen that the Company's position of control over its army did not change a great deal between Wellesley's governorship in the early 1800s and that of Dalhousie in the 1850s. The Company simply could not gather taxes or guarantee internal peace without its assistance. Nor could it control the size of the force in any effective manner. By 1820 the Indian army numbered approximately 300,000 men, still made up predominantly of sepoys officered by Europeans. This figure was supplemented by royal forces, limited to no more than 40,000 in service in India by the 1813 charter. The Europeans were always in charge of the artillery, for fear of mutiny or insurgency. But the fact remained that loyalty of the sepoys in the Indian army proved the key to the effectiveness of this force which stood as one of the largest standing armies in the world at that time. The sepoy redcoat was the agent of pacification on the ground, and, if required, the means of persuasion in the tax system. Indeed, the whole military edifice rested on the ability of the Indian peasant farmers and artisans to produce sufficient wealth for its day-to-day needs. This army was not supported by the British taxpayer at all. It is little wonder then, that the economic position of the mass of the working people in India barely improved in the period from 1813 until the Great Rebellion. By contrast, those involved in the fighting units and logistical support for the army often did quite well indeed. This divergence of interest became manifest in the events of 1857–58.

In these circumstances, any singular assessment of the impact of the army on the Company's history in this period is fraught with difficulties. The fate of the army and the Company were so closely intertwined by the 1820s that viewing them as separate entities often makes no sense at all. The legacy of Dundas and his Scottish patronage networks ensured the perpetuation of an ever-expanding source of offices and emoluments in India: offices the Company found impossible to limit or differentiate between their civil or military provenance. The duties of the Company resident and local military officer frequently overlapped; the role of the military engineer and public works official often coincided, and the office of tax-gatherer and pacifier very rarely existed apart. The Indian army was the

Company's largest financial headache but its men were also the pillars of Company authority. The army was known to cause social dislocation and yet what would Company rule in India be without the security it offered? How could so few bureaucrats rule vast territories on the sub- continent without this military insurance? The Indian army needed to be reformed and controlled but all efforts in this direction had failed. Resources continued to be consumed by this vast fighting force to the Company's detriment, and nothing could be done about the problem until catastrophe struck in 1857. The proconsular state in India, as it evolved under titular Company rule after 1813, was driven forward first and last by the army.

ANGLICISM VERSUS ORIENTALISM

In light of the military machine and its overwhelming demands on the revenues of India, it might be thought that little room was left for Company initiative or other affairs. To a degree this was the case, for all Company efforts at revamping the administration of Indian territories after 1813 were dogged by lack of funds and ever-present debt. Nevertheless, a major change of emphasis did take place during this period in the Company's administrative policies towards the people under its charge. Moreover, it was a change that had profound effects on the British role in India as a whole. Up to 1813 the predominant view and practice favoured by Company administrators in India had been one known as orientalism (Green and Deasy Jr 1985). The purpose of Company rule in the view of Orientalists was that Indian institutions and culture should be left alone as much as possible. Company activity at points of contact with the native peoples should be limited to revenue or security issues; designed, in the last analysis, to promote acquiescence to the British presence. This mode of thought can be traced back to Burke, Cornwallis and Shore and, despite Wellesley's regency period of military adventurism, the policies of the Company and state reflected the views inherent in this benevolent approach. Colleges for Sanskrit teaching and Islamic education founded in the time of Hastings were continued and supported financially by the Company into the nineteenth century. The courts of Indian princes in subsidiary alliance with the British were also encouraged to patronize native arts and culture as a means of preserving the past and offering emollients to the rougher edges of Company rule.

After 1813 it could be said that this picture began to undergo a drastic revision. The impetus was provided by a changing view in Britain of the government's responsibilities to the people and societies under its charge. Reform movements sprang up in the 1820s and 1830s seeking to cast off the old methods of paternalistic supervision and replace them with a more interventionist and constructionist regime. There were both practical and spiritual elements to these movements, and three, in particular, are worthy of note: evangelicalism, utilitarianism and liberal free-traders (often referred to as radicals). The history of these groups in the domestic British setting has been well-documented of late. They were not linked in any formal way, but their aims and aspirations often overlapped (Hilton 1988). In looking at the impact of the ideals transported by these groups to British overseas possessions, certain policies and initiatives emerge that do mark a break with past practices. In Canada this change became associated with Lord Durham's report, responding to the rebellions there in 1839. In India the new approach appeared most emphatically under the governorship of William Bentinck (1828–35). The one common thread that bound evangelicals, utilitarians and liberals together in India was their overriding desire for change and reform. In their view, orientalism had served the people of India and the Company's interests poorly, and the time had come for a spiritual, constitutional and social conversion or rejuvenation along western lines. Nothing brings out this contrast between the old and the new regime from 1793 to 1856 better than the portraiture of the proconsuls sent to govern India. The pictures of Cornwallis and Wellesley speak of authority expressed through regal, military splendour with uniforms and decorations to the fore. Representations of Bentinck and near contemporaries, like Dalhousie, on the other hand, convey the Victorian reform ethic: steely-eyed figures in black frock coats with sober accessories – men of business who meant to get the job done.

Of this reform triumvirate, the evangelical missionary societies operating in India were new to the scene. The Company had been successful in the past at keeping the religious reformers seeking conversions in India at bay. After the charter renewal of 1813, however, exclusion ended and their presence became official policy. Historians differ as to the long-term effect that missionaries had on the native populations. Some, like David Fieldhouse, believe their presence proved an irritant for the Company but, overall, they made few converts and exercised little influence in the day-to-day affairs of British India (1982: 283–4). Others, like Bernard Porter and Chris Bayly, see the missionaries as social disruptives, forcing alien values and spiritual teaching on a resistant population and the sepoy army units (Porter 1984: 31; Bayly 1989: 146-7).

Not all missionaries shared the same vision of what their role in India should encompass. Their differences of creed alone dictated that. As in Britain, there was a whole range of denominations seeking souls to convert in India, from Baptists, Scottish evangelicals, Anglican missionary zealots, right through to Jesuits in Calcutta itself (A. Porter 1987–88; Ballhatchet 1978–79). On certain moral imperatives, however, most British missions stood united. They were in India primarily to offer the benefits of western religions and education to a suffering mass of humanity, oppressed, as they saw it, by centuries of superstition and ignorance about spiritual and worldly affairs. Underpinning this assurance was a burden of guilt shared by many early Victorian thinkers that Britain held Indian territory in trusteeship. The terrible events involved in the conquests of the Company army required absolution, and this could only be achieved by devotion to the spiritual well-being of all the people under British supervision.

In and of itself this philosophical outlook seems quaint, even bizarre today, and many seasoned Company administrators took the same view at the time. The Company had resisted the potential for antagonism between Christian proselytizers and Hindu/Muslim teachers for what seemed solid political reasons – social unity and peaceful rule. However, under the changed outlook in Britain and India of the 1820s and 1830s, this missionary zeal took on a special significance for Company rule in India. As the late Eric Stokes explained in a brilliant essay (1980) on the subject of bureaucracy and ideology in India and Britain at this time, the moral fervour dovetailed nicely with the public spirit of utilitarians and liberals when it came to reforming Company rule. All these groups, for one reason or another, wished to change the way the Company treated the native population. They believed that in westernizing India the spiritual lives of those 'in trust' to British care would be improved. Meanwhile profits and markets for industrial goods and consumer items from Britain would rise exponentially. The drive of those saving souls in tandem with the entrepreneurs trying to create brave new civic worlds and consumer markets, produced an intoxicating climate for many Company servants who came to India after 1813. In the age of Bentinck's Governorship, in particular, many new thinkers came to see India as some sort of living laboratory, ripe for testing every reform idea currently fashionable.

In the language of modern analysis what transpired was an attempt at social engineering. After Bentinck's appointment as Governor in

1828, the Company entered an age of social and economic planning on a scale that it would have considered anathema a generation earlier. No one reading the records of this period, however, can doubt that the Company possessed the raw talent in its ranks to undertake such a task. This was a very literate and knowledgeable bureaucracy. From studying the exquisite maps and reports done by the Survey of India to the detailed accounts of Company residents and district officers, it is possible to discern a care and professionalism for the responsibilities of government that many modern democracies would be unable to match.[3] 'It was a period', to use the words of Eric Stokes, 'mainly of paper planning – of law codes, educational schemes, scientific land revenue systems, railways, irrigation projects, and the like' (1980: 154). These plans were set in motion with enormous confidence and a belief that the British way was the best and only way to proceed. The success of its government and institutions, confirmed in contemporary eyes by the passage of the Great Reform Act in 1832 and the technological leadership that Britain was providing to the world, revealed the true path to progress and the superiority of British guidance on that route.

To appreciate the faith that all these movements placed in changing the nature of Company rule for the better, there is no need to look further than the debate on education policy. It has certainly been well discussed in histories of British India, not least because the towering figure and intellect of Thomas Babington Macaulay is involved. Macaulay was appointed to the Bengal Supreme Council created by the India Act of 1833. He served for five years in that capacity and spent his time on meticulous examinations of judicial procedures and the question of education in the Company's territories. His labours on the judicial side produced a draft penal code in 1835. The code was enacted after the 1850s, forming, in turn, an essential foundation stone of modern Indian law (Clive 1987: 465–66). The work achieved on education proved no less compelling or far- reaching, going right to the heart of the anglicism versus orientalism discourse. To Macaulay the old Company policy of preserving and protecting Indian language and culture was redundant in the British Victorian world of improvement and progress. His idea was to abandon past practices and embark on the westernization of Indian élites under Company supervision, and the message was carried in the form of a 'minute on education' dated 2 February 1835, sent to Governor-General Bentinck.[4]

To call this document a minute is rather misleading as it suggests something brief. Macaulay's observations on education actually ran to several pages of incisive prose and a characteristically biting critique of the matter at hand. He offered broad opinions on all issues relating to education in India, and specific actions to be taken to resolve what he believed to be a crisis of learning and lack of modernization in India. The root of the problem lay with the Company's old policy of encouraging native languages which were archaic, containing 'neither literary nor scientific information, and are moreover so poor and rude that, until they are enriched from some other quarter it will not be easy to translate any valuable work into them'. The enrichment could come, in Macaulay's scheme, through the adoption of the English language as the means of instruction and commercial exchange in the Company's territories. Macaulay pointed to the examples of antiquity and early modern Russia to demonstrate his point that societies can emerge from 'ignorance' through teaching modern languages, like English, 'in which the greatest mass of information has been laid up'. In summing up, Macaulay pleaded with the Governor-General to throw off the old policy of orientalism and grasp the nettle of spreading English by a direct effort at education of the people of India in the language of the modern, western state. The logic of the argument appeared crystal clear to Macaulay. Company funds in this field should be spent 'in teaching what is best worth knowing, that English is better worth knowing than Sanskrit or Arabic, that the natives are desirous to be taught English . . . that it is possible to make natives of this country thoroughly good English scholars, and that to this end our efforts ought to be directed'.

The prevailing mood of confidence in the superiority of British institutions and culture could not have been more clearly stated. Macaulay caught the sense of destiny many of his peers experienced when encountering the ideal of trusteeship in India. They sought, and to some extent, achieved a break with the past and were encouraged to do so by the higher echelons of the Company administration who expressed sympathy for the goals of Macaulay and his like. Only the previous year, Bentinck himself had written down his own reflections on reform in India, revealing that he was of the same mind as Macaulay on the critical move from orientalism to anglicism. He expressed 'entire dissent from the opinions of those who think it better that the natives should remain in *ignorance*,' for the simple reason that 'I cannot recognize the advantage of ignorance to the governors nor the governed . . . let them have the means provided by our greater intelligence, of discovering their errors.'[5] No doubt existed in the minds of the reformers, whether liberal, spiritual or utilitarian, that the Company should be the agent of social change.

Scholarly opinion on this matter, however, has been less consensual. Many historians believe, in fact, that in essential philosophy, people like Macaulay were anti- imperialist. They had no time for territorial conquest and its attendant ceremonials and debt. Yet here they were occupied in the paradoxical task of making India an efficient, well-run imperium for the British crown. A secondary debate has also developed over the utility of these reforms in the long term: how did they affect the course of Anglo-Indian history? In truth, it is a highly contentious question to address. Much scholarship of the twentieth century that might be termed anti-colonialist or imperialist has seen this period of British rule through the Company as disastrous for the cause of progress in India. Actions like the introduction of English Common Law in many civil and criminal processes, the westernization of Indian education by means of English language instruction, and the outlawing of certain traditional Hindu practices, such as *sati* (widow-burning) and *thuggee* (ritualistic banditry), have been held responsible for creating severe divisions within native societies. Such divisions, in turn, halted the natural rise of India's economy and people to the position of a modern industrial state, as its producers served the markets of a distant colonial overlord rather than the nascent national interest.

There is certainly evidence to support these arguments. The Company's reforms did introduce alien values and legal philosophies to India. Its westernizing efforts did give rise to a class of Indians, known derisively as *babu*, who were neither wholly of the English world into which they had been drawn nor still part of the culture they left behind. Legal and judicial reforms perhaps caused more distress and aggravation than any other novel policy brought forward by the Company prior to the Great Rebellion. Last, missionary work was, at its worst, proof to the learned élite of Hindu and Muslim society of insufferable British condescension on matters of Indian custom and tradition. Up to 1857 British missions actually made few converts, but they wished to interfere at all levels of society in order to civilize and raise the morality of a people lost to what they viewed as antiquated religious sophistry. They were cultural imperialists and generally supported the Company's more radical economic and social reforms as a means to achieve their own spiritual ends. At best, missionaries were vociferous irritants always on display and always ready to preach about the benefits of the British way: 'Hence', as Bernard Porter expressed it so well, 'the paraphernalia of blouses and tea parties and Methodist hymnals which went along with mission stations and their converts, as "tokens of civilisation" ' (1984: 24).

Of late other schools of thought on the reforming impulse in these years of Company rule have been more circumspect. They do not deny that the Company's administration penetrated the societies under its control, but caution that it was more patchy and constrained than initial examination would indicate. Two or three problems are normally cited to explain this revision. First the utilitarian view of governing India rested, as it did in Britain, on a concerted effort at the centralization of power. This effort failed in India not only because of opposition from native powers but also from divided purpose amongst the British. Liberals, orientalists and their sympathizers in the Company's employ or simply at work in India, did not want centralization at all for both philosophical and economic reasons. Too much power at the centre destroyed the natural balance of constitutional forces and would eventually wreck opportunities for profits. As in Britain, the utilitarians in India had lost this battle over centralization by 1850 (Stokes 1959: 234–43). Second, and more important, the Company was never able to carry reform as far as it wished, for the simple reason that it had no money. The 1830s and 1840s were times of economic and trade depression in India, and the Company's revenues suffered accordingly. Debt accruing from military operations on the frontiers of Company rule simply made the situation worse. In consequence, many of the planned changes to the legal system, for example, had to be phased in over a number of years or postponed until after the Great Rebellion. Other plans for extensive public works simply had to be abandoned altogether. Financial stringency and fiscal retrenchment became the overriding goals of the Company's bureaucracy after 1833 and, in such circumstances, it is unrealistic to talk of large-scale, unchecked spending on reforms or grandiose public projects for westernizing India (Bayly 1988: 120–8).

The latest research suggesting caution is helpful in explaining why the upheavals of 1857–58 affected certain segments of Indian society more profoundly than others. Points of contact between reformed Company policy and the people of India were ubiquitous, assuming many forms and eliciting different experiences. Constraints and practical problems also reveal why the Company's zeal for such reform policies diminished so severely by the 1850s. Yet the argument about the legacy of these years rages on. Whatever the conclusions historians reach, the remnants of what Bentinck and his servants sought to achieve persist to this day. The use of the English language, modern Indian law and the bureaucratic state are ever-present reminders in the late twentieth century of the impact of this period of Company rule on India. Reaching a consensus on the history of these years may never be possible because the debate echoes with the guilt of a colonial past. The tendency for western historians to see something beneficial for India in this period of Company activity is deeply entrenched: the inclination for Asian scholars, on the other hand, is to present the modern age, before independence in 1947, as one long struggle against oppression. These divisions are no longer so rigid or nationalistic as they once were, for the simple reason that at the core of interpretative analysis of this topic lies the vexed question of progress and its place in any historical narrative.

No matter how this issue is settled in the end, historians of the East India Company must view these analytical cleavages as emphatic evidence of how far down the road from a trading organization that body had travelled. Anglicism versus orientalism had never been an issue in the past, for the Company possessed the influence and power to resist such notions of change. Left in 1813 with the task of reinventing its administrative function in India, however, the Company became the unwitting agent of social change in the territories under its control. The movements for reform generated in Britain and transplanted to India, left the Company, yet again, bereft of control over its own destiny. One more function corrupted meant one more nail had been hammered into the coffin of Company business.

COMPANY TRADE AS AN APPENDAGE

It seems slightly ironic in hindsight that the Company should be left after 1813 with no responsibility for or direction over trade in India. After all, this was where it had all begun: the Company originally traded anywhere in the East but India. For a brief period the Company retained its monopoly on the tea trade to Canton. But enjoyment of these privileges proved to be shortlived. The charter of 1833 removed all commercial activities from the Company, throwing the whole trade of the East open. Why the Company was left with this appendage of its traditional trade function between 1813 and 1833 is something of a mystery at one level. The anti-monopolists had carried all before them when the charter came up for renewal in 1813, so why not the China trade too? Moreover, there was the added incentive that the tea trade was extremely profitable, and continued to be so for the Company until 1833. In 1813–14 the Company sold some 29.5 million pounds of tea and by 1833 this figure had risen to 33 million. These sales brought in over £4 million per annum to the Company's treasury and, incidentally, provided the state with about 7 per cent of total public revenue through excise and other duties. Those who have studied the trade thoroughly point out that it was one of the most cost-efficient and well-run enterprises that the Company ever mounted (Mui and Mui 1984: 136–8). The tea monopoly defied the critics' usual arguments about slack direction and waste, and its very special structures, using super-cargoes in Canton, worked to perfection throughout the last twenty years of the monopoly.

In terms of performance, therefore, nothing changed in the tea trade controlled by the Company in this period. And to understand why it lost the monopoly in 1833 and not 1813 requires a broader analysis than merely looking at the economic model of that particular pattern of exchange. In the first place the tea trade provided ancillary opportunities for profit-taking that began to attract the attention of British merchants in the 1820s and 1830s. The original pattern of exchange had involved metals, usually silver, being taken from London to Canton in exchange for tea. Over time this practice had been deemed too draining on the Company's exchequer, and its servants in India had developed a new mode of trade in goods produced in India itself and then shipped to Canton via Calcutta. The particular Indian products in demand in China were opium and cotton piece goods. Developing this country trade, as it was known, saved the Company a great deal of hard cash, as well as offering the chance for subsidiary patterns of trade and discounting to develop between producers and merchants in India. British merchants who could involve themselves in such activities saw an opportunity for profit in the primary market of exchange in the East and then further chances for profit from delivering the tea to London. Some even saw the chance of controlling the trade at both ends, and began growing tea on plantations in Assam (northern India), cutting out the Canton connection and traditional supply mechanisms in one fell swoop.

If the profit motive was not sufficient as part of the campaign to break the monopoly by 1833, there was also a philosophical one. Adam Smith had predicted eighty years earlier that when monopolies had run their course, the nation would benefit from throwing them open to competition from all merchants. By the 1820s there was hardly any interested party who did not feel this way about the tea monopoly. Whether it was run efficiently or not did not matter any more as a point of debate. Worse still from the Company's viewpoint, practically no one within its ranks was prepared to mount a public defence of the monopoly in these years. The decision to end the monopoly of tea was taken by the government as early as 1825 and Wellington, the prime minister, informed a very acquiescent Directorate of this decision in 1829 (Phillips 1961: 181–90). The subsequent inquiries of the House of Lords and Commons before the charter renewal in 1833 merely confirmed the course of action already decided upon.[6] The triumph of the anti- monopolist mood and free trade crusade that gathered momentum from the mid-1820s on could not have been more complete. As one correspondent in London told Bentinck in December 1833, it was a sad time for the Company, and the forces at work in dissolving its monopoly might yet rue the day for this sudden change:

> Though I think the abolition of the China monopoly was inevitable and that it never would have done for us to have gone on trading in competition with the public as a system, I fear, and believe, the sudden and entire stop put to our commercial relations with China, will tend materially to injure our assets, to enhance our responsibilities and to produce mischief which might have been avoided by a more gradual change.[7]

These comments revealed a prescience lacking elsewhere. The opium wars and constant military and naval expeditions to protect the China trade in the future did nothing whatsoever to improve profits from tea. In this instance economic principles were bought at a higher price than the old monopoly. To believe that the Company could have escaped its fate in 1833 when all its commercial activities ceased, is, however, unrealistic. The prevailing atmosphere favouring reform and change infected the civil and political world in Britain and India, and could not be prevented from influencing economic thought and policy. One of the most elementary means of analysing just how powerful these forces for change appeared to the Company at the time, is to examine the statutes passed in 1833 affecting its operations in the East apart from the charter renewal. In the month of August alone, laws were passed on the better administration of justice; allowing Protestant dissenters to take special oaths for the India service; for the regulation and restructuring of customs and dues; for the encouragement of British private shipping and navigation; controlling the registration of British vessels in the eastern trade; to abolish slavery in all British possessions and colonies and, of course, to wind up the tea trade monopoly, setting out the terms of its future development.[8] Each of these new laws bears witness to a changed conception in

Britain of the Company's role in India and the East. No organization could have resisted this revolution in thinking about Britain's interests in the East and the demands for open markets and chance for profit on the part of British merchants and manufacturers. The year 1833 did mark the end of the East India Company's trading mission originally undertaken in the reign of Elizabeth I. A further charter renewal in 1853 merely confirmed the abandonment of its former powers, purpose and expertise.

DEMISE

The forces that made it impossible for the Company to continue as a trading entity made sure the bureaucratic function did not endure either. The reforming efforts of the Company's servants after 1833 and the necessity of reinventing a role for the organization, now that it was no longer a trading entity, foundered, as ever, on the inability to control military expenditures. In an odd way the Charter Act of 1833 guaranteed this sabotage, as clause 39 stated 'that the superintendence, direction, and control of whole civil and military government of all the said territories and revenues in India shall be and is hereby vested in a Governor-general and counsellors, to be styled "The Governor-general of India in Council" '.[9] The authors of this passage might well have put proconsul at the end of the clause too, for these civil and military powers vested in such an executive body amounted to the same thing. This combination of ultimate civil and political authority was a trend foreshadowed elsewhere in the East. The aggressive campaigns of James Crawfurd in Ceylon in the 1820s and Stamford Raffles in Malaysia in the 1820s and 1830s, in particular, demonstrated how quickly the old trading imperatives of the British had been exchanged for autocracy by force of arms and racial condescension.

Faced with such concentrations of power at the top, the problem for the Company then became its impotence when the army blundered into confrontations with the indigenous population. Prior to the Great Rebellion there were many manifestations of popular dislike for the military men in India. Insurgency and banditry, especially in the north-east, were coupled with a disaffection amongst the native élites being deprived of traditional powers and status within their own societies. The resentments touched on small issues, such as the decision in 1835 to discontinue the use of Persian in official communication and records, to the more serious economic problems in the trade depression years of the 1830s and 40s. As the Company sought to reform the internal affairs of Indian trade and production, casualties occurred and these were exacerbated by the downturn in the economy. Cottage industries were destroyed, land reform displaced peasants and urban development went ahead regardless of old ties and structures. No matter how hard the British tried, even to the point of changing land assessments after a revenue conference in 1847, it proved impossible for them to turn India into the booming economy desired by the reformers after 1833. The majority of peasants remained poor and the economy stagnated until the 1850s when world trade picked up and the Company recanted many of its plans to westernize India under duress.

The overriding problem of the army remained, however, as the one constant irritant to both the people of India and Company government. It existed as the Company's force in name only, being ruled over by military men with no connection at all to mercantile endeavours. Since 1784, or even earlier, the army had been at odds with the Company's economic goals and this situation never changed up to 1857. In the intervening years the Company's distaste for the army grew while its ability to control military activity declined. A bureaucratic department of state, which is what the Company amounted to at the time of the Great Rebellion, simply could do nothing to influence the course of events where the army was concerned. Indeed, reading over the mass of literature on 1857–58 two factors appear uppermost: the folly of the British government in allowing the Company army to develop as it did and the hopelessness of the Company's civil branch of government to do anything constructive in the face of the onslaught begun by the Bengal army at the outset of the Rebellion. In most of the histories of the events of 1857–58 there is an implicit acknowledgement of these facts when discussing causation and consequences. Historians use particular language to describe the bloody and gory events of the Rebellion, and the words of the East India Company are not often included. The British army, British India and British interests are the significant phrases, replacing those that would have described the Company's role in events seventy-five years earlier.

In view of this approach, there is very little to be learned specifically about the Company's history in detailed discussions of the Rebellion and transfer of formal rule in India to the crown in 1858. Nevertheless, it is worth raising some of the broader themes in the Company's decline, leading up to the outbreak of hostilities between British forces and the Indian rebels. When Disraeli reflected on the events of the Rebellion, he made the sensible analytical comment that long-term grievances, as well as short-term disasters, must have been at play to cause such an eruption. Of these, the most pertinent are the social and economic factors. The Great Rebellion was, to all intents and purposes, a localized affair. The most intense feelings and resentments arose amongst soldiers in the Bengal army, enhanced as it was by Muslim elements from Awadh, recently conquered by the British. The fighting itself became centred in Bengal and areas north-west of the Ganges delta. Why this was so is commonly believed to rest with the fact that the reforming impulse under the Company's aegis after 1813 was most severely applied in these places. Territories controlled by the Madras and Bombay presidencies retained more of the old structures of local government, taxation and production. In other words, local Company administrators in these presidencies did not abandon the eighteenth-century heritage so readily. They resisted the reform mania that gripped the Council and its servants in Calcutta and, in consequence, reaped their more peaceful rewards in 1857–58.

A second factor related to localization concerns how quickly the Rebellion in the North turned into a race war. In many places Hindu and Muslim forces tried to wipe out all Europeans and all their traces, attempting, at root, to obliterate the recent humiliating episode of Indian history. In response the British inflicted terrible reprisals, acts of inhumanity born out of an outrage fuelled by feelings of racial and cultural superiority. To understand how these animosities developed, there is no need to look further than the attitudes of Wellesley, Metcalfe, Macaulay, Dalhousie and the various missionaries who had always considered India and its people backward and in need of modernization. In 1856, for example, Dalhousie could still write with remarkable assurance and obliviousness that 'My parting hope and prayer for India is that . . . the Presidencies and provinces under our rule may form, in each successive year, a happy record of peace, prosperity and progress.'[10] In the seventeenth and eighteenth centuries such beliefs would have appeared quite out of place with the Company's philosophy of trading with partners from fortified bases. Indeed the Company had kept missionaries at bay for so long for that very reason. It is little wonder then that after taking Delhi and Agra in 1857 the Rebels sought to restore the old Mogul emperor to his ancient throne and power. They wished to turn the clock back to a previous era where those dreadful reformers from Britain had not existed, and Company rule had appeared in a far different form from its Victorian incarnation.

As a final word it must be said that to make any generalizations about the Great Rebellion, other than that it brought the Company down, is fraught with dangers. The debate goes on to the present about its origins and meanings and may never be resolved. Commenting on the work of Eric Stokes (published after his death) on these events, Chris Bayly wrote that everyone should be alerted to the 'complexity and variability of social movements in an ancient agrarian society' (Stokes and Bayly 1986: 226). This appears sound advice indeed to students of this period not least because it reflects the realities of the Company's experience in India. In effect, the East India Company had always alerted itself to the complexities of India up to 1784, but lost its way thereafter. The Company and its servants of the nineteenth century, deprived of the trading mandate, had the temerity to ignore the forces at work in the agrarian society under their control. In fact, they went further and tried to remodel the economic and social structures of that ancient society, paying in the end a terrible price for their arrogance. In retrospect it can be seen how the decline of the Company's trading mission in the wake of rising militarism sealed the fate of two centuries' work, building wealth for the country and its mercantile classes. What may never be known, however, is why the Company's bureaucratic shell was allowed to exist until 1858 when it had long ceased to have meaning as a trading power. Perhaps it was nothing more than the seductive romance of the original enterprise with its exotic products and the mystery of nations in eastern seas that kept the attachment to the Company name alive. Even the brutality of the Rebellion in 1857–58 could not then, and has not since, dented the enthusiasm of artists, story-tellers, amateur historians and, latterly, Hollywood producers, for the Raj. The mystique of the East India Company flourishes and the profound impact of its experiences in Britain, India and the East are evident to this day.

NOTES

1. Hough, *Political and Military Events in India* I, x.
2. *Life and Correspondence of Charles, Lord Metcalfe*, I, 477.
3. *Historial Records of the Survey of India*, first four volumes covering the years 1777–1848.
4. *The Correspondence of Lord William Cavendish Bentinck*, II, 1403–13; all the quotations in the paragraph that follows are taken from this source.

5. Ibid., p. 1286.
6. *Parliamentary Papers*: Inquiry into Affairs of E.I. Co. and the trade between Great Britain, the East Indies, and China. Report of Select Committee of House of Lords with Appendix (1830), and Select Committee of House of Commons on China Trade, and affairs of E.I. Co. Reports; with Minutes of Evidence, and with Appendices (1830–32)..
7. *The Correspondence of Lord William Cavendish Bentinck*, II, 1154.
8. *The Law Relating to India and the East India Company*, pp. 430–60.
9. Ibid., p. 421.
10. Muir, *The Making of British India*, p. 378.

Postscript

The formal transition of the Company's interests to the state in 1858 brought to an end the most remarkable phase in Anglo-Indian history. The story of how this trading organization became an imperial power with its own armed forces is exceptional in its own right, but there are many more lessons still to be learned from the Company's unique past. In the general context of British history, the Company's role in the development of overseas trade, the advance of empire and the evolution of the modern bureaucratic state is now more broadly accepted and appreciated. In addition, the immense impact of the Company's activities at the centre of operations in London has at last begun to permeate the written texts and overviews dealing with these years of British expansion. More needs to be done, however, because the most striking and rewarding aspect of studying the East India Company's experience is that it confounds nationalist histories of one sort or another.

The Company, in fact, represented a force for the globalization of trade and cross-cultural contact before that phraseology became fashionable in our post-modern world. Its ships and sailors traded across oceans and continents, carrying products mundane and exotic, that paid little heed to national boundaries, treaties or even diplomatic imperatives. This trade created its own economic universe, inhabited by a mercantile élite and 'oceanic proletariat' that are only just beginning to be understood today (Linebaugh 1992: 126; Reddiker 1987). The Company formed a central pillar of the consumer society that developed in Britain and its wider trading and colonial world in the Atlantic and eastern seas. The ties of business and credit emanating from these relationships were frequently strained, as problems in Ireland and America bore witness. Nevertheless, the ties endured and expanded, and the Company's full part in this global drama has yet to be revealed.

No less important the Company followed the vanguard of early modern European nations seeking contacts with alien cultures, political systems and trade networks in order to expand the opportunities for economic growth and profit. In this process the motive behind Britain's territorial conquests in the East, or what is often referred to as the will to empire, is laid bare. The Company's experience illustrates how complex, opportunistic and paradoxical the dynamic of empire-building could be. Although a great deal has now been written on this topic by both Asian and western scholars, no agreement has been reached on the causation and legacy of the Company's transition from trader to sovereign power in India. This dissension has certainly been helpful in keeping this field of study alive and kicking. Many students working with the excellent archival material and massive secondary literature now in existence continue to produce books, articles and popular histories in efforts to settle old arguments and open new debates.

Less well studied is the impact of the Company's experience in the East on Britain itself. Only over the last two decades or so has a literature emerged that seeks to trace the changes taking place in Britain in reaction to the Company's rise in the East. Here would seem an area of the Company's history that warrants further attention. The picture being painted by present-day historians of the vibrant consumer society and buoyant industrializing economy of eighteenth- and nineteenth-century Britain could undoubtedly be heightened by more focus on the East India Company's business. Scholars in the past, such as Lucy Sutherland, and those of today, like Huw Bowen, have already demonstrated how the Company's tentacles reached into the nation's political institutions, economic structures and social fabric. This approach has enriched the understanding of the Company's place in the course of Britain's development over the whole period of its operations and points the way for further rewarding findings. Last, but by no means least, the East India Company's history is instructive to all those interested in the broader role of history in the development of modern societies, as it defies the pernicious periodization of the past that has so gripped a good deal of modern scholarship and writing.

Thus the Company story provides a means of examining the links between the pre- and post-industrial worlds, and the movements of peoples and products that characterized the whole dynamic of British expansionism. In writing this study it has been these larger themes, many of which can only be hinted at, that have made this effort at bringing the Company's past to a wider audience so compelling. The full implications of this fascinating episode in the history of Britain and the wider world have yet to be revealed and understood. In particular we need to explore further the relationships established through the agency of the East India Company between Britain, India and other societies in the Orient. These encounters proved to be two way affairs. How Britain influenced India and the East is well documented, but how India and the East influenced Britain is not so clearly understood. This is a matter for regret and points the way to future research and writing in this field. A deeper understanding of the forces at work in the course of British history will emerge if this work is undertaken. In the words of E.M. Foster, who understood this dynamic as well as any observer in this century, 'You can make India in England apparently, just as you can make England in India'. (*A Passage to India*, Penguin Edition, London, 1989, p. 90).

Bibliography

The following bibliography covers all sources used in the text. It includes a section on printed primary documents and then another on secondary sources covering books, articles and theses. Though not cited directly in this study for reasons of space and accessibility, the manuscript sources for the study of the East India Company are voluminous. The majority are located in the India Office, Waterloo, London – a branch of the British Library. For those interested in pursuing this avenue of investigation into the Company's past, there is a very good reference tool by Martin Moir, entitled *A General Guide to the India Office Records* (British Library Publications, London, 1989).

For those looking for official documentation that is already in print the magnificent series of volumes by Madden and Fieldhouse, *Select Documents*, listed in the first part of the bibliography, is invaluable for presenting the official view of eastern enterprise. In terms of the Company's history in the early period to 1750 the work of Professor K.N. Chaudhuri is necessary reading. His studies referred to below, specifically *The English East India Company* and *The Trading World of Asia*, present the statistical details and a global context to the development of the Company that is quite unique. For the later period the work of three or four scholars stands above the rest for basic information. Professor Peter Marshall, whose career has been devoted to bringing a deeper knowledge and understanding of British India to a wide readership, is absolutely required reading. Professor Marshall has opened many of the debates that dominate the field of Anglo-Indian history today, especially his essays, 'British Expansion in India' and 'Empire and Authority', and he is still pioneering a greater analysis of this dynamic in his contribution to the 'Modern Cambridge History of India' – cited here as, *The Bengal Bridgehead.* The work of Professor Chris Bayly stands in similar importance to modern scholarship on the Anglo-Indian past. He is general editor of the latest 'Cambridge History of India' and has produced one of the most stimulating studies on British imperialism, covering the heyday of the East India Company's years, entitled, *Imperial Meridian.*

This is not a static field, however. It will be obvious from the dates of many of the works used in this study that new research by younger scholars is also being produced that contrives to enrich the field. On the Company, in particular, Dr Huw Bowen has contributed much fine work on the impact of the Company's growth on Britain itself: *Revenue and Reform* is a distillation of the new explorations into the Company's history. Professor Kathleen Wilson's essay further proves how the rewriting of Britain's imperial experience in the East and elsewhere can change the whole view of the nation's past in the Hanoverian period. This is a theme that interests me very much, and I have pursued it throughout the book in the citations of my own work and that of others, as well as in the arguments put forward.

None of this is intended to belittle the contributions of writers and scholars of all types who have been fascinated by the Company's history in the past. The bibliography that follows remains select because it is impossible to comprehend, let alone list, the number of works in the English language alone that cover the East India Company's experience and demise. I have tried to include all the best of the early works, supplemented by the most recent research and publications on the Company and Anglo-Indian history in general.

REFERENCES APPEARING IN THE NOTES

(a) Parliamentary and Official Publications

Calendar of State Papers: East Indies, 1513–1629. vols 1–4, 6, 8 London 1862–84.

Cobbett, W., *Parliamentary History of England from 1066 . . . to 1803.* 36 vols, London 1806–20.

Historical Manuscripts Commission: Lords MSS: 14th report Appendix, Part vi, II, London 1903.

Historical Manuscripts Commission: Egmont MSS. vols 1–3, London 1923.

Journals of the House of Commons.

Journals of the House of Lords.
Parliamentary Papers. East India Company Reports from Committees of the Lords and Commons: 1808–12, 1813, 1830–32.
Statutes of the Realm. 12 vols, Reprint, London 1810–22.
Pickering, D., *Statutes at Large.* vols 1–10, London 1771.

(b) Printed Primary Sources, Collected Documents, Older Works and Theses

Auber, P., *An Analysis of the Constitution of the East India Company with Supplement.* London 1826.
The Correspondence of Lord William Bentinck: Governor-General of India 1828–1835. ed. C.H. Phillips, 2 vols, Oxford 1977.
Birdwood, G. and Foster, Sir W., *East India Company Letter-book 1600–1619.* London 1892.
Bowen, H., 'British Politics and the East India Company, 1766–1773'. University of Wales Ph.D. thesis, 1986.
Cawston, G. and Keane, A.H., *Early Chartered Companies (A.D. 1296–1858).* London 1896.
Fort William–India House Correspondence: And Other Contemporary Papers Relating Thereto, 1764–1766. ed. C.S. Srinivasachari, vol. IV. Delhi 1962.
Historical Records of the Survey of India. ed. R.H. Phillimore, vols 1–4, Dehra Dan, India 1945–48.
Hough, W., *Political and Military Events in British India From the Years 1756 to 1849.* 2 vols, London 1853.
The Law Relating to India, and the East India Company; with Notes and an Appendix, 2nd edn, London 1841.
Laws and Standing Orders of the East India Company. London 1621.
Lawson, P., 'Faction in Politics: George Grenville and His Followers 1765–1770'. University of Wales Ph.D. thesis, 1980.
McGilvary, G.K., 'East India Patronage and the Political Management of Scotland 1720–1774'. Open University Ph.D. thesis, 1989.
McCulloch, J.R., *Early English Tracts on Commerce.* Reprint, Cambridge 1970.
Madden, F.W. and Fieldhouse, D.K. (eds), *Select Documents on the Constitutional History of the British Empire and Commonwealth.* vols I–III, Connecticut and New York 1985–87.
Malcolm, Sir J., *The Life of Robert, Lord Clive: Collected from the Family Papers Communicated by the Earl of Powis.* 3 vols, London 1836.
Marshall, P.J. (ed.), *The Writings and Speeches of Edward Burke; Volume V – India: Madras and Bengal 1774–1785.* Oxford 1981.
The Life and Correspondence of Charles, Lord Metcalfe; Late Governor-

General of Jamaica and Governor-General of Canada. ed. J.W. Kaye, 2 vols, London 1854.

Mill, J., *The History of British India.* London 1858.

Muir, R., *The Making of British India 1756–1858: Described in a Series of Dispatches, Treaties, Statutes and Other Documents, Selected and Edited with Introductions and Notes.* Manchester 1915.

Newman, A.N. (ed.), *The Parliamentary Diary of Sir Edward Knatchbull, 1722–1730.* Royal Historical Society Publications, Camden 3rd series, London 1963.

Nicholls, J., *Recollections and Reflections, Personal and Political, as connected with Public Affairs during the Reign of George III.* 2 vols, London 1819–20.

Seeley, Sir J.R., *The Expansion of England.* Reprint, Chicago, 1971.

Stevens, H. (ed.), *The Dawn of British Trade to the East Indies as recorded in the Court Minutes of the East India Company, 1599–1603.* London 1886.

Taylor, W.S. and Pringle, J.H. (eds), *The Correspondence of William Pitt, Earl of Chatham.* 4 vols, London 1838–40.

Thirsk, J. and Cooper J.P. (eds), *Seventeenth-Century Economic Documents.* Oxford 1972.

Horace Walpole: Memoirs of King George II. ed. J. Brooke, 3 vols, New Haven 1985.

The Letters of Horace Walpole, Fourth Earl of Oxford, ed. Mrs Paget Toynbee, 16 vols, London 1903–05.

BOOKS AND ARTICLES

Andrews, K.R., 1978. *The Spanish Caribbean: Trade and Plunder 1530–1630.* New Haven.

Anon., 1698. *A Letter Concerning the* ***East India*** *Trade to a Gentleman.* London.

Appleby, J., 1978. *Economic Thought and Ideology in Seventeenth-Century England.* Princeton.

Arasaratnam, S., 1986. *Merchants, Companies and Commerce on the Coromandel Coast.* Delhi.

Arbuthnot, Sir A.J., 1888. *Lord Clive: The Foundation of British Rule in India.* London.

Ballhatchet, K., 1978–79. 'Missionaries, Empire and Society: The Jesuit Mission in Calcutta, 1834–1846', *Journal of Imperial and Commonwealth History*, 17.

Barber, W.J., 1975. *British Economic Thought and India 1600–1858: A Study in the History of Development Economics*. Oxford.

Bayly, C.A., 1988. *Indian Society and the Making of the British Empire*. Cambridge.

Bayly, C.A., 1989. *Imperial Meridian: The British Empire and the World 1780–1830*. London.

Bayly, C.A., (ed.), 1990. *The Raj: India and the British 1600–1947*. London.

Bhattacharya, S., 1954. *The East India Company and the Economy of Bengal*. London.

Birdwood, Sir G., 1891. *Report on The Old Records of the India Office with Supplementary Note and Appendices*. London.

Bowen, H., 1986a. ' "Dipped in the Traffic": East India Stockholders in the House of Commons 1768–1774', *Parliamentary History*, 5.

Bowen, H., 1986b. 'The East India Company and Military Recruitment in Britain, 1763–71', *Bulletin of the Institute of Historical Research*, 49.

Bowen, H., 1988. 'A Question of Sovereignty? The Bengal Land Revenue Issue, 1765–67', *Journal of Imperial and Commonwealth History*, 16.

Bowen, H., 1989. 'Investment and Empire in the later eighteenth century: East India stockholding, 1756–1791', *Economic History Review*, 42.

Bowen, H., 1991. *Revenue and Reform: The Indian Problem in British Politics 1757–1773*. Cambridge.

Bowen, M., 1981. *Empiricism and Geographical Thought: From Francis Bacon to Alexander von Humboldt*. Cambridge.

Boxer, C.R., 1969. *The Portuguese Seaborne Empire 1415–1825*. London.

Boxer, C.R., 1980. *Portuguese India in the Mid-seventeenth Century. Delhi*.

Brenner, R., 1976. 'Agrarian Class Structure and Economic Development in Pre-Industrial Europe', *Past and Present*.

Brenner, R., 1982. 'The Agrarian Roots of European Capitalism', *Past and Present*.

Brewer, J., 1976. *Party Ideology and Popular Politics at the Accession of George III*. Cambridge.

Brewer, J., 1989. *The Sinews of Power: War, Money and the English State, 1688–1783*. London.

Bryant, G.J., 1978. 'Officers of the East India Company's Army in the Days of Clive and Hastings', *Journal of Imperial and Commonwealth History*, 6.

Bryant, G.J., 1986. 'Pacification in the Early British Raj, 1755–85', *Journal of Imperial and Commonwealth History*, 14.

Callahan, R., 1972. *The East India Company and Army Reform 1783–1798*. Cambridge, Massachusetts.

Cannon, J., 1969. *The Fox–North Coalition: Crisis of the Constitution 1782–84*. Cambridge.

Catron, F., 1708–09. *The General History of the Mogul Empire, From the Foundation by Tamerlane to the Late Emperor Aurangzeb*. London.

Chaudhuri, K.N., 1965. *The English East India Company: The Study of an Early Joint-Stock Company*. London.

Chaudhuri, K.N., 1978. *The Trading World of Asia and The English East India Company*. Cambridge.

Chaudhuri, K.N., 1985. *Trade and Civilization in the Indian Ocean*. Cambridge.

Cherry, G.L., 1953. 'The Development of the English Free-Trade Movement in Parliament, 1689–1702', *Journal of Modern History*, 25.

Child, Sir J., 1693. *A Discourse Upon Trade*. London.

Clark, K., 1969. *Civilization: A Personal View*. London.

Clive, J., 1987. *Macaulay: The Shaping of the Historian*. Cambridge, Massachusetts.

Cohen, S.P., 1971. *The Indian Army: its Contribution to the Development of a Nation*. California.

Colley, L., 1976. 'The Mitchell election division, 24 March 1755', *Bulletin of the Institute of Historical Research*, 49.

Colley, L., 1982. *In Defiance of Oligarchy: The Tory Party 1714–1760*. Cambridge.

Colley, L., 1984. 'The Apotheosis of George III: Loyalty, Royalty and the English Nation', *Past and Present*, 102.

Colley, L., 1986. 'Whose Nation? Class and National Consciousness in Britain, 1750–1830', *Past and Present*, 113.

Cressy, D., 1987. *Coming Over: Migration and Communication between England and New England in the Seventeenth Century*. Cambridge.

Davenant, C., 1696. *Essay on the East India Trade*. London.

Davies, G., 1959. *The Early Stuarts 1603–1660*. Oxford.

Davies, R.R., 1990. *Domination and Conquest: The Experience of Ireland, Scotland and Wales, 1100–1300*. Cambridge.

Defoe, D., 1719. *A brief state of the question, between the printed and painted callicoes and the woollen and silk manufactures*. London.

Dickson, P.G.M., 1967. *The Financial Revolution in England: A Study in the Development of Public Credit, 1688–1756*. London.

Dodwell, H.H., (ed.), 1929. *The Cambridge History of India*, v. Cambridge.

Douglas, A.W., 1969. 'Cotton Textiles in England: The East India Company's Attempt to Exploit Developments in Fashion 1600–1721', *Journal of British Studies*, 8.

Fieldhouse, D.K., 1982. *The Colonial Empires: A Comparative Survey from the Eighteenth Century*. London.

Foster, W., 1924. *The East India House: Its History and Associations*. London.

Foster, W., 1933. *England's Quest of Eastern Trade*. London.

Fryer, J., 1698. *A New Account of* ***East India*** *and* ***Persia****, in Eight Letters*. London.

Furber, H., 1976. *Rival Empires of Trade in the Orient 1600–1800*. Minneapolis.

Gill, C., 1961. *Merchants and Mariners of the Eighteenth Century*. London.

Green, W.A. and Deasy Jnr, J.P., 1985. 'Unifying Themes in the History of British India 1757–1857: An Historiographical Analysis', *Albion*, 17.

Guha, R., 1983. *Elementary Aspects of Peasant Insurgency in Colonial India*. Delhi.

Guy, J., 1984. 'The Tudor Age (1485–1603)', in K.O. Morgan (ed.), *The Oxford Illustrated History of Britain*. Oxford.

Guy, J., 1988. *Tudor England*. Oxford.

Headrick, D., 1981. *The Tools of Empire: Technology and European Imperialism in the Nineteenth Century*. Oxford.

Hilton, B., 1988. *The Age of Atonement: The Influence of Evangelicalism on Social and Economic Thought, 1795–1865*. Oxford.

Hunter, W.W., 1899–1900. *A History of British India*, 3 vols, London.

Ingram, E., 1981. *Commitment to Empire: Prophecies of the Great Game in Asia 1797–1800*. Oxford.

Jack, S.M., 1977. *Trade and Industry in Tudor and Stuart England*. London.

Keay, J., 1991. *The Honourable Company: A History of the English East India Company*. London.

Keirn, T. and Melton, F.T., 1990, 'Thomas Manley and the Rate-of-Interest Debate 1668–1673', *Journal of British Studies*, 29.

Kenyon, J.P., 1986. *The Stuart Constitution 1603–1688*. 2nd edn, Cambridge.

Lawson, P., 1982. 'Parliament and the First East India Inquiry, 1767', *Parliamentary History*, 1.

Lawson, P., 1986. 'The Missing Link: The Imperial Dimension in Understanding Hanoverian Britain', *Historical Journal*, 29.

Lawson, P., 1989. ' "Arts and Empire equally extend": Tradition,

Prejudice and Assumption in the Eighteenth-Century Press Coverage of Empire', *Studies in History and Politics*, 7.

Lawson, P. and Phillips, J., 1984. ' "Our Execrable Banditti": Perceptions of Nabobs in Mid-Eighteenth-Century Britain', *Albion*, 16.

Legaut, F., 1708. *A New Voyage to the East Indies*. London.

Lenman, B.P., 1968. 'The Weapons of War in Eighteenth-Century India', *Journal for Studies in Army Historical Research*, 66.

Lenman, B.P., 1987 (Feb.). 'The East India Company and the Emperor Aurangzeb', *History Today*. London.

Lenman, B.P. and Lawson, P., 1983. 'Robert Clive, The "Black Jagir" and British Politics', *Historical Journal*, 26.

Levine, D. and Wrightson, K., 1991. *The Making of An Industrial Society: Wickham 1560–1765*. Oxford.

Linebaugh, P., 1992. *The London Hanged: Crime and Civil Society in the Eighteenth Century*. New York.

Macaulay, T.B., 1830. 'Essay on Lord Clive' in Macaulay, *Essays*, reprint 1888, Edinburgh.

Malcolm, Sir J., 1836. *The Life of Robert, Lord Clive: Collected From the Family Papers Communicated by the Earl of Powis*. 3 vols, London.

Marshall, P.J., 1965. *The Impeachment of Warren Hastings*. Oxford.

Marshall, P.J., 1968. *Problems of Empire: Britain and India, 1757–1813*. London.

Marshall, P.J., 1975a. 'British Expansion in India in the Eighteenth Century: A Historical Revision', *History*, 60.

Marshall, P.J., 1975b. 'Economic and Political Expansion: The Case of Oudh', *Modern Asian Studies*, 9.

Marshall, P.J., 1976. *East Indian Fortunes: The British in Bengal in the Eighteenth Century*. Oxford.

Marshall, P.J., 1981. ' "A Free though Conquering People": Britain and Asia in the Eighteenth Century'. Unpublished lecture.

Marshall, P.J., 1987a. *Bengal: The British Bridgehead, Eastern India 1740–1828*. Cambridge.

Marshall, P.J., 1987b. 'Empire and Authority in the Later Eighteenth Century', *Journal of Imperial and Commonwealth History*, 15.

Marshall, P.J. and Mukherjee, R., 1985. 'Debate: Early British Imperialism in India', *Past and Present*, 106.

Marshall, P.J. and Williams, G., 1982. *The Great Map of Mankind: British Perceptions of the World in the Age of Enlightenment*. London.

Misra, B.B., 1959. *The Central Administration of the East India Company 1773–1834*. Manchester.

Morison, S.E., 1978. *The Great Explorers: The European Discovery of America*. Oxford.

Moss, D.J., 1976. 'Birmingham and the Campaigns against the Orders-in-Council and East India Company Charter, 1812–13', *Canadian Journal of History*, 11.

Mui, H.C. and Mui, L.H., 1984. *The Management of Monopoly: A Study of the East India Company's Conduct of its Tea Trade 1784–1833*. Vancouver.

Mui, H.C. and Mui, L.H., 1989. *Shops and Shopkeeping in Eighteenth-Century England*. Montreal.

Mukherjee, R., 1974. *The Rise and Fall of the East India Company*. New York.

Mukherjee, R., 1982. 'Trade and Empire in Awadh, 1765–1804', *Past and Present*, 94.

Mun, T., 1621. *A Discourse of Trade from England into the East Indies*. London.

Mun, T., 1628. *The Petition and Remonstrance of the Governor and Company of Merchants of London Trading to the East Indies*. London.

Mun, T. 1664. *England's Treasure by Foreign Trade, or the Balance of our Foreign Trade is the Rule of our Treasure*. London.

Nightingale, P., 1969. *Trade and Empire in Western India, 1784–1806*. Cambridge.

Ovington, J., 1696. *A Voyage to Surat in the Year 1689*. London.

Parker, G., 1988. *The Military Revolution: Military Innovation and the Rise of the West, 1500–1800*. Cambridge.

Parker, J., 1965. *Books to Build an Empire: A Bibliographic History of English Overseas Interests to 1620*. Amsterdam.

Parry, J., 1981. *The Age of Reconnaissance: Discovery, Exploration and Settlement 1450 to 1650*. California.

Peers, D., 1990. 'Between Mars and Mammon; The East India Company and Efforts to Reform its Army, 1796–1832', *Historical Journal*, 33.

Phillips, C.H., 1961. *The East India Company 1784–1834*. Manchester.

Phillips, J., 1985. 'A Successor to the Moguls: The Nawab of the Carnatic and the East India Company, 1763–1785', *International History Review*, 7.

Phillips, J., 1988. 'Parliament and Southern India, 1781–83: The Secret Committee of Inquiry and Prosecution of Sir Thomas Rumbold', *Parliamentary History*, 7.

Plumb, J.H., 1967. *The Growth of Political Stability in England 1675–1725*. London.

Pollexfen, J., 1697. *England and East India Inconsistent in their Manufactures*. London.

Pollexfen, J., 1698. *A Letter concerning the* ***East India*** *trade to a Gentleman*. London.

Porter, A., 1987–88. 'Scottish Missions and Education in Nineteenth-Century India: The Changing Face of "Trusteeship" ', *Journal of Imperial and Commonwealth History*, 16.

Porter, B., 1984. *The Lion's Share: A Short History of British Imperialism 1850–1983*. London.

Rabb, T.K., 1967. *Enterprise and Empire: Merchant and Gentry Investment in the Expansion of England*. Cambridge, Massachusetts.

Reddiker, M., 1987. *Between the Devil and the Deep Blue Sea*. Cambridge.

Rogers, N., 1989. *Whigs and Cities: Popular Politics in the Age of Walpole and Pitt*. Oxford.

Russell, C., 1971. *The Crisis of Parliaments: English History 1509–1660*. Oxford.

Sacks, D.H., 1990. 'Office and Calling: The Problem of Monopoly in Early Modern England'. Unpublished Paper.

Said, E.W., 1978. *Orientalism*. New York.

Scammell, G.V., 1989. *The First Imperial Age: European Overseas Expansion c.1400–1715*. London.

Schama, S., 1987. *An Embarrassment of Riches: An Interpretation of Dutch Culture in the Golden Age*. New York.

Scott, W.R., 1910–12. *Constitution and Finance of English, Scottish and Irish Joint-Stock Companies*. 3 vols, Cambridge.

Smith, A., 1776. *An Inquiry into the Nature and Causes of the* ***Wealth of Nations***. London.

Spear, P., 1983. *A History of India*, vol. 2, London.

Stokes, E.T., 1959. *The English Utilitarians and India*. Oxford.

Stokes, E.T., 1980. 'Bureaucracy and Ideology: Britain and India in the Nineteenth Century', *Transactions of the Royal Historical Society*, 30.

Stokes, E.T. and Bayly, C.A., 1986. *The Peasant Armed: The Indian Revolt of 1857*. Oxford.

Sutherland, L.S., 1947. 'The East India Company and the Peace of Paris', *English Historical Review*, 42.

Sutherland, L.S., 1952. *The East India Company in Eighteenth-Century Politics*. Oxford.

Thieme, O.C., 1982. *By Inch Candle: A Sale of East India House, 21 September 1675*. Minneapolis.

Wallerstein, I., 1980. *The Modern World System II: The Consolidation of the European World Economy, 1600–1750*. New York.

Watson, I.B., 1980a. 'Fortifications and the "idea" of force in early English East India Company relations with India', *Past and Present*, 88.

Watson, I.B., 1980b. *Foundation for Empire: English Private Trade in India 1659–1760*. Delhi.

Williamson, J.A., 1961. *A Short History of British Expansion: The Old Colonial Empire*. London.

Wilson, K., 1988. 'Empire, Trade and Popular Politics in Mid-Hanoverian Britain: The Case of Admiral Vernon', *Past and Present*, 121.

Wolpert, S., 1989. *A New History of India*. London.

Wrigley, E.A. and Schofield, R.S., 1989. *The Population History of England*. Cambridge.

Maps

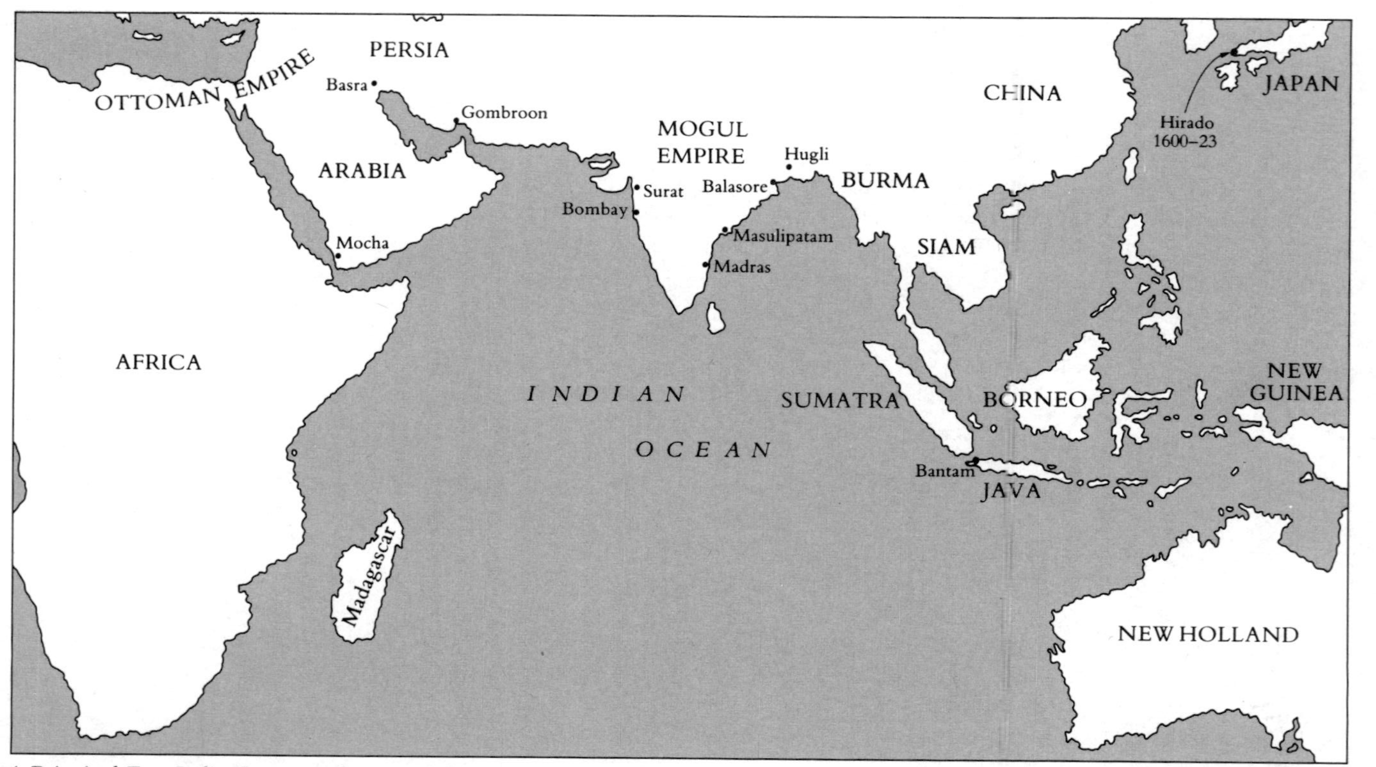

1 Principal East India Company bases and factories *c.* 1600–50

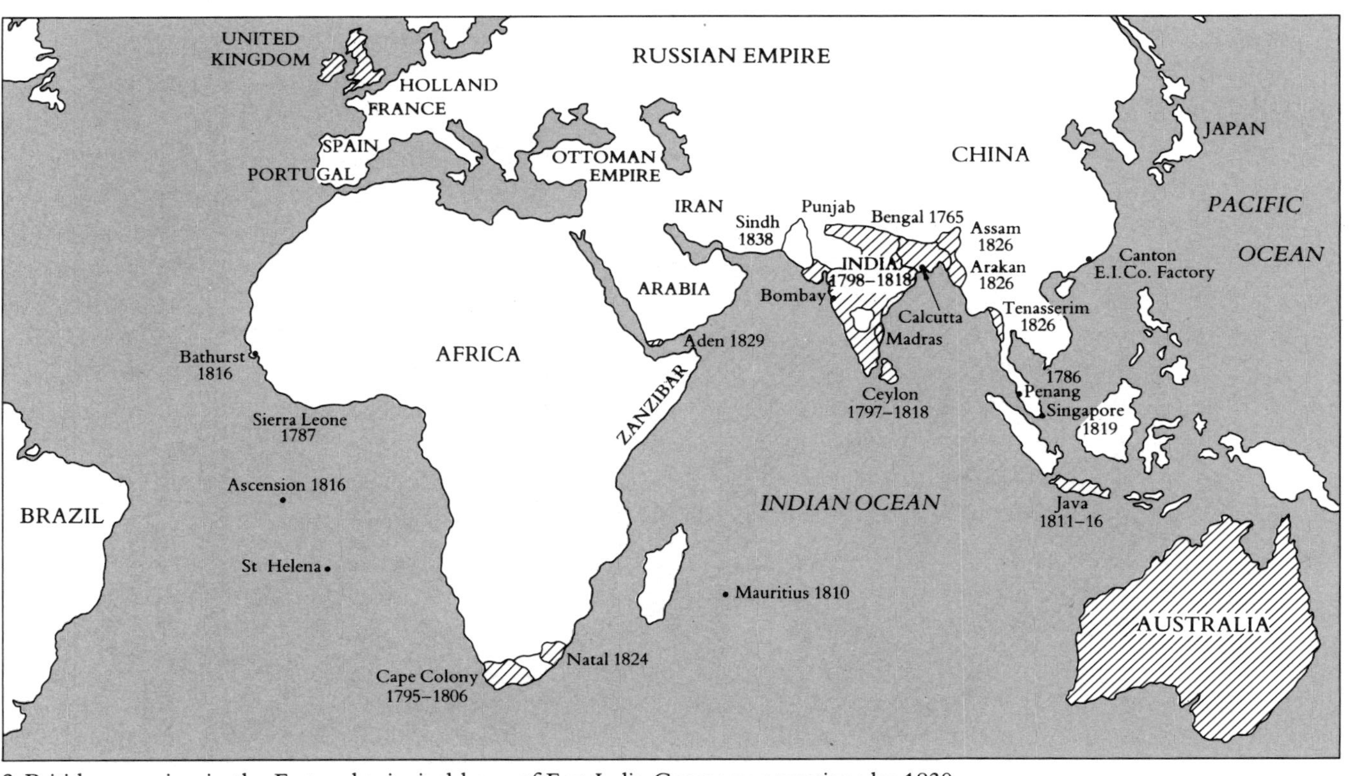

2 British expansion in the East and principal bases of East India Company operations by 1830

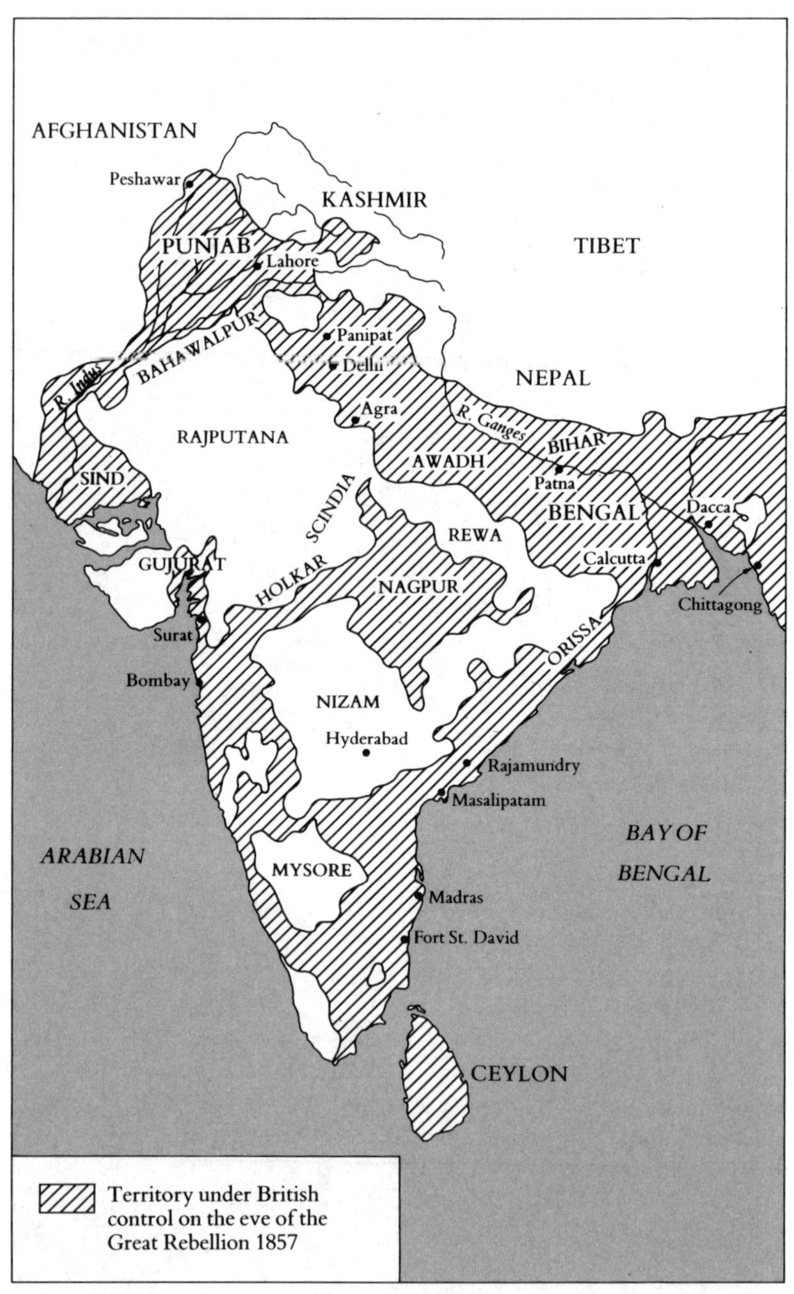

3 British India and Ceylon, 1857

Index